DEC 3 0 70

D0712741

POLITICAL
LEADERS OF
LATIN AMERICA

Richard Bourne

POLITICAL LEADERS OF LATIN AMERICA

Che Guevara

Alfredo Stroessner

Eduardo Frei Montalva

Juscelino Kubitschek

Carlos Lacerda

Eva Perón

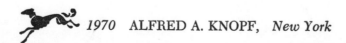 1970   ALFRED A. KNOPF,   *New York*

Acknowledgments

The opinions throughout this book are my own, and none of the persons or institutions whose help I gratefully acknowledge here are in any way responsible. My first debt of gratitude is to the *Guardian* and its editor, Alastair Hetherington, and to the Brazilian government, thanks to whom I first became acquainted with Latin American affairs. In 1965 the Brazilian government awarded me one of two scholarships then available to young British citizens and the *Guardian* permitted me six months' leave of absence in Brazil to enjoy it. Subsequently, in 1967, both the Brazilian and the Chilean governments assisted me with air fares to their countries in a shorter trip to gather material for this book.

Among individuals to whom I am indebted are: Senhora Vera Pacheco Jordão, former Brazilian cultural attaché in London, and Mrs. Raquel Braune, the kind and long-serving assistant cultural attaché at the same embassy; Señor Fernando Debesa, cultural attaché at the Chilean embassy in London; Jane Braga of Reuters, Henry Hogg, a *Daily Express* correspondent, and Carlos Widmann of the *Süddeutsche Zeitung*, with whom I had hours of discussion in Rio de Janeiro, David Bravo, free-lance correspondent, and Richard Gott, the *Guardian's* correspondent in Santiago; Professor David Joslin and Mr. Adrian Johnson, who had the kindness to read the manuscript; and my wife, Juliet, who accompanied me in 1967, and has been amazingly tolerant of my Latin American mania.

April 1969   R.B.

Contents

POLITICAL
LEADERS OF
LATIN AMERICA

Introduction

The "feel" of politics in Latin America

Latin America, stretching through twenty republics from the Rio Grande to Tierra del Fuego, is a convenient collective name for nations with diverse ethnic and cultural characteristics. Setting aside the traditional British, French, Dutch and North American territories in and around the Caribbean all the republics officially speak Spanish, with the exceptions of Portuguese in Brazil and Creole French in Haiti. But in spite of the diversity of these Latin countries, and their very different states of economic development, they share certain attitudes toward politics and its conduct. On the whole, political life is regarded as important and highly respectable. This is not to say that Latin American countries do not enjoy the pleasures of periodic cynicism about their governors, or that stories of graft and peculation of public funds are always unfair and untrue. But about politics there still hangs an aura of elite distinction that in Britain was dying by the end of the nineteenth century: that to serve in public life is the most honorable and significant contribution a man can make for his country's good. Hence politics has an attraction both for the scions of old established families and for aggressive individuals of immigrant or poor parentage who wish to prove their merit. It is the only career for which other respectable personages in a Latin American society—generals, lawyers, doctors, writers—are often willing to forsake their duties. As a distinct, high-status occupation in its own right it offers rewards sufficiently attractive to outweigh the insecurity of political office. Posts with embassies abroad, jobs with the United Nations and international agencies, directorships with companies controlled by supporters, are all reasonable expectations for a prominent politician. In addition, there are countless opportunities for graft, ranging from the patronage of jobs in the public service to the power to obtain official permission for industrial or other developments, or the power to award contracts.

Respectability for politics is much abetted by the traditionalism of the "quality" press in many Latin countries, a traditionalism that has survived the arrival of tabloid papers, news magazines, radio, and television. The old-fashioned quality papers have a nineteenth-century delight in printing many columns daily of speeches and dry political doings, without necessarily illuminating the subject. Many of the papers are flagrantly partisan, though TV and radio are often less so.

The degree to which politics is open to public view, and hence to public participation, varies enormously in the different Latin countries. In Chile, for example, though the decision-making processes of the Communist Party may not always be as clear as day, the public is probably as well informed about the taking and purposes of political decisions as any Western European population. But in Brazil or Paraguay, where the armed forces are either in power or very close to it, political decision-making is much more obscure. Though a Paraguayan, by chance or word of mouth, might know the gist of a discussion between General Stroessner and his cabinet on a particular day, he would not get more than a superficial account officially. No one would tell him regularly, even in a partial way, the most important political facts of the régime—the current state of relations between the President and the army officers or the Colorado Party. In Brazil, a much more sophisticated state where the press is less backward than in many countries, there are still aspects of political maneuvering in both civilian and military circles which are distinctly under-reported.

The stability of the party system varies among the different countries; but one facet of the personal patterns of leadership which coexist with even well-established parties is the clique that surrounds the leader. Sometimes such a clique is formed purely for political admiration, but very often the prospect of jobs to be shared out if the leader takes power is also a factor. Whereas the Chief of Staff, a Stroessner, or a Castello Branco in Brazil, intervenes with a ready-made cadre of surrounding officers, civilian leaders have to create their own. On their quality the leader is enormously dependent; in Chile, for example, although the group around Frei which came to power with him in 1964 seemed well endowed with intellectual ability, some of them were unprepared to grapple with the political and administrative difficulties of running a government.

In Latin America one is very aware of politicians as a separate class, pursuing a specialized business, and using in public a rather high-flown vocabulary to describe it. The rhetoric of liberty, equality, justice, and national independence is endlessly invoked. On the whole, these practitioners are of middle to upper status in the community and the numbers of peasants or manual workers who become involved are few. This is partly a function of the small part that the latter have played in the system in the past. A complex of factors has been responsible, including the lack of institutional means by which they may focus their strength (though sometimes manual workers' unions are long established, they are by no means all-powerful, and countries like Brazil and Chile only began large-scale unionization of peasants in the sixties) and literacy qualifications which have kept them off the electoral register. Lower-income groups have traditionally been used for street demonstrations or as threats by which politicians are able to extract or refuse concessions from privileged groups. But though the participation of these groups may be indirect, the whole population of these countries is normally aware of the consequences of political change as a result of patronage: in Colombia, where the traditional parties are Liberal or Conservative, or in Uruguay, where they are Blanco or Colorado, the jobs of many thousands of people may be affected by a change of administration. Where labor is plentiful and jobs are in short supply, such bureaucratic patronage is important.

The history of government since independence

Most of the Latin American countries emerged from the womb of colonialism in the first decades of the nineteenth century. The small Creole class that won independence, and fought over the inheritance for several more decades, acquired from Spain the absolutist attitudes of monarchy, and the rigid structures of the Catholic Church and a colonial bureaucracy. Many vital traditions in Spanish America may be traced to this time: the heroic role of the armed leader exemplified by Bolívar and San Martín, the leanings to dictatorship that this could imply, coupled with an attachment to idealist constitutions of a dogmatic liberalism that were ignored or perverted by events. The turbulent postindependence period threw up *caudillos*—military leaders who could offer protection in return for near-absolute loyalty—all over the continent, and produced struggles between centralists and federalists in the huge and unsettled new states. Many of the *caudillos* were despotic and uncultured, like Rosas in Argentina, but the creation of viable governments, amidst anarchy, particularism, and the racial and linguistic divisions between the descendants of the Conquistadores and the Indians, was often due to their arms and resolve.

In this process Brazil and Cuba were two notable exceptions. Portugal had never succeeded in achieving the bureaucratic control over its American empire that Spain had in hers, and the actual achievement of independence, in 1822, occurred peacefully under royal leadership in Brazil. This accident, which created a Brazilian Empire that lasted until 1889, gave a continuity and a legitimacy to government which contributed to the conciliatory and nonideological strain in the Brazilian political tradition. Cuba was different in that fighting for independence from Spain lasted on and off from 1868 to 1901, and independence was guaranteed by the United States's victory in a war which also ousted the Spaniards from the Philippines and Puerto Rico. The result was that although Cuba was nominally independent, the

Platt Amendment[1] and the U.S. base in Guantanamo ensured a persistent U.S. influence in Cuban affairs which was understandably resented by patriots.

The constitutions adopted after independence were influenced by the Hispanic monarchical tradition, by the example of the strong Presidency and balancing Congress adopted in the United States half a century earlier, and also by some of the democratic notions of the French Revolution. In the period of lawlessness that followed in many states, all constitutional provisions were breached; but by the late nineteenth century a strong executive Presidency was the accepted norm, theoretically elected by a narrow and literate franchise, and assisted by a bicameral legislature. But there were plenty of experiments; between 1830 and 1895 Ecuador alone had eleven constitutions. Throughout much of Latin America the nineteenth-century parties were those of Liberals and Conservatives. Generally, though not always, the Liberals represented the interests of the towns and the metropolis. They tended to be anticlerical, to extend the range of their support downwards into the urban middle sectors, and to uphold a centralist constitution with strong guarantees for individual liberties. The Conservatives tended to the opposite—to be rural, clerical, landowning, and federalist. But neither party nor ideological distinctions were immutable, and family loyalties and regional associations also played a significant part. Both the personal popularity of individuals and the political activity of army factions confused the evolution of parties.

Whereas in the nineteenth century Latin America had been generally prepared to accept its role as a producer of primary products—beef in Argentina, coffee and sugar in Brazil, sugar in Cuba, and bananas and other fruit in Central America—and the interests of the towns were those of importers, bureaucrats, and

---

[1] The Platt Amendment to the new Cuban constitution was passed while U.S. troops still occupied the island. This allowed U.S. forces to intervene "in the interests of the Cuban people" whenever the U.S. President saw fit.

the professional classes rather than of manufacturers and workers, the twentieth century saw a growth in the desire to industrialize. Just before and around the turn of the century the southern countries in particular, and most notably Argentina and Brazil, received a considerable wave of immigrants from Europe. These came from Italy, Germany, and Eastern Europe, as well as from the Iberian mother countries, and they brought a new impetus to urban living and new expectations. The combination of pressure to industrialize—fostered by the disruption in the flow of manufactured goods from traditional sources during the First World War—with some immigration created demands for a wider suffrage and social and trade-union legislation.

In Argentina in 1912 the Saenz Peña law was passed, requiring every man aged eighteen to enroll for military service and to register as a voter. Voting was made secret and compulsory. The result of this law was a period of Radical hegemony, associated particularly with Hipólito Irigoyen, which diminished the political power of the landed oligarchy and brought recognition of labor's right to form unions. A code of wages and hours for factory workers was introduced. In the first two decades of the twentieth century José Batlle y Ordóñez in Uruguay was advocating compulsory suffrage and mass education, the state operation of banks and public utilities, and advanced social security and labor legislation. At the same time he wrote a constitution which sharply reduced the powers of the President, who now had to share them with a nine-man elected council—a constitution that was in force until the 1960's, when intense inflation and political factionalism were held to necessitate a strong executive President.

The progress of social reforms and the growth of mass parties were extremely uneven over Latin America as a whole. Governments were especially unsettled in the Central American republics, not least in the canal republic of Panama, whose independence from Colombia was proclaimed under U.S. auspices in 1903. But it was in Central America, in Mexico, that a confused but real social revolution broke out in 1911 that was the first of its kind to occur in the Americas. After almost a decade of intermittent warfare and political confusion the revolution came to solidify in a near-monopoly party (after several changes of name it is now known as the Partido Revolucionario Institucional), and in the 1930's it adopted nationalization of the oil fields and an agrarian reform at home and a nationalist stance in foreign affairs. But there was still room for private enterprise in the Mexico of the PRI, and by the 1940's and 1950's the party was being used impartially by peasant, labor, and bourgeois groups for the arbitration of their differences. In late 1968 the corruption and repression of this regime resulted in dramatic student protests which overshadowed the Olympic Games.

The Mexican Revolution had strong Indianist overtones, and by the 1930's other countries with large unintegrated Indian populations, such as Peru, were becoming concerned about the racial, linguistic, and cultural barriers that divided the Hispanicized upper class from the Indian peasantry. APRA,[2] whose leading light was Haya de la Torre, attempted to combine the Peruvian middle sectors, labor, and the peasantry in a tightly organized, semirevolutionary party which now—after over thirty years of existence in which it has largely shed its Marxism and become conservative—is still regarded with suspicion by Peruvian aristocrats. APRA and the similar Acción Democrática in Venezuela exemplified the growth of more tightly knit parties by the mid-twentieth century. The degree of discipline among party members was comparable to that shown by European party members.

In 1969, however, there were still many countries in which parties were fuzzy and personalities were all-important. Ecuador was a small country of which this was true. Brazil also lacked a solid party structure. The parties abolished by the Brazilian military régime in 1965—the União Democratico Nacional, the Partido Social Democratico and the Partido Trabalhista Brasileiro—were largely alliances of state political machines stiffened with some national figureheads. But they did not represent fixed

[2] Alianza Popular Revolucionaria Americana.

ideological positions or any guaranteed voting strength for a party irrespective of its candidates. The essential weakness of this structure was shown by the proliferation of small parties and interparty alliances.

By the 1960's, although the power of individual governments might alter according to circumstances, the power of government in general throughout most of Latin America had enormously increased. Increased industrialization, substantial sectors of nationalized industries in several countries, and the impetus to central planning given by the United Nations Economic Commission for Latin America and the Alliance for Progress, were added to the integrative effects of improved domestic communications to make central governments ever stronger. The transfer of power was symbolized in the new constitution adopted for Brazil after the military revolution of 1964 which formally abandoned federalism and changed the country's name from "United States of Brazil" to "Brazil."

Constitutions, elections, and voting

Extreme centralization of power in Latin American states is the norm, although state governors, *intendentes*, and the like may provide centers of local authority, particularly in the largest countries. The typical Latin American constitution provides for a directly elected President who is also Commander in Chief of the armed forces. The 1940 constitution of Paraguay, for example, provides that the directly elected President, who may be re-elected and who is also Commander in Chief, may appoint ministers of state, members of the Supreme Court, and other officials, and may dismiss councillors of state; he may declare a state of siege in an emergency; he may make laws by decree during a parliamentary recess and veto bills passed by the Chamber of Deputies. These are obviously enormous powers, and elsewhere some limits are placed on the Presidency. In Mexico and many other countries it is illegal for a President to stand immediately for re election, and in Chile, for example, a presidential veto may be overturned by two thirds of Congress.

But while a powerful executive is usual, the means of election vary considerably. Not all states match Mexico, where there is universal suffrage for citizens over twenty-one, or eighteen, if they are married. Several countries, including Chile and Brazil, have a literacy qualification. But in the early 1960's it was estimated that nearly half of Brazil's adult population was illiterate, while even in relatively advanced Chile some sixteen per cent of the population over fifteen was illiterate in 1960. Literacy qualifications naturally tend to reduce the expected support for reforming parties or individuals, keep the underprivileged out of electoral politics, and give a special political bite to adult literacy campaigns and educational spending. The age structure of most Latin American countries, where the birth rate has been high, makes the voting population often as little as half of the total population. Where this is coupled with a restrictive literate franchise, as in Brazil, it is quite normal for only a quarter of the total population to go to the polls. The Brazilian suffrage has been restrictive in an extraordinary manner: not only have illiterates and servicemen been excluded, but while voting is compulsory for men and employed women aged eighteen to sixty-five, it is optional for unemployed women within that range and for both sexes over sixty-five.

While election of Presidents is usually direct (though indirect election was provided for in Brazil under the 1967 constitution), the election of deputies and senators may take many forms. Argentina, Chile, and Brazil are among countries using proportional representation, while Peru, for instance, used the system of a simple majority vote until the 1968 revolution.

If voting is theoretically free, it remains true that in many parts of Latin America voters are under strong pressures to vote in a particular way. This occurs not only in dictatorships like Paraguay, where opposition parties may only be semitolerated and there is a tradition of terror against opponents, but also in apparently democratic countries. In both rural and urban areas there may be patrons who direct voters and operate as brokers, able to negotiate for so many votes in dealings with the parties. In rural areas in Brazil, for example, a landowner or employer may cast his employees' votes in return for money or other reward. He may or may not pay his men for their votes. This tradition persists because landworkers recognize that their masters have greater power to alter their lives than politicians and, perhaps, because they identify their own interests with those of their employers. In urban areas patronage works in other ways. The cohorts of federal, state, or municipal officials may be under orders to vote for the continuance of the existing regime, and may be offered credible rewards for their loyalty. Given the strong powers of Latin American governments in the labor and social-welfare fields, it is not unusual for bidding to develop for the votes of trade unions and other groups. In this case a trade-union leader may instruct his members to vote in a certain way in response to favors received or expected.

Several parties—outstandingly the Christian Democrats in Chile and the Peronists in Argentina—have sought to take advantage of the votes to be gained in the slums that surround all big cities in Latin America. The slums are formed partly of country people, on their way to urban living and an industrialized money society, and partly of town dwellers for whom there is no pre-existing accommodation. In such places, where sanitation, schools, and communications are in a parlous state, it is possible for a local leadership to deliver the overwhelming majority of votes in a particular direction. In this twilight world politics and corruption and gangsterdom may fuse: one of the most notorious cases concerns the Tammany-type rule of Tenorio Cavalcanti, "the gunman of Caxias," who held sway for a decade up to the mid-sixties in an industrial suburb on the outskirts of Rio de Janeiro. His home was like a fortress, yet he ran as a working-class candidate for the governorship of Guanabara in 1960 and made a creditable showing by coming in third.

Since class systems in Latin America are not uniform and parties do not stand for fixed ideologies, it is not surprising that voting does not follow a straightforward sociological pattern. In the early 1960's, for example, one could see the strange spectacle of the PTB, apparently the most left-wing party in Brazil and committed to some degree of land reform, winning power in rural states by the same manipulation of landlords' and tenants' votes that was practiced by the conservative parties. In the slum barrios on the outskirts of Lima one might see APRA, the Acción Popular of Belaúnde Terry, and UNO, the Union Nacional Odriista of the ex-dictator, Manuel Odría, competing on equal terms.

Looked at in detail, however, some voting patterns do conform to relatively simple social categories. In Chile the presidential election of 1964 which brought Frei to power showed women and middle sectors favoring him to a significant degree over his Socialist opponent, Allende. The following year, in Rio de Janeiro, the election for the governorship of Guanabara showed a surprisingly clear-cut division in which the bulk of lower-income voters opted for Negrão de Lima, the candidate of the PTB and PSD, while the bulk of middle- and upper-income voters supported Flexa Ribeiro, the candidate of the UDN.

Parties in politics now

Parties in Latin America are best analyzed in terms of individual countries, although attitudes and policies from one national figure may be extensively borrowed elsewhere. Only two political movements currently pretend to be organized on a Latin-America-wide basis—the Communists and the Christian Democrats—although the Peruvian APRA party has a family relationship with Venezuela's Acción Democrática. (It is doubtful how much stress should be put on this last link now; although the two parties shared revolutionary origins and a concern to integrate the Indians and peasants into the community, and subsequently espoused democratic methods, they have diverged since.)

The Communists, whose mainstream tradition in Latin America is nonrevolutionary, have suffered from successive schisms. In

the 1920's and 1930's they suffered from the activities of Trotskyists, and in the 1960's they have been seriously weakened by
the hostility among Moscow, Peking, and Havana. While the
quarrel between Moscow- and Peking-liners has been about the
relative prospects of the parliamentary and revolutionary roads
to power, the men of Havana have added to the discord by emphasizing the place of guerrilla warfare in the capture of power
and by welcoming the support of non-Communist revolutionaries.
In most countries the Moscow adherents have kept an advantage
over those of Peking, but at a cost of confusion in their own
ranks and diminishing influence outside them. Peru, for example,
saw the appearance of two parties with an identical name—the
Partido Communista Peruano.

Divisions over the role of guerrillas caused a mass boycott
by orthodox Communist parties of the Cuban-inspired Organization of Latin American Solidarity meeting in Havana in 1967,
and a bitter public polemic between the Cuban and Venezuelan
Communist parties. The Venezuelan party had for a while supported the guerrilla Fuerzas Armadas de Liberación Nacional,
whose best-known leader was Douglas Bravo; but although these
fighters had achieved some local successes, the party acquired
a more moderate leadership which was increasingly doubtful of
the chances of long-term victory. Much to the annoyance of
Havana, this leadership cut off help for the guerrillas—and was
even accused of betraying them to the government—and declared
itself against the armed way.

The country with the strongest and most homogeneous Communist party is Chile, where a considerable parliamentary representation makes a parliamentary road to power a genuine possibility. It is no coincidence, therefore, that the Chilean Communists
are least interested in the armed way, which is a source of division with their erstwhile allies of the Chilean Socialist Party. The
latter, more nationalistic and more prone to the influence of
charismatic leaders of the Castro type, have become enthusiastic
admirers of the Cuban way—even operating an OLAS office in
Santiago—although they have yet to transform their words into

guns at home. In some of the biggest countries, like Brazil and Argentina, Communists of all sorts are few in proportion to the total population, and of restricted influence.

If it is true that the Communists do not work in any coordinated or uniform way, the same is equally true of the Christian Democrats. In some manner Christian Democrats now have political formations in most Latin American countries. Apart from Chile, where their success in attaining power under President Frei has offered a beacon to sympathizers elsewhere, they command strength also in Venezuela, Peru, and El Salvador. In December 1968 Dr. Rafael Caldera, of the Christian Democratic party, COPEI, was elected President of Venezuela with a less than one per cent plurality over Acción Democrática. His domestic program is much more conservative than Frei's. The Chilean example suggests that, working from a basis in social Catholic ideology among Catholic-oriented sectors of the population which would now reject traditional conservatism, Christian Democrats would like to establish coherent and far-reaching movements.

An interesting feature of the Chilean party is its breadth of approach: not only was a mass party set up, but individual interests and especially the "marginal" [3] populations on the edge of the cities were catered to, while a concurrent attempt was made to seize power in the student and trade-union movements. But the zig-zag course of the actual Frei administration in Chile may well reduce the attractiveness of Christian Democracy in the hemisphere as a whole and, though the Catholic hierarchies have appreciated the need for social change in some countries, their support can not be guaranteed everywhere. Early attempts to inject Christian Democracy into Brazilian politics were notably unsuccessful: although both Jânio Quadros, President in 1961, and Juarez Távora, a presidential candidate in 1955, were connected with a small nucleus describing itself as Christian

---

[3] "Marginal" is a key word in Christian Democratic literature. Though often used for shanty dwellers in cities, it may extend to all those who are poor or feel they have no stake in society.

Democratic, it was clear that this was just one more small group in Brazil's multiparty system rather than the core of a serious political movement.

In their pursuit of power Latin American parties often adopt alliances and discard ideologies in a way that would be regarded as somewhat shocking elsewhere. Curious alliances, for example, may be cited from pre-Castro Cuba, where the old Communists at one time explicitly supported Batista in return for influence in the labor movement; from Argentina, where Arturo Frondizi, the Intransigent Radical, came to power with the votes of the Peronists, although throughout the reign of the Peróns both Frondizi himself and the Radicals in general had been the most persistent opponents of the régime; or from Peru, where in the 1960's APRA formed a pact with the party of the ex-dictator General Manuel Odría, who had done his best to obliterate it. The attitude toward policy and ideology may be indicated by two examples from Argentina: General Perón, in his second term of office, attempted to negotiate an agreement with a U.S. company to conduct oil exploration, although national control of national resources had been one of the main planks of his government's platform; in 1958 the Intransigent Radical Party (UCRI) had campaigned for a state-planned economy with nationalization of electric power and petroleum, immediate agrarian reform, opposition to Roman Catholic and private universities, and an anti-imperialist foreign policy; but by December 1960 a party convention explicitly abandoned all this and instead wanted respect for private property, cooperation between state and private education, and more foreign capital. (In Chile in the mid-sixties another old-established Radical Party was moving in the opposite direction.)

Such sharp changes of line reflect and contribute toward the continuance of the institutional weakness of democratic politics in the Latin American countries. They are made easy where parties represent neither a coherent social interest nor a distinct ideology, and their leaderships are under little obligation to adopt consistent tactics in their efforts to gain power. An added factor making for inconsistency of policy and allies is the

Latin American tradition of personalism: where supporters' prime allegiance is to a person, not a party or set of ideas, the leader may feel free to take whatever course he considers likely to bring him immediate advantage. More than in developed, pluralistic societies, control of the executive and the patronage and employment it provides is a vastly exciting prize in a Latin American state, where other sources of wealth and power may be few. In some cases strange alliances are a response to a bloodstained history—the best recent example is the accord between the Liberals and Conservatives of Colombia, which pledged their combined support to presidential candidates nominated alternately by each party after political violence between them had killed an estimated 200,000 people between 1948 and 1957.

In this situation it is not surprising that party loyalties should sometimes be weak. There are exceptions, of course. The quasi-monopolistic PRI of Mexico, the strictly drilled APRA in Peru, are in their different ways strong parties, while in Colombia and in Argentina, where the persecuted Peronists fought several elections under different names after 1955, it was obvious that loyalties were strong. But elsewhere this was not the case. Brazil, for example, never succeeded in building a strong party structure after the overthrow of Vargas in 1945 and the election of Jânio Quadros, a man not really beholden to any party, showed the frailty of the parties in the 1960's. In Bolivia the Movimiento Nacionalista Revolucionario—which was founded in 1941 with a radical program of nationalization and land reform and came to power in 1952 after an uprising—had become hopelessly divided by the 1960's. By the time General René Barrientos led his successful coup in 1964, the MNR was ready to collapse. Chile also offers a case of the rapid desertion of traditional parties—the Radicals, Liberals, and Conservatives—by their voters between 1958 and 1964, making possible the upsurge of the Christian Democrats.

Eclectic populist parties, often endowed with a charismatic leader, were a strong feature of the 1940's. The Peronists in Argentina led by the Peróns, the MNR and Paz Estenssoro in

Bolivia, APRA and Haya de la Torre in Peru, Acción Democrática and Rómulo Betancourt in Venezuela, and the Partido Trabalhista Brasileiro of Getúlio Vargas in Brazil were all parties of this type. Phrases and ideas were drawn freely from Marxism, Fascism, Catholicism, and liberal democracy as the occasion prompted; promises of nationalization and drastic social change accompanied by a reassertion of nationalism were not always honored when these parties formed governments, but they colored the emotional atmosphere. Both the Peronist and PTB parties were founded as instruments of dictatorial leaders, and in the others too, inner party democracy was sometimes open to doubt.

Armies in politics now

In most Latin American countries the armed forces have a high degree of influence over the direction of national politics, even outside their professional interests. In Brazil and Argentina—to take two of the most powerful countries, which in 1969 both had military governments—their respective armed forces regard themselves as entitled to a veto over the choice or tenure of a President. In 1962 the Argentine military removed President Frondizi after he had permitted Peronists to take part in elections in which they obtained thirty-five per cent of the votes. In 1966 the military deposed President Arturo Illia for similar reasons. In Brazil, both Presidents Kubitschek and Goulart were only permitted to take office after compromises with the armed forces, and in 1964 the troops removed Goulart. In several of the larger countries—including Venezuela, Peru, and Colombia—the military have exercised direct control within the last twenty years. In even the most "democratic" states—Chile and Uruguay—the regional tradition of army intervention has been so strong that within the last five years, there could be speculation, which did not amount to more, on the possibility of direct military interference at moments of politicoeconomic weakness.

How has this degree of power arisen, and how is it used?

Thanks to the fact that independence from Spain was won by military means, and the fact that the new states often survived internal anarchy by force of arms, the armed forces have traditionally been associated with patriotism and the maintenance of domestic order. It is common in Latin American countries now, and defended on grounds of patriotic duty and the integration of the masses into national life, for there to be conscription. Though the period may be short and some youngsters may avoid it, this military service may be used for teaching literacy, hygiene, and other essentials that an inadequate school system has failed to provide. But of course in no familiar military sense—no Latin American country can truly be described as under threat of attack in spite of guerrilla movements as in Guatemala and Venezuela—is there any need for conscription. One may even suspect that covert aims of compulsory service are to indoctrinate the rest of the population with the superiority of the status, ethos, and "mission" of the military, and to minimize unemployment by keeping young men off the labor market.

The Latin American armies may in some ways be compared with slightly superior police forces. Where in France or England gendarmes or policemen would be called out to control political demonstrations, in Latin America this task may well devolve on the troops. The police themselves are not always efficient and may lack status. In Paraguay, for example, it is customary for an army general to be imposed as the Chief of Police. In Brazil and states where militarized police exist at a state or municipal level, and might be used by local political leaders against the central authority, the army is inevitably regarded by the national government as the ultimate guarantee of its power.

Important as is their possession of the physical weapons of repression, the military leaders in Latin America claim something even more crucial: to be in command of the only cohesive, disciplined group of people in the state.[4] Given the structural weak-

---

[4] An interesting sidelight on the military reputation for discipline and administrative competence is the common use of officers for bureaucratic jobs in civil life.

nesses of many Latin American societies—divisions between ethnic groups, as in the Andean countries, or sharp class antipathies, as in Argentina—and the indiscipline of many political parties and even civilian governments, this claim may have some substance. On the other hand, the very involvement of the military in a directly political cause can break this cohesion and transfer political divisions in the nation at large into the heart of the armed forces themselves. This, in Brazil for example, has proved a real check on the timing and nature of military intervention. But it is quite apparent throughout much of Latin America that, in spite of or possibly even because of all the contacts with U.S. officers since the Second World War, the military remain a law unto themselves, unwilling to recognize the supremacy of civilian control.

The actual percentages of national budgets devoted to the armed services are often veiled. But the following figures,[5] given for 1940 and 1958 respectively, indicate the rough position for some countries: Argentina 18 and 25; Brazil 24 and 28; Colombia 16 and 17; Chile 26 and 22; Cuba 22 and 17; and Mexico 21 and 10. By comparison with European countries these figures are high, and it is interesting to note that the only one of these states to have achieved a sharp reduction in defense outlay over this period was Mexico, where an effectively one-party system gave unusual continuity and authority to the civil power. Given the quite frequent overstaffing of the officer corps in Latin American armies (in Paraguay, it has been said, there are as many generals as in the United States) and the defective and regressive taxation structures which are equally common, it is clear that the

---

[5] The 1940 estimate was published by the *Inter-American Statistical Yearbook* (New York: Macmillan; 1940), and the 1958 estimate was given in *Visión* magazine for December 5, 1958. Several factors combine to make accurate, comparable figures hard to obtain. In *Latin America and the Caribbean*, edited by Claudio Veliz (London: Anthony Blond; 1968), Alistair Hennessy quotes generally lower figures for defense spending as a percentage of national budgets in 1964: Argentina 15.6, Brazil 11.4, Colombia 15.3, Chile 11, and Mexico 9.6. For Cuba, alleged to have the best-equipped forces in Latin America, Hennessy records that such figures are not available.

officer class, in particular, has a favorable financial status. The biggest Latin American army is Brazil's, with approximately 200,000 men and taking three per cent of the gross national product.

In spite of their political weight, however, these forces are not generally large. In Colombia, where the Commander in Chief, General Rojas Pinilla, made himself dictator from 1953 to 1957, the troops under him—increased in numbers and given special benefits as they were—amounted to only about thirty thousand in a population of over ten million. To this extent it is obvious that military intervention in politics relies on a degree of acceptance by the civil population that would be surprising in other types of society. The special place of the armed forces means that their influence may extend in many directions. In Argentina, for example, they are in charge themselves of certain "strategic" industries, while in Brazil they provide some of the best technical education facilities.

The military efficiency of these forces has scarcely been tested in recent years, although Brazil, for example, sent an expeditionary force to Italy in the Second World War, contributed troops to the Organization of American States force in the Dominican Republic in 1965, and has taken part in UN peace-keeping forces in Suez and elsewhere; Colombia had a frigate and a battalion serving in Korea in 1950. On the whole, the military equipment is obsolete by NATO or Warsaw Pact standards, and it was not until 1967 that the United States offered supersonic F-5 aircraft for sale to Latin American governments—after it became known that Peru was ready to buy supersonic French Mirages. Weaponry easily gives rise to jealousy between services and countries. Perhaps the most ludicrous case involved a British aircraft carrier, bought and refurbished by Brazil at a cost of well over $200 million in 1956, and subsequently disputed between the air force and navy.

The United States, which had some 100,000 servicemen stationed in Latin America during the Second World War, has been the predominant supplier of arms and military advice ever since.

Military cooperation, originating in an Emergency Advisory Defense Committee which later became the Inter-American Defense Board, both based in the United States, has been continuous since the 1940's. It is normal for senior Latin American officers to have received some training in the United States and since Fidel Castro took power in Cuba, officers have been trained by U.S. experts in antiguerrilla warfare particularly. The United States, which has bilateral military agreements with many of her southern neighbors, is estimated to account in aid for only about five per cent of the total they spend on their armed forces. But the links with the Pentagon add to the prestige of the Latin American military at home.

The social composition of the officer class varies in different countries. It is generally agreed that the Brazilian army is more inclusive than the Argentine, and in most states the navies are usually more highborn, and conservative, than the armies. In Bolivia, after the 1952 revolution, one of the main objects was to create a new army in which landowning interests would have little place and where peasants and workers could be officers. The growth of professionalization has encouraged the growth of corporate political ideas which may conflict with the extraprofessional political influences always tugging at the military. In Brazil the "Sorbonne" 6 school in the army developed its own brand of anti-Communism, which reached fruition in the intervention of 1964, while in Peru the "Nasserist" officers, who believed in the necessity of national modernization, temporarily gave their support to President Belaúnde Terry's modernizing measures.

It was significant, however, that the issue on which the army ousted President Belaúnde in October 1968 was a nationalist and "Nasserist" one: it complained that he had accepted inadequate terms in establishing Peruvian ownership of oil fields belonging

⁶ The "Sorbonne" was a nickname given to a group of officers associated with the Escola Superior de Guerra (Higher War College, founded 1949) in Rio. They were hostile to the corruption in civil politics and believed Brazil had to have a pro-Western, hence pro-United States, foreign policy.

to the U.S. International Petroleum Company, and expropriated the fields soon after the coup. The purposes of military intervention have varied according to the political conditions of individual states, but in recent years there has been a trend away from personalist military leaders—like Perón in Argentina, Odría in Peru, Rojas Pinilla in Colombia, or Ibáñez in Chile—who tried to build up nonmilitary support on the basis of their ideas and character. This kind of situation was liable to have a shattering effect on the cohesion of the armed forces themselves, where officers became obliged to make political choices in their professional life. Lately, in Brazil and Argentina, the interventions of Marshal Castello Branco and General Carlos Onganía have been different in style: while both were keen to transform the political system and economy, they were not anxious to set up parties of which they were personal leaders. They were content to rest their strength entirely on the armed forces while employing civilian technicians, like economists, to make the alterations they wanted. This perhaps was a more mature and surgical approach to intervention, though it remained to be seen whether it entirely avoided the dangers of politicization of the army or produced any better answer to the old problem of intervention: at what point should the military withdraw from government?

It is rare for the military to support a government of the left with enthusiasm, if only because their own privileges and the links some officers have with landowners and others make them vulnerable to genuine reform programs. Nevertheless, they may tolerate reformist governments—as they did a Popular Front government in Chile in the forties and, for a brief period, the Goulart regime in Brazil in the sixties. In some countries the bulk of the officer corps has become obsessed with keeping certain parties out of power; phobias against APRA in Peru and the Peronists in Argentina (in spite of Peronism's military history) are cases in point.

Occasionally military intervention is directly related to the profit of the military as a caste. Sergeant Fulgencio Batista's NCO take-over in Cuba in the thirties had this kind of motivation, and some of the activities of Brazilian officers—notably the memorandum of eighty-two colonels to Vargas in 1954 when they were worried about their salary differentials—have a trade-union aspect. Where the military have state power it is normal for them to benefit in salary and status (the classic coup is followed by dismissals and promotions) and, significantly, they may also do well when a civilian government is weak and dependent on their approval.

The actual modes of intervention vary. One such is the classic barracks revolt (*cuartelazo*) which can take power in a small country like Ecuador or Paraguay with small warning and on trivial personal pretexts. In such cases rapid removal of the existing government, domination of the streets with a show of force, and a quick announcement of the success of the coup on a radio station will suffice. In larger countries, where garrisons may be separated by hundreds of miles and civil war is a real possibility if success is not attained simultaneously across a wide area, a longer build-up is necessary. Intricate planning is required, although the fact that the military has its own communications network makes it possible to carry on a great deal of this undetected by civilian authorities. At the same time, a period of civil disorder, financial chaos, or governmental instability is often necessary to provide a consensus among the military that action is required, as well as some degree of civic tolerance for such action. In contributing to such a period of excitement, talk of a possible coup is obviously no hindrance. Hence the interventions that brought Castello Branco and Onganía to power in Brazil and Argentina were successful partly because they were no surprise.

Subsequent removal of military regimes occurs in many ways. Obvious economic or political failure may cause them to collapse, strikes and student demonstrations may prove they have lost their power to coerce, and they may be replaced by further military action. In the case of Cuba, when Fidel Castro took over, Batista suffered from all these factors. All juntas suffer because their legitimacy is always open to question, and they are sometimes unstable because of service rivalries among the officers who compose them. There is something inherently temporary and insecure about a junta: a committee is unlikely to secure the loyalty of an army and people, or even stay loyal to itself, for long in Latin America.

Politics and economics

Due to a combination of rapid population growth, insufficient industrial base, and a dependence on a handful of exportable primary products which are vulnerable to swift, adverse turns in the terms of world trade, the economic problems of Latin America are both urgent and deep-rooted. They are magnified because islands of developed consumer societies tend to coexist inside large populations enduring poverty, and the latter may still be outside a money economy. In some states there is a clear regional distinction. Brazil contains both the sophisticated entrepreneurial city of São Paulo, and Indian tribes subsisting on hunting and fishing in the Amazon jungles; and an annual income per capita in the city of Rio de Janeiro which is ten times as great as that in the desolate northeastern state of Piauí. The dependence on primary products may be illustrated by the case of Bolivia, which in 1966 was still getting seventy per cent of its foreign exchange from the export of tin, most of which is smelted in Bootle and Hull, in England, rather than in the Andes. Even Brazil, with one of the most advanced industrial bases in Latin America, still gained over forty per cent of its export revenue from coffee in the same year.

It is scarcely surprising, therefore, that politics in these countries are affected by contrary impulses: on the one hand, there is a tremendous urge to industrialize, diversify, and improve material living standards; on the other hand, the groups associated with the primary export products and importers urge that nothing be done to upset existing trade. Hostility to the international purchasers of primary products, to the privileged domestic groups, and to the foreign companies and advisers who might provide the techniques necessary for domestic growth, ebbs and flows in waves of nationalization and recrimination. Attempts at immunizing industries or states from the effects of deteriorating terms of world trade—which had severe effects on many developing countries in the 1950's and 1960's—have taken such varied forms as the Cuban-Soviet sugar agreement of 1960, the International Coffee Agreement, and the Latin American Free Trade Area. Import substitution—the domestic production of goods formerly imported—has been seen by some as the magic solution to Latin America's economic ills. World wars, sudden collapses of primary exports, and devaluations have achieved some import substitution spontaneously, and it was a planned part of LAFTA's regional philosophy. But overall, such factors as restricted internal markets, a shortage of development funds, and technological backwardness have made for a disappointingly meager record of regional progress.

Although individual countries are exceptions, Latin America as a whole saw a slowdown in economic growth from the fifties to the mid-sixties. Because of a poor growth in exports and the worsening terms of trade the purchasing power of Latin American exports in terms of goods imported rose by only twenty-three per cent from 1950 to 1962.[7] In the decade after the Second World War important industrial complexes were set up in a climate of optimism; but the faltering performance in the subsequent decade coincided with a growing realization of the region's backwardness relative to the U.S. and European economies. Political weakness in Argentina and Brazil in the early sixties was closely interrelated with a declining growth rate per capita.

Peru, Mexico, and the Central American Common Market were among the exceptions to this undynamic pattern in the late fifties and early sixties. Peru's improving growth rate per

---

[7] This figure is taken from *A Latin American Common Market?*, by Sidney Dell (Oxford University Press; 1966), p. 10. Certain other economic statistics are taken from the same source.

capita in this period was accompanied by heavy investment from the United States, Japan, and Australia, and a dangerous dependence on a single boom industry, fishmeal. From practically nothing eleven years earlier this industry was providing a quarter of the nation's exports by value in 1966. The Central American Common Market, consisting of Guatemala, El Salvador, Honduras, Nicaragua, and Costa Rica (with a total population of some thirteen million in 1965), had succeeded in increasing gross national product per capita by almost a third (to U.S.$281) in the fifteen years up to 1965. Mexico, whose steady growth had many admirers at least until the Olympic riots in 1968, had almost a three per cent per capita growth rate from 1950 to 1965.

In spite of the strains involved in Cuba's wholesale alteration of trading, the Economic Commission for Latin America was crediting it with a high growth rate in the first years after the revolution. But for Latin America as a whole the attempts to persist in a high growth rate in spite of the poor performance of exports and the insufficient injections of outside finance and the inefficiency of local saving resulted in a crisis level of foreign debt. In the early sixties service payments on foreign debts were consuming a fifth of the exports of Argentina, Brazil, and Chile. It was, therefore, the first objective of the new regimes of Generals Onganía and Castello Branco and President Frei to "reschedule" those debts, or obtain new loans to cover them. Not only was the mortgaging of exports calamitous at this level, but the policies of the International Monetary Fund and the World Bank reflected the belief of many aid givers in the 1960's that monetary controls and curtailed growth were necessary to stabilize the finances of recipients.

A high rate of inflation has been an unsettling feature of certain economies in recent years, notably those of Argentina, Brazil, Chile, Colombia, Peru, and Uruguay. The astonishing height to which this could jump is illustrated by Argentina, where the average yearly increase in the cost of living was 66.9 per cent from 1955 to 1960. Two schools of economic thought—the monetarists who thought that monetary policy was at fault, and the structuralists who considered that the whole structure of the economy must be overhauled to bring inflation within more acceptable limits—have disputed both causes and remedies. Whereas the former have analyzed wage and cost pressures and deficit financing by governments, the latter have commented on the need for widespread social and industrial changes, the disparity of development between urban and rural sectors, and the low level of capital formation. The argument still continues, and the governments of high-inflation countries have only had partial successes in curbing the phenomenon; but while in Brazil inflation has accompanied both growth and stagnation, growth in Mexico has gone forward with very little inflation.

The psychological and political effects of inflation are far-reaching. Governments have been expected at the same time to curb inflation and maintain growth, to make sure that wages for which they are responsible neither contribute to the inflationary process nor lag behind the cost of living. But if inflation has regularly embarrassed governments in power, there is little evidence that opposition parties have any more satisfactory solutions.

Unemployment and underemployment are a common feature of Latin American economies, although statistics are unreliable. In many states at least half of the population is employed in agriculture, in which seasonal periods of idleness are usual. In the cities the problem takes several forms: in absolute terms there are not enough viable jobs for the population of working age, so that there is a great temptation to invent jobs of limited economic value, a general tendency to underemployment, and a countervailing attempt by individuals to work at more than one job in the same day. "Bogus" jobs, which may actually retard the development of an economy, include anything from an inflated bureaucracy to street hawkers and house servants.

The sorriest sight in some countries is of occupations in relatively advanced industries, which in Europe or North America would promote full employment and high wages, employing less than the optimum number of men at less than optimum wages.

In Brazil in 1961, for instance, only two of the firms producing trucks achieved an output equal to more than half the potential of one shift. This underutilization of capacity to make goods for which, by comparison with developed countries, there is an absolute shortage, is part of a vicious circle; a small home market due to limited purchasing power results in inefficient production and a high-cost finished product. This kind of experience is central to the frustrations of underdevelopment and it is not surprising that North American and European companies responsible for introducing sophisticated industries should bear the brunt of local disappointment. One disturbing trend in some countries where there is severe urban unemployment is that foreign companies seem more willing to start capital-intensive industries than labor-intensive ones. Advances in technology make such industries an increasing feature of developed economies, and the complexities of labor legislation in Latin America can dissuade outsiders from introducing labor-intensive processes under their own management. Employment problems in the cities are aggravated by two overriding pressures: first, the Latin American population is growing at a rate of nearly three per cent a year (and faster in poorer countries like those of the Central American Common Market than in richer ones like Argentina); and second, the large urban centers, due to internal migration and better health services, are growing even more rapidly.

The urge to industrialize and substitute imports, combined with the examples of the European Economic Community and Free Trade Area, have inspired in Latin America several attempts to achieve economic growth by the establishment of larger, integrated markets. Political solidarity has played a part but the objectives have been mainly economic. The two chief vehicles for this movement have been the Central American Common Market of five states which signed a treaty in 1958 providing for a free-trade area after ten years, and the Latin American Free Trade Area, now with eleven member countries, which was founded by the Treaty of Montevideo in 1960. Although the Central American Common Market has been disappointing in the rate at which it has established new heavy industries, its success in light industry and trade liberalization has been considerable. LAFTA, on the other hand, although it managed to increase trade between member countries from six per cent of their total trade in 1961 to eleven per cent in 1965, has been felt to have virtually no effect on local growth rates. The rapid progress achieved in this period was largely confined to the trading of agricultural goods, countries were highly defensive about their protected industries, and the complex system of negotiation failed to induce urgency.

In particular, the Treaty of Montevideo was unsuccessful in promoting two critical aspects of growth: the establishment of new industries that need a multinational market to be viable, and the trading of new products that had not traditionally appeared in intra-LAFTA trade. Huge variations in tariffs, lack of regional financial and communications services, and disparate degrees of interest among member countries were extra hazards in the early sixties.

By the late sixties two different phenomena were observable: a theoretical commitment to integration by national leaders was universal, and had been emphasized by the Punta del Este meeting of Presidents in 1967; but disappointment with the actual progress of LAFTA was leading to more emphasis being placed on two subgroups—the Andean group of Chile, Bolivia, Peru, Ecuador, Colombia, and Venezuela, and the Plata Basin group of Bolivia also, Paraguay, Uruguay, Brazil, and Argentina. There was no guarantee that these groups would make rapid progress either.

Behind the politics of Latin America rests a concern as basic as the need for a job and objects to spend one's money on. This is food. It would be wrong to suggest that millions face famine in the way they may in the Indian subcontinent, although the diet of some groups—such as the Indian peasantry of the Andean plateau—may be very poor in content, and drought areas in northeast Brazil can know hunger. The problems in Latin America are nevertheless serious, principally ones of diet, inefficient distribution, and a growth in production that scarcely outstrips population increase. The political effects show up in varying ways, from the embarrassment of meatless days in Argentina under the Peróns and after, in a country where a high consumption of cheap beef is a tradition, to the drain of food imports on Chile's balance of payments in the 1960's, when agricultural experts are certain that better use of resources could make the country a net exporter. In a situation like Chile's, agrarian reform becomes an issue for economic as well as social reasons.

Over Latin America as a whole, Food and Agriculture Organization statistics show that agricultural production per capita was ominously stable from 1952 to 1965. In Argentina and Uruguay, two traditional exporters that had fallen behind in agricultural technique, the figures showed a fall in output per capita between the early fifties and 1965. In Cuba the fall in the same period amounted to over a quarter.[8] Even countries where output had risen, like Brazil, still suffered problems of shortages in the cities due to poor distribution. Mexico is one Latin American country that has achieved steady agricultural growth in recent years, and it has been in the forefront in the adoption of new, heavy-yield grain varieties.

Politics and sociology

Uniting the politics and economics of Latin America is a complex sociology embracing the heirs to quite distinct civilizations —European, indigenous Indian, and African. In certain areas the strains involved in this fusion of peoples and cultures are not yet worked out. In the Andean countries, for instance, when

[8] See *The State of Food and Agriculture 1968*, FAO, Rome, Annex Table 2B, per capita food production. Comparison of this report with its 1967 predecessor shows that figures on this table are still being revised, even for the early fifties, and they should therefore be used cautiously. The Cuban fall has worsened from a fifth (1967 report) to over a quarter (1968).

Indian communities organize invasions of big estates, they are in some sense avenging their post-Conquest subservience to a European system of estates which incorporates their communal lands. Simultaneously the process of acculturation goes on as Indians come down from the sierra to Lima, cut off their pigtails, and speak of themselves as no longer Indian. On the other side of South America, in Brazil, the population of the *favelas*, the shanty towns of Rio de Janeiro, is overwhelmingly Negro. Although Brazil is not nearly so color-conscious as the United States, it is inevitable that Negroes at some point will begin an active struggle against a state of affairs in which most of them are underprivileged.

The most impressive single trend in Latin American society now is the rate at which it is becoming urbanized. São Paulo proudly proclaims that it grows ever bigger, and by December 1967 it had over seven million people living in its metropolitan area. But the same kind of explosion is occurring in much smaller towns all over the continent. Whereas in 1950 only Argentina and Chile had more urban inhabitants than rural, this is rapidly becoming true of Peru, Colombia, and Brazil also. The reasons are not far to seek: the disparity between urban and rural living standards makes migration to the cities a popular alternative to revolution or destitution. A city seems to be somewhere where anyone can make a fortune, and represents social opportunity to those in the countryside.

Inevitably this migration adds to the demographic pressures on the cities; in spite of Pope Paul's ruling on contraception in 1968, birth control, sometimes encouraged by radical priests, is a growing trend in Latin American cities; but in the first generation ill-educated arrivals from the land tend to have large families.

Though the cities may have a settled social structure, they also have built-in tensions. For the arrivals from the land there may be severe disappointments: life on the margins of the cities, with poor housing and the struggle to earn enough money to live, is not inspiring. Factory workers in these cities form a defensive aristocracy of labor. They are in a privileged position compared with the others who are scrambling to make a living in service or marginal occupations, and they know it. Like their employers they may look for support to the state, and they share the same need for protection from the industrial competition of more advanced economies.

All these fears and frictions, and the downright poverty of the urban lower classes, make fruitful material for a politician who understands the complex of demands: in the forties both Perón and Vargas cultivated these fields, and in Brazil the experience of Goulart and Leonel Brizola in the early sixties showed how combustible they could still be. But it would be wrong to imagine that politicians have it all to themselves. Traits of fatalism, and cynicism about politicians, may reduce their impact and much of the passion may be exhausted in religion. It is noticeable in Brazil, for example, that religious sects—Protestant, spiritualist, and voodoo—thrive among the urban lower classes.

But if the lower social groups in the cities are often unhappy, the same is true of the middle sectors. Though they may not be well defined socially, they tend to associate themselves with the professional classes—the doctors and lawyers—and tend to have links with the army officers, the men of standing in the country towns, and the accountants and functionaries of the big rural estates. Such middle groups are easily frightened, and may be buffeted about by high rents and the pressures of inflation. Only in certain places, perhaps São Paulo or Mexico City, are they confident enough to commit themselves outright to free-enterprise capitalism and to adopt the liberal competitive ethic. The older values of these groups, deriving from the army and the liberal professions, and behind them the rural estates, were essentially undynamic, and it is understandable that, in Brazil, they should be attracted by the leadership of a Carlos Lacerda, who offers them protection from lower-class pressures. It is from among the children of such groups that the revolutionary students in the universities come and it is among them that Christian Democracy attempts to win its converts. The essential promise of the Christian Democrats is that they can offer security to all classes by incorporating depressed groups on the margins of literacy, of cities, or of a modern economy into the system. In several countries the middle sectors have a schizoid relation with the military: they see them as the last bastion of their security and at the same time they are embarrassed by them in government and provide their leading opponents.

With houses in the big cities and large estates in the countryside, the still-powerful landed oligarchs are men of influence in both areas, despite the growth of industry. In Latin America as a whole it has been estimated that two per cent of the population owns over half its wealth, largely accounted for by rural landownership. Even in Chile, a country with substantial middle sectors and a relatively advanced industrial establishment, the power of landed wealth is still very great. The harder a Latin American government tries to diversify its economy and industrialize, the more, in the short term, is it likely to depend on its primary products. Even in Fidel Castro's Cuba and Perón's Argentina an emphasis on industrialization had to be followed by a recognition that agriculture was the immediate basis of the economy, and the source of capital funds for other developments. Beneath the landowners the rural social system varies, containing both highly dependent peasants, insecure farmers of tiny uneconomic patches, and a whole gamut of rural debtors and creditors.

In this area of Latin American society, still statistically the greatest sector, land reform is an issue, and leftists who take their inspiration from Havana and Che Guevara have made it the basis for guerrilla movements. Although the Alliance for Progress is committed to fostering agrarian reform, the phrase is a marvelous catch-all that may be interpreted in many ways. Some countries, like Paraguay, think it is enough to settle landless peasants on untilled land. Others, like Brazil, may permit peasants to take over estates that have gone bankrupt and in the meantime spend years on a massive land survey which postpones the political decisions involved. Even the handful of countries that have carried out "genuine" land reforms may surprise observers: in Cuba the cooperatives became effectively state-collective farms in which the peasants had little more say than in the days of the old private estates, while in Mexico, where the land had been divided among the peasants, increased production has been explained recently by the covert amalgamation and commercialization of the farms.

The problems of instituting land reform, even if a government has the ability to stand up to the oligarchs involved, are fiendishly difficult. The first decision must be whether to offer compensation or whether to expropriate. If a government offers considerable compensation, it will find itself with an expensive commitment and no structural change in the position of the wealthiest classes—though their wealth may have been transferred from the land to the cities—while if there is to be no compensation, there may be no logical stopping point, as the Cuban Revolution found, on the road to complete expropriation of the economy. Then, related to this, a government must decide whether to encourage, countenance, or prohibit peasant invasions of the estates. Such invasions have a long history in Latin America, the recurrent product of resentments against particular landlords or the desperation of the peasants. In Mexico, Bolivia, and Cuba spontaneous peasant invasions and take-overs at a time of general excitement helped to ensure the reality of agrarian reform, while the Chilean Christian Democrats specifically stated in their land-reform legislation that invaders and squatters could not benefit from it. There is obviously every difference between a reform largely effected by the political pressure of the peasants themselves and one organized from the top down to suit the political and economic convenience of the government. The land reform schemes engendered by the Alliance for Progress were all in fact of the second type.

Further problems of land reform concern the measures necessary to increase production of food and other commodities and the best method of management of "reformed" farms. By no means the least possibility is that surplus farm production may fall, simply because the peasants feel entitled to feed themselves better. One of the main fallacies of the wave of thinking characterized by the Alliance for Progress was to imagine that a social revolution in the countryside could be achieved without revolutionary methods, simply through the work of a smattering of politically neutral technicians.

If the path of the agrarian reform is hard, it is not necessarily easier for an agrarian guerrilla. In the decade following the success of the rebel army in Cuba there have been attempts in most of the Latin American countries to imitate it. In some, such as Argentina and Brazil, the efforts were trivial or ludicrous. In others, like Venezuela, Guatemala, and Colombia, they became an enduring feature of the polity, though by 1968 only Guatemala seemed to hold out any hope of triumph. In Bolivia, in 1967, the elimination of the band led by Che Guevara damaged the morale of would-be guerrillas throughout the hemisphere. Local factors—personalities, organizational and ideological jealousies—hurt the guerrilla movements, and their "constitutional" opponents were increasingly well prepared to meet them.

Moreover, the actual rural sociology, as Che Guevara came to recognize, was not entirely favorable for Castroite guerrillas. In many places the peasant psychology was *petit bourgeois:* a peasant was willing to fight for an agrarian reform only if this meant he and his family had a larger acreage to till. It was up to the guerrilla leadership, and the momentum of ideas in the guerrilla band, to attract peasant soldiers for a wider cause and away from concern for personal property. Therefore, an actual distribution of lands to landless peasants—as happened in Venezuela, for instance, where 66,000 peasant families got lands between 1960 and 1964—could cut at the roots of this potential ideological metamorphosis.

Another difficulty for the guerrillas was the frequent inability of rural people to distinguish between ideological guerrillas and bandits. Given the long history of banditry in Latin America, where laws have not been enforced in the countryside and land hunger and injustice have caused men to take to theft and brigandage, this was understandable. Romance and an aura of the poor versus the rich are essential to this tradition of banditry, as is shown, for instance, by the tales about Lampião, a twentieth-century bandit in northeast Brazil; and men joined Castro in the Sierra Maestra for adventure and a license to rob. Hence peasants would feel ambivalent about the ideological guerrillas. While they might sympathize with them, they might also fear them.

External restraints on political behavior in Latin America

Though Latin America sometimes looks isolated from the outside, and one may hear archaic notions of Manchester liberalism or feudalistic patronage from her politicians, the politics of the region operate under several external restraints. The most obvious, where countries are dependent on a handful of export products, may be economic. In the second half of the 1950's, for instance, the problems of Brazil's politicians were compounded because the world supply of coffee, which had been unprepared for the postwar resurgence of demand, once more exceeded it and prices fell. In 1968, when the Chilean government of President Frei was severely embarrassed at home, a sharp drop in the price of copper on the London Metal Exchange added to its afflictions.

More generally, Latin America is increasingly open to the ideas of the rest of the world thanks to the spread of television, transistor radios, and improving literacy rates. Such awareness may result in anything from university student riots in Rio de Janeiro and Mexico City in 1968, partly inspired by the student unrest in Europe and North America, to a more subtle awareness of the need to emphasize technology in Latin educational systems. But two external influences deserve closer inspection: the United States of America and the Roman Catholic Church.

United States policy and attitudes to Latin America have undergone several changes since the enunciation of the Monroe

Doctrine in 1823, from paternalism through the annexation of half of Mexico in the war of 1848 and President Franklin Roosevelt's Good Neighbor policy in the 1930's and the "partnership" envisaged by President Kennedy's "Alliance for Progress." If official U.S. attitudes are a strange amalgam of idealism, contempt, frustration, and defensive self-interest, the Latin Americans have an equal diversity of views about the United States. Its apparent materialism is both rejected and envied, its power alternately resented and sought.

The power relation between the United States and Latin America is one of enormous disproportion. Though this has become more evident since the First World War, when the United States became a major world power, it has been a fact since the early nineteenth century, when the Spanish Empire fractured into multiple parts, each lacking that remarkably dynamic material culture and political continuity which consolidated the geographical vastness to the north. The position by the 1960's was such that Brazil, the biggest Latin American state in population (some eighty million) and in area larger than the United States minus Alaska, had a total income only roughly the same as Australia and New Zealand combined; while Argentina, which in 1930 had been wealthier than Canada or Australia and which in 1950 had had a higher per capita income than France, had been far outdistanced by these.

In the 1960's it was clearer than before that the strength of Latin America as a whole, in its relations with the United States, lay mainly in its weakness. Whereas U.S. corporations, with a choice of investment opportunities, would almost always prefer to put money into Western Europe, Canada, or Australia, the U.S. government after the Cuban Revolution decided that it was strategically essential to do more south of the Rio Grande. Although U.S. private investment in Latin America was worth about $10 billion in the mid-sixties, and was not increasing rapidly, a tenth of this sum was going south from the United States annually under Alliance for Progress programs (though this was less than five per cent of contemporary U.S. spending in Vietnam). At the same time the United States began to encourage the Latin American drive for economic integration and political cooperation, recognizing that it was less likely to be a threat than a prospect of escape from economic and political stagnation.

Formally the United States is linked to Latin American nations by various bilateral treaties and in the Organization of American States, a weak institution which was nevertheless recognized by the United Nations when the latter was founded. The OAS, by the Rio Treaty of 1947, has certain military characteristics, and it was certainly regarded by the United States in the height of the Cold War as assisting in the quarantine of the Western Hemisphere. But it is doubtful how much military weight it could be made to bear now. After the U.S. intervention in Santo Domingo in 1965, to which Chile and Mexico were opposed, efforts to create a standing OAS "peacekeeping" force were encouraged by the United States and Brazil. But they came to nought, and President Johnson, who did his best for Alliance for Progress funds in Congress and was sufficiently aware of the importance of Latin America to want to confer with Latin American Presidents in 1967 and with Central American ones in 1968, had little respect for the OAS.

Within the last decade Western Europe, Russia, Japan, and, at least where revolutionaries are concerned, China too, have all given increasing aid and showed more interest in the region. But for Latin American governments the U.S. relationship is still the most important. Latin American opposition forces, particularly of the left, often blame the United States for the establishment or survival of unpopular regimes. Yet apart from a few familiar cases, like the Central Intelligence Agency's interventions in Guatemala in 1954 and Cuba in 1961, or the Marines in the Dominican Republic in 1965, the evidence suggests that the influence of the United States does not match her strength.

The relationship between the United States and the Latin

American countries is infinitely subtle. Where governments support the United States, it is only so far as is justified by their own interests, and the United States cannot compel them—unless they are exceptionally weak—to take decisions they resent. This becomes clear in cases of both pro- and anti-North Americanism. The pro-U.S. orientation of Brazil after May 1964 was adopted for internal political reasons, but it did not mean, as Washington would probably have liked, that the military regime would go further than it wanted in presenting a façade of democracy. The military coup in Peru in October 1968 was partly provoked by the fact that the pro-U.S. President, Belaúnde Terry, seemed to be offering too good a price for U.S. oil fields. U.S. policy is something violently counter-productive, as in Argentina in 1946, when the U.S. "blue book" on the Nazi inclinations of the military regime there proved an asset to General Perón.

More often, the U.S. practice of attempting to maintain good relations with Latin regimes of all types falls foul of their successors. In Brazil, in 1964, Ambassador Lincoln Gordon, who had exerted himself to patch up affairs with the awkward Goulart administration, subsequently found himself singing the praises of the military dictatorship which replaced it. Such a rapid adjustment inevitably tended to damage U.S. standing all round. Perhaps the worst case of this sort, in its results for the United States, was in Cuba where, after blowing hot and cold over the Batista regime for years, the Eisenhower government cut off arms supplies to the dictator within a year of his fall. The belated decision undoubtedly helped Fidel Castro's rebels, yet it was hardly sufficient to mollify them. A confusing factor, for Latin Americans, is the multiform character of the U.S. presence in their countries. Among the distinct groups at work in most is the embassy, representing the State Department, the military mission, representing the Pentagon, the employees of private U.S. firms, the aid men of various sorts, and the Peace Corps; it would be a travesty to suggest that the influence of all these points in the same direction, although there is evidence that seemingly objective U.S. technicians attached to ministries may work in a coordinated way for a U.S. policy.

The influence of the Roman Catholic Church, in a region in which more than 200,000,000 people may be described as its followers, is as profound as it is sometimes elusive. No politician, not even a Fidel Castro, can be unaware of it, and those who do battle with it, like Juan Perón, may find that it is they who suffer. Traditions concerning the Church vary from one country to another. But two factors stand out over Latin America as a whole at present: significant sectors of the Church are now anxious for social change, and its own character is changing in response to demographic and other pressures. In the past, in spite of drastic outbursts of anticlericalism and secularizations of Church property, the Church in most of Latin America has been generally associated with the rural oligarchy and the social status quo. There have always been exceptions, of course, since the time Bartolomé de las Casas challenged the Conquistadores themselves in order to protect the Indians. But although Rome itself had begun to show an interest in social questions, and individuals like Jacques Maritain excited some Catholic intellectuals in Latin America in the 1930's, the Church there as a whole was a byword for social conservatism until the 1950's.

However, in that decade, with the self-discovery of the Third World and economists analyzing the ills of underdevelopment, the younger and more conscientious churchmen in Latin America began to preach the need for radical social changes. Active in this new movement were substantial elements in the Chilean and Colombian churches and outstanding individuals like Dom Helder Camara, at that time Archbishop of Rio de Janeiro. Of great significance in this context was the Papacy of John XXIII and his farsighted social encyclicals—*Mater et Magistra* and *Pacem in Terris*. This ideological transformation has continued in the 1960's and has affected politicians and the general public way beyond the ranks of the Christian Democrats; in Colombia,

Father Camilo Torres chose to throw in his lot with guerrilla revolutionaries and became a martyr.

Pope Paul, in the course of his pilgrimage to Colombia in 1968, made clear his support for sweeping social change in Latin America. A sign of the growing radicalism of the Church in Latin America was a degree of public questioning of his encyclical on birth control that would have been inconceivable fifteen years before.

Changes occurring in the organization of the Church may prove equally important. At present there is about one priest to every 5,700 inhabitants of Latin America (in Honduras the ratio is nearly one to 16,000), and the manpower situation is worsening rapidly as the population expands. Over the last fifteen years the number of priests has increased by about twelve thousand while the population has risen by some fifty million. In certain countries, of which Brazil is one, the Church is already extremely dependent on foreign-born priests. In order to meet this situation the Church is adopting new media of communication with the faithful—radio, television, and so on—and placing more emphasis on the role of the laity. Both of these developments may have far-reaching effects.

In Brazil, for example, the Church-sponsored Movimento de Educação de Bases has been using radio to conduct literacy campaigns in the rural areas, while the growth of Catholic Action —Catholic worker, student, and family groups—in nearly all the countries has entailed a reassertion of Catholic ideals at all levels of the community. The latter bodies do not, of course, necessarily all point in the same political direction. Whereas in Brazil in 1964 Catholic women's groups and students were among those campaigning to get rid of the Goulart government, in Chile in 1967 Christian Democratic and Catholic students were advocating political cooperation with the Communist Party. Throughout Latin America the Church still has a powerful place in the educational system, controlling many of the best schools and universities, and able to propagate its version of social reconciliation to a large section of the young elite.

Bureaucratic and other restraints on political behavior

Before leaving the subject of restraints on politicians it would be worthwhile to examine some of the internal restraints under which they work. It is often a matter of surprise that in countries where change of government by coup d'état is the norm, there is seldom much bloodshed. Deposed presidents are rarely shot; they usually go into exile, in many cases after a stay in a foreign embassy that gives them asylum in their own country. There are several reasons for these conventions. The first is that where the armed forces are united in making a coup d'état, opposition usually seems fruitless. This obviously gives the military an ultimate advantage in all dealings with a civilian president. Where the coup d'état is directed against a military president or junta, as happened at the fall of Juan Perón, there may be a longer period of doubt before it becomes clear which side possesses the larger share of military and public support. But even then the casualties are rarely heavy and the defeated are not given to desperate last stands. This is because it is repugnant to comrades in a professional army to decimate each other when the "sides" they belong to may be quite arbitrary, the result of calculations by superior officers, and the issue at stake is not some transcendent issue of ideology but merely which clique of men shall enjoy the perquisites of political power.

Where resistance is neither prolonged nor painful, a retreat into exile by the defeated leaders serves valuable purposes: for the victors it saves them the embarrassment of a trial, a martyrdom, or a living center of resistance within their own territory, and for the vanquished it means a period of recuperation without making compromises of any sort with the new regime. In fact, the exile has a long and respectable history in Latin America, and certain cities in recent years, like Montevideo and Santiago, have been almost universities for exiles where people from different countries have exchanged ideas and matured their political concepts.

However, for the supporters of a defeated regime who stay behind, there may be many penalties. The Brazilian military regime after 1964 withdrew the political rights for ten years of hundreds of political opponents. Some were sent to prison and then gradually released. More serious can be the wholesale transfer of patronage, ranging from municipal appointments to university professorships, which may suddenly threaten thousands of people with poverty. Press and political opposition may be curtailed. In Mexico recently controls over newsprint have discouraged the press from pursuing an opposition line, and in Brazil, after the 1964 revolution, fear of outright closure caused a marked reduction in opposition from *Ultima Hora,* a stalwart supporter of the overthrown regime. By 1969 all Brazilian papers were reduced to self-censorship after the Costa e Silva government had introduced a most restrictive press law. Latin American governments also make use of emergency or "state of siege" powers to curb opposition; such powers may make it easier for police to make arrests and prohibit political meetings. Where opposition is penalized in these ways, of course, the mere growth of an effective public opposition becomes a sign of the weakening of an existing regime.

No sketch of the environment in which Latin American politicians work would be complete without consideration of the bureaucracy, the professional servants of government. On their shoulders lies the burden of translating the grandiose visions, the short cuts to development, into reality. When a regime falls, it is among them that there may be the most drastic changes. Historically, in most of Latin America, their roots go back to those patient local officials who laboriously transcribed the minutiae of colonial administration for the benefit of Spain's Council of the Indies, and a preoccupation with paper documents and clerical details remains a weakness among many civil servants. Their offices are notoriously used in some countries as ways of adding to employment, or repaying political supporters, without much correlation between the type of task that needs doing—if it needs doing at all—and the candidate for the post.

In Uruguay, where the unusual system of conciliar government gave partisans of both the Blancos and the Colorados access to patronage, and state intervention in the economy and social services had a long tradition, overstaffing had become a national scandal by the mid-sixties and was blamed as one cause of inflation. Throughout the region the European view of civil servants—in which they are ideally nonpartisan, professional servants of the country, irrespective of government in power—is far from being paramount. But this is not to say that Latin American bureaucrats, in the widest sense, are all inefficient. Argentina, for example, was the first country in the world whose police fingerprinted the entire population. Though some might regard this as sinister in a country with a history of authoritarianism, it meant, for example, that when doubts arose over the identity of the man believed to have been Che Guevara, killed in Bolivia in 1967, the Argentine police could give an objective test.

Taking one country, Brazil, it is possible to see both the faults and the triumphs of administration in underdeveloped Latin America. If one arrives by sea at a port, for instance, one is met by complicated customs formalities and unloading procedures involving much paper and several officials. No matter, one hires a *despachante*, who circumnavigates the lot. Such an arrangement provides plenty of work for both officials and *despachantes*, but a visitor may be forgiven for thinking that this was the object of the regulations rather than the speedy flow of goods and passengers. At another extreme lie the operations of the Brazilian Coffee Institute, which is staffed by highly qualified personnel, responsible for framing and operating a highly complex system of taxes and subsidies to growers of different qualities and costs, and capable of negotiating the first successful world commodity agreement with powerful consuming countries and rival producers. Brazilian administrators run the gamut from the hopelessly inefficient with sinecures, appointed by patronage, to the diplomats only allowed to enter the foreign service after stiff exams (though until recently a dark skin or Jewish ancestry added crucial minus marks). Because of the ingrained cronyism of Brazilian politics, rationalization of the bureaucracy—though one of the professed aims of the 1964 military government—is difficult: instead of outright abolition of an institution composed of the appointees of a previous regime, the all-too-frequent practice is to set up a new one having only slightly different functions.

Efforts to improve the quality of the civil servants are now being made in many countries, as part of the attack on problems of infrastructure to which the Alliance for Progress has given support. Among early gains to be expected are increased collection of taxable revenue, removal of bureaucratic obstacles to increased trade, and more accurate basic statistics. In time, this must have a beneficial effect. At present, of course, the inefficiency of public servants may be compounded by the inadequacy of communications: in Brazil there are said to be many towns living in a permanent state of illegality because the official gazette posted to them always arrives so late, while critical government decisions have been held up because of a shortage of telephone lines between Brasília and Rio de Janeiro. New types of technical experts are being introduced into Latin American administration at an accelerating rate—economists, sociologists, scientists and "planners" of all sorts—but, as in advanced industrial countries, it is not clear that they are being placed in the most desirable relationship with politicians and other administrators. There are dangers that such people may just become an extra factor making for confusion and bureaucratic infighting, and may be disillusioned themselves if politicians have not the will to implement their technical recommendations.

With the encouragement of the UN Economic Commission for Latin America and other bodies, central economic planning units have been established in most Latin American countries. Mexico, Chile, and Brazil are among those which have experimented with sophisticated economic policies and regional development programs. The relationship between politicians and planners varies, but it is generally true that it is tending to grow closer and more productive with time. One of the curiosities of

Latin America is the harmony that has sprung up in places like Brazil and Argentina between military governments and economic planners: the former welcome the systematic, apparently politically neutral remedies of the latter, while the latter feel it may be possible to impose policies by force which would fall foul of the prejudices or constituents of civilian politicians.

Political figures in Latin America

The politicians of Latin America are a varied and colorful breed —some honest, some corrupt, some brave, some cowardly, some far-sighted and others obtuse. There is every difference between "Papa Doc" Duvalier, the dictator of Haiti who has even turned voodoo into a weapon of terror, and former President Belaúnde Terry of Peru, who is alleged to have defied the dictator General Odría by marching through Lima draped in a Peruvian flag; between Rómulo Betancourt of Venezuela, who was so devoted to the constitutionalism of liberal democracy that he evolved a doctrine by which Venezuela would not recognize unconstitutional regimes in other countries, and Getúlio Vargas of Brazil, whose extraordinarily pliant philosophy allowed him, as a dictator with Fascist leanings, to declare war on Mussolini and later run for election as a democratic presidential candidate. All these, and many more, deserve analysis, and the figures discussed in this book are inevitably personal choices. Together they are the means to many insights into the issues perturbing Latin America, into the way politics is conducted, as well as being of great interest in their own right as six key figures of recent history.

Che Guevara, famous all over the world since his death in 1967, had for some years been the living symbol of the Cuban Revolution's hemispheric, if not worldwide, implications. In Latin America his career has for years been followed because of the Cuban guerrillas' success in defeating a regular army, because the trials of building a new form of Communist state in an underdeveloped Latin country were of interest to all, because of his concern with ethical issues, and because he was prepared to commit his own life to the revolutionary cause elsewhere. His own frank and humorous personality added to his appeal. But, though he was the idol of "revolutionary" students and handfuls of alienated bourgeoisie or militant peasants, the curiosity and sympathy which millions felt for him did not necessarily mean a willingness to adopt his methods. It has yet to be seen whether his death will be the liberating myth that Fidel Castro has hoped, or whether it will prove a definitive setback for the armed way of revolution. But his significance is unquestionable. He is the representative *par excellence* of the view that conditions in Latin America are so inhuman, so much dependent on the interests of United States imperialism, that only warfare and bloodshed offer hope of improvement.

President Frei of Chile represents an almost polar opposite. He stands for the assertion that democracy, of the European or United States variety, is the right path for the underdeveloped countries of Latin America. Whereas Che rejected the traditional elements like the Church, the middle class, and the existing division of property, Frei, through Christian Democracy, wishes them to achieve a reformation. In spite of the Yankee rhetoric of the Alliance for Progress, Frei's line on the role of democracy is still a qualified view among rulers in the region, and may long remain so. His catch-phrase about a "revolution in liberty" has inspired continual debate: if there is to be a revolution, can there be liberty, or if there is to be liberty, could there possibly be a revolution? Most observers would say the President has erred more on the side of liberty than of revolution. But Christian Democracy is an important doctrine, unfinished, and liable to evolve in continuing response to Latin American conditions. Although now wedded to parliamentary forms of democracy, the Chilean variety has Fascist and conservative influences embedded in its roots and has flirted with both Socialists and Communists; it is conceivable that in extreme circumstances Christian Democracy might short-circuit the democracy and draw on regional and clerical traditions of authoritarianism to impose its revolutionary changes. (Dr. Rafael Caldera, the new President of Venezuela, has come to terms with the followers of the ex-dictator Pérez Jiménez to build a congressional majority.)

President Stroessner of Paraguay offers a further contrast. He symbolizes the continuation of the dictatorial tradition in modern Latin America, and the military propensity for taking over civil power. His fascination, and his significance, lie in his survival as an apparently traditional military ruler in a country with a harsh capacity for dismissing strongmen who fail to make the grade. Stroessner is, in fact, extremely sagacious in detecting his own interests—and maintaining them by manipulation of the army and the Colorado Party—and he is not totally oblivious to Paraguay's. He is not only an example of how an army man may come to power in a Latin American state, and of how once there he may prove hard to dislodge, but he represents that conservative attitude to Latin American problems which is still widespread in all sectors of society. He genuinely believes that stable government and the inculcation of patriotism and religion should be the main objectives of a ruler, and that zeal for immense material progress or social change is self-defeating and harmful.

The two Brazilians here, Juscelino Kubitschek and Carlos Lacerda, give some insight into the idiosyncratic politics of Latin America's largest nation, whose population will reach 100 million within a decade, and whose natural resources are as yet scarcely touched. They have been on opposite sides for most of their political lives, yet both have worked within a fragile political system, at once the target of military intervention from the center right and of attack from demagogic workers and radical forces of the left which are not necessarily bound by the constitution. Left and right do not perfectly reflect Brazilian politics, but whereas Lacerda frequently called for military intervention to counter the populist followers of Vargas, Kubitschek sought their votes and consistently maintained that the wilder ones could be tamed without recourse to the army.

The debate between them concerning the pace and possibilities of change in a developing country was of the utmost importance, and not only for Brazil. Although Kubitschek did not stand for a social revolution as such in his Presidency, his policy of radical progress in industrialization had wide implications; the battle over agrarian reform and the labor unrest under his successor but one, President Goulart, were in some respects a logical result of his policies. When the army deposed Goulart, it was an indication not only of the failure of the latter, but of the extent to which civilian control of the military under Presidents Kubitschek and Quadros had failed to become a reality. As for Lacerda and his supporters, their disillusionment with the military regime founded in 1964 might possibly mark the end of that yearning for army rule by the conservative middle sectors which so bedeviled Brazil's transitory experiment with democracy after 1945.

Finally, this book examines the heroine of Argentine nationalist populism, Evita Perón. Not only is her career a demonstration of the cross-currents that flavor mass politics in a relatively advanced Latin American country, but her work still stands. Though she died as long ago as 1952, her legend, interwoven with that of her husband, contributes to the enduring stalemate in Argentine politics. As long as the Peronists manage to get about thirty per cent of the vote in anything like a free election, and as long as other sectors of political life—especially the military—fear them above all, Argentina seems condemned to insecure civilian governments or army rule. In no other Latin American country since her death has a woman wielded so much political power. It was "Saint" Evita, the working girl, who enabled Argentina's burgeoning urban proletariat to identify its cause with the personable General Juan Perón. Though the paths of the military and the Peronists have become opposed since her death, this conjunction was of great importance while it lasted; a spirit of authoritarian nationalism, instilled under a dual personalist leadership, both gave the military a sense of mass support and the workers a sense of power and of integration into the life and affairs of the nation. In its way Che Guevara's efforts to maintain a revolutionary consciousness among postrevolutionary Cubans, by encouraging many of them to join militias and postulating eternal strife between the "free lands of the Americas" and Yankee imperialism, had a similar aim: to offer wider civilian groups a share in Latin America's glittering heritage of militarism in return for patriotic obedience.

Che Guevara

Death

The world took several days to believe the truth: that on October 9, 1967, Che Guevara, the legendary Argentine lieutenant of Fidel Castro in Cuba, had met his end after a small guerrilla engagement in southeast Bolivia. The unwillingness to believe that one myth, nurtured by his mysterious disappearance from Cuba two years before, could be so definitively killed by the Bolivian army—of all Latin American regular armies the one with the most consistent history of defeat—was reinforced by the rapid disposal of the body by the Bolivians. Roberto Guevara, the dead man's brother and a lawyer, was told on the 12th by the Bolivian Commander in Chief, General Alfredo Ovando Candia: "Sometimes one does not arrive in time. The Armed Forces have cremated his body." The whereabouts of the ashes were not disclosed. But enough outsiders had seen the body of the dead guerrilla when it was flown into Vallegrande by helicopter from La Higuera, near which Che had been captured, for his identity to be beyond doubt. At least one[1] of the foreign journalists who saw the body had seen him alive in Cuba and testified that, although thinner as a result of his jungle existence, the face with its black, wispy beard was unmistakably the same. His fingerprints were unofficially checked with those held in the Argentine records, and they tallied.

However, behind Bolivian equivocations over public display of the body, the prevention of contact between the press and soldiers who had actually taken part in the action near La Higuera, and the subsequent sealing off of the village from

[1] Richard Gott of the *Guardian*, October 11, 1967.

journalists, lay growing doubts about the official account that Che had died as a result of wounds received in battle. Careful reconstructions of the circumstances of his death[2] indicate that he had been captured with only a leg wound on October 8, when the guerrilla group of seventeen had been surrounded by the army in a narrow wooded canyon which leads into the Rio Grande. He had been trying to escape with a tin miner named Willy and, with a Peruvian guerrilla who was taken in the same engagement, they were kept overnight at La Higuera before being dispatched on the signed orders of General Ovando and President Barrientos. Che, who had been put in a schoolroom which was afterwards demolished, was shot first by Sergeant Mario Terán, and others also fired at him. The military medical report prepared by Dr. Moisés Abraham showed that Che had been killed at least twenty-four hours after capture and his body contained seven bullet wounds. These included mortal wounds in both lungs and a shot through the heart, as well as a massive contusion on the back which could have been caused by a rifle butt. Two Cuban exiles and CIA men, Eduardo Gonzales and Felix Ramos, were reportedly active in the period after his capture.

Che, of course, had written his own epitaph. In his letter to the executive of OSPAAAL (Organization of Solidarity of the Peoples of Asia, Africa, and Latin America) the previous April he had said: "Wherever death may surprise us, it will be welcome, provided that this, our battle cry, reach some receptive ear, that another hand stretch to take up weapons and that other men come forward to intone our funeral dirge with the staccato of machine guns and new cries of battle and victory."

Obituaries even in the bourgeois West were on the whole

---

[2] Among published reconstructions are those by Michele Ray in *Paris Match*, December 27, 1967, by Richard Gott in the *Guardian* of March 14, 1968, and by Fidel Castro in his introduction to Che's *Bolivian Diary* (Cape Lorrimer Edition, 1968), pp. 19–20. One of the first to report the discrepancy between the medical and military accounts of the time of death was Paul L. Montgomery, Latin American correspondent for *The New York Times* on October 12, 1967.

friendly. In Cuba, where national mourning was declared, Fidel Castro produced a long eulogistic oration in the Plaza de la Revolución on October 18. He praised Che's skill as a guerrilla, his industry, his devotion to revolutionary ideals, and his boundless faith in moral values. "We should say that he saw, with absolute clarity, moral resources as the fundamental lever in the construction of Communism in human society," he added. Cubans and Latin Americans in general should look on him as a model:

> No other man of our time has carried the spirit of internationalism to its highest possible level as Che did. . . . National flags, prejudices, chauvinism, and egoism had disappeared from his mind and heart. And he was ready to shed his generous blood spontaneously and immediately, on behalf of any people, for the cause of any people.

Cuba at once started "Plan Che," a project to bring the island's waste land into cultivation, and declared 1968 "The Year of the Heroic Guerrilla." In Moscow, where two hundred Latin American students demonstrated outside the U.S. Embassy, *Pravda* published a surprisingly generous obituary considering Soviet-Cuban differences. "Comrade Guevara died for the great cause of liberating the peoples from oppression and exploitation. He will remain in our memory as a man of great moral integrity and amazing selflessness," stated the Politburo, led by Kosygin and Brezhnev. In Bolivia itself, Régis Debray, the French Marxist philosopher on trial for alleged guerrilla activities, abruptly changed his plea to guilty and the harried remnant of the guerrilla group began its long trek to the Chilean frontier.

Origins, family, and early wandering

The man who was to exercise such a pull on the imagination of his contemporaries was born on the night of June 14, 1928, in Rosario, Argentina. His parents, whose marriage later fell apart, were Ernesto Lynch Guevara, a chunky, obstinate man of all trades of Irish-American and Argentine descent, and Celia de la Serna, a romantic woman of Spanish descent who was to take great delight in Che's adventurous life. Guevara Senior had a radical, libertarian outlook, and his family kept on the move in varying economic circumstances as he tried his hand at shipbuilding, maté-tea growing, farming, and real estate, before settling down as an architect and civil engineer. The young Ernesto had two brothers and two sisters, and the family moved from Misiones, in northern Argentina, to Buenos Aires, to Alta Gracia and Córdoba in the mountains, and then back to Buenos Aires.

On the whole, the Guevaras had a bourgeois standard of living and aspirations. At the age of two Che had his first asthma attack—the weakness was to dog him for the rest of his life—and it was partly on his account that they all moved to the healthy air of Alta Gracia. There he took up sports, swimming, golf, rugby, and shooting, initially perhaps for his health, but soon because he found he could excel as an athlete. There too he developed a wanderlust, cycling and motorcycling for hundreds of miles across Argentina in his early teens.

His health, ability, and sense of independence combined to give him a unique education. He did not attend primary school regularly, though his mother and brothers and sisters gave him lessons at home. He read widely as an adolescent—Baudelaire certainly and quite likely Marx. When, in the forties, he entered medical school in Buenos Aires, he did not attend classes regularly, partly because he disliked having "Justicialism," the official Peronist ideology, rammed down his throat. As a teen-ager he was a good mathematician, but it was probably idealism, kindled by the obvious sufferings of the Argentines he had seen on his travels, that attracted him to medicine. In addition, his own experience with asthma, and the sight of his paternal grandmother —ironically a U.S. citizen—dying from cancer, may have been personal factors in his choice.

He became interested in leprosy and tropical diseases (he attempted to manufacture an insecticide for sale in 1950), and it was to find out more about them that he and an old friend, Alberto Granados, set out on a prolonged tour of Latin America by motorcycle and on foot at the end of 1951. He mixed with peasants and left-wing students, looked at pre-Conquest remains and leper colonies; this trip gave his mind continental horizons. The pair reached Chile via Patagonia, then traveled to Peru, saw the Amazon at Iquitos, were expelled from Colombia because of their reputation for political activism, and after a collection by students, managed to get to Venezuela. "In Iquitos," Granados said afterwards, "we were football coaches and earned enough money for our plane fares. In Bogotá they deported us."

Granados stayed in Venezuela, and Guevara, traveling in a plane loaded with thoroughbred horses, spent a month in Miami. He had very little money, and it is tempting to think that this short stay may have given wings to his anti-Americanism. From Miami he went home. There his anti-Peronism and revolutionary impulses led him to take part in an abortive anti-Peronist conspiracy led by General Menéndez. At this time, it is said, both he and his father were working independently in anti-Peronist plots. His powers of concentration and industry were shown at their best when, in less than a year, he had succeeded in passing his medical exams in more than ten subjects. He graduated as a doctor in March 1953.

He never, however, practiced in Argentina. Whether he was actually expelled by the Peronist secret police or whether he disliked the prospect of working in a profession exposed to strong pressures from an alien regime when the whole of Latin America beckoned, is uncertain. In any case, after graduating he left Buenos Aires with the intention of joining Granados in Venezuela and working in the Cabo Blanco leper colony. One suspects that revolutionary politics, rather than medicine, were already his chief concern, for he passed from left movement to left movement, via Bolivia, Peru, Ecuador, Panama, and Costa Rica, before reaching Guatemala at the end of 1953.

At the time Guatemala was the most exciting place for a radical to be in the Americas. The country was poor—between 1925–9 and 1950–4 the per capita product had actually decreased by

19.2 per cent on average each decade—and its politics had been dominated by the extensive interests of the U.S. United Fruit Company and other foreign concessionaires for many years. From 1945 to 1951 President Juan José Arévalo had alarmed the U.S. State Department by redistributing wealth through social security and educational programs, by permitting legal Communist activity, and by squeezing the U.S. firms. Under his elected successor, Colonel Jacobo Arbenz, the process and the alarm went further, though it is doubtful whether he was the crypto-Communist of U.S. mythology. The high point of Arbenz's development program was an agrarian reform which distributed some 1.5 million acres within two years—some of it land belonging to United Fruit. Precisely what Guevara did in Guatemala in the six months before Arbenz was overthrown by the CIA-supported Colonel Castillo Armas is a little obscure. Differing accounts have it that he was either an inspector of the land reform program (for which he could have had no technical experience) or that he worked on allergies in an infirmary. His economic situation was precarious.

By his own account, he fled to Mexico a couple of months after Arbenz's fall. But it appears that he attempted to join a group willing to fight after the regular army had transferred its allegiance to Castillo Armas, and that he spent some time in the Argetine Embassy before making his escape. In Mexico City, he and a Guatemalan he had met on a train, Julio Roberto Cáceres Valle, scratched out a living as street photographers. They had no labor permits, so their situation was strictly illegal.

Naturally Che was once more attracted to revolutionary circles and in the summer of 1955, after an introduction from Raúl Castro, he was accepted as expedition doctor to the Cuban Revolution after a famous all-night discussion of world politics with Fidel. Fidel, who had been released from his imprisonment in Cuba after the failure of the assault on the Moncada barracks two years before, had now gathered his supporters in Mexico to prepare for the invasion of the island.

Che—his Argentine nickname was a generalized form of address equivalent to something like "Mac"—was an experienced man of twenty-seven when this fruitful meeting took place. He was a trained doctor, he had a good grasp of leftist politics in many Latin American countries, and he had witnessed the defeat of the Arbenz government. As a doctor's vocation tends to require idealism, so a professional awareness of the differences in health between the poor (such as the Andean Indians) and the rich who could afford physicians must have sharpened his realization that class divisions foster suffering. As a man who knew the left in various countries, he must have realized the common need for social revolutions and he must have learned from the left's failures.

Was he at this time a member of the Communist Party? In 1959 he said that he had never been a party member and, though Batista's forces had referred to him as an "Argentine Communist" when he had been in the Sierra, to all outward reckoning he could scarcely have been described as such—at least until the middle of 1961, when the ORI (Organizaciones Revolucionarias Integradas), the forerunner of the United Party of the Socialist Revolution, later renamed the Cuban Communist Party, was born. It is possible that Guevara was a Communist in 1955, but if so it is extremely doubtful that party allegiance restricted either his independence of mind or freedom of action. He must, of course, have known individual Communists well by then, but at that stage neither local Communist parties nor the Soviet Union nor Communist China had a bright image in Latin America. It seems more likely that he was an anti-American, anti-imperialist, Socialist revolutionary—versed in Marx and Lenin in all probability— but nothing more concrete. The Arbenz episode had discredited a traditional Communist popular-front tactic because it had resulted in a counterrevolution instead of a revolution. This taught Che two lessons: that a successful revolution cannot be achieved without the destruction of the regular army, and that the United States in the fifties was, in defense of its geopolitical and financial interests, indeed the enemy of any far-reaching Latin American revolution.

Doctor to the Granma *expedition*

Che was extremely lucky to have been chosen for the Cuban expedition: Fidel Castro was averse to collecting a ragtag army of diverse nationalities for his invasion. He wanted it to be a Cuban affair. Even Albert Bayo, a Cuban and onetime Spanish Republican general who gave the expedition's members weapon and tactical training on a ranch in Mexico, was left behind when the small vessel *Granma* sailed. The inner relationship between Che and Fidel may never be known in its entirety, between a towering, eloquent personality determined to be the leader of the Cuban Revolution and a man who believed in social revolution as the supreme good, to whom an individual was of no importance beside an idea, and whose romantic vision was supported by a firm grip on practical details. But Fidel trusted him at once and, as Che states in his book, he was put in charge of personnel under Bayo. "I had been linked to him [Fidel], from the outset, by a tie of romantic adventurous sympathy, and by the conviction that it would be worth dying on a foreign beach for such a pure ideal," he wrote.[3] Che was a star pupil of Bayo's academy, but the understanding was that in Cuba he would be the expedition's doctor.

The party was due to sail in March 1956. Mexican police, however, arrested Fidel, Che, and many of the other members, and precious time and money had to be spent on getting them out. Later Che, whose illegal activities in Mexico made him vulnerable anyway, said that he had suggested to Fidel that he be left behind; but the former would not hear of it. On November 25, after further scares with informers and police, eighty-three persons, including sailors, set off, ill-equipped with arms, in the *Granma*, for the coast of Cuba.

After seven hungry and seasick days on board, the party landed at a place named Belic, in eastern Cuba. It was a most

---

[3] Che Guevara: *Reminiscences of the Cuban Revolutionary War*, translated by Victoria Ortiz (Monthly Review Press: New York; George Allen & Unwin: London; 1968), p. 38.

inauspicious beginning, for the invasion occurred in daylight and
was observed by a coast guard cutter, and it happened a couple
of days after Frank País, Fidel's urban lieutenant, had organized,
in the city of Santiago, extremely successful riots which had
come close to capturing the Moncada barracks also. After three
days' marching through swampy country in which nearly all
the medical supplies were lost, the exhausted invaders were surprised by Batista's planes at Alegría de Pío. Most of them were
killed, and Che himself was wounded in the neck and chest. He
has recounted that in the moment of attack he faced a crucial
choice: he could carry either a medicine pack or a cartridge case,
but not both. He took the cartridges.

  With the group dispersed and demoralized, Che and four
others made a pledge to fight to the death. His ingenuity stood
out in these conditions: he even used the tiny pump of an anti-
asthma vaporizer for extracting badly needed water from little
puddles in the rocks, and he attempted, ineffectively, to mix
sweet and salt water for drinking purposes. Although the five,
who shortly became eight, were hungry and had no idea where
to meet other survivors, and though planes and army troops
were continuing to search the vicinity, Che discouraged them
from entering peasant houses in order that they should not be
seen.

  But his influence was not strong enough. On his own account,
they approached three houses and, after nine days of wandering
without much more food than crabs and sugar cane, their despair
and hunger were such that they knocked on a peasant's door at
Puercas Gordas. By pure good luck the peasant welcomed and
feasted them, and passed them on to contacts through whom they
were reunited with Fidel Castro in the Sierra Maestra. However,
Che's intuition that to call on an unknown peasant was wrong
proved fully justified. As a result of local gossip a sick comrade
who had been left behind was captured, along with nearly all
the guns and ammunition with which the guerrillas had incautiously parted. Two important guerrilla maxims—constant mistrust and the need to preserve one's weapons at all costs—were

thus borne in on him by early experience. When Che's group joined up with Fidel's a few days later, the rebel army amounted to fifteen—or twenty-one after a few more days, when some more stragglers appeared; but it was more than the twelve of legend.

It soon became apparent that Che was too valuable a man in too many directions to be regarded just as the expedition doctor. He was Fidel's indispensable aide, particularly responsible for developing the morale of the army. This was not an easy task, as Che explains in his *Reminiscences,* as individuals were constantly joining and leaving. Apart from Fidel, Raúl, and himself, few of the guerrillas had much in the way of education, or a clear understanding of what they were fighting for. Sierra peasants who joined them might think they were participating in some form of banditry, and urban recruits sent up by the July 26 Movement's helpers in the cities were hopelessly unprepared for the rigors of guerrilla life. Early in 1957 Fidel announced that the three crimes punishable by death were insubordination, desertion, and defeatism, and these were the enemies Che had to fight. Treachery threatened the guerrillas; on one occasion Fidel shared his blanket at night with a man armed to kill him. Desertion occurred continually, carrying with it the risk that a deserter might, voluntarily or involuntarily, give away rebel positions to the Cuban army and remove one of the precious guerrilla weapons. Fidel had to dismiss men who could not endure the privations.

But the area in which the guerrillas were operating, the Sierra Maestra, was difficult country for pursuit, and gradually, in small clashes, they built up confidence and experience. In an attack on a small barracks on January 17, they killed two and wounded five—Che threw a grenade—and in late May they succeeded in overrunning a well-defended seaside post at El Uvero. Che with a machine gun crew filled a gap in the semicircle of attackers. At the cost of six dead and nine wounded among the guerrillas, they wounded nineteen, killed fourteen, and took fourteen prisoners. After this battle Che, whose minimal medical equipment made it hard for him to offer much succor to the wounded, was left in charge of their withdrawal—his first independent guerrilla command. When he and Fidel were reunited in July, by which time the rebel army totaled about two hundred men, he was promoted to command of the Second Column, with the rank of major. His duties as doctor, for which he had already been given an assistant, were then transferred to another.

By this stage Che was a good shot and, apart from the agonies he suffered from asthma, physically well adapted to guerrilla life. The most hazardous period of the insurrection—in which, on several occasions, a handful of unconfident troops could easily have been annihilated—was past. Che's efforts at tooth pulling and doctoring among the peasant communities of the Sierra deepened his identification with a popular revolution. But it is most improbable that his ideological lectures to the troops consisted of advanced courses in Marxism-Leninism, even though he himself may have been increasingly convinced that a real social revolution could have no other anchor. The peasant soldiers were fighting for security of land tenure or a share of the landlords' property. Many of those who gave comfort to the rebels, like the Babún estate owners, did so to earn favors of a future government, or as a sort of protection payment in the meantime. In his ideological work among the rebels—which included teaching a man to read and answering all manner of questions—he concentrated on fostering an unprogrammed revolutionary consciousness and a will to win.

Che as guerrilla in Cuba

As commander of the Second Column, later named the Fourth, he entered on the period of seventeen months which was to make his guerrilla reputation. To start with, he had only seventy-five men, known as "the dispossessed peasants," he was in touch with Fidel about once a week by messenger, and he was to operate to the east of Mount Turquino, while Fidel, who retained over-all command, operated to the west. Until early 1958

Che's troops were, on the whole, limited to small-scale actions in the Sierra. Liaison with urban supporters was poor, and there were even muddles with the other guerrillas: shortly after Che's column separated from the rest, he asked Fidel's permission to attack a barracks at Estrada Palma, and then discovered from a government broadcast that it had been burned down by Raúl Castro (actually Guillermo García had led the attack).

At this period the guerrillas did not venture down from the mountainous Sierra, while Batista's army was extremely cautious about chasing them. Support from the local peasantry increased all the time. Guerrilla tactics were not especially sophisticated, since the number of men involved and the weapons were nearly always few. A sudden raid on an isolated post, or an ambush of an enemy patrol—Fidel would appear in one area and Che's troops would lie in wait for the troops sent to catch him—wore down the morale of Batista's regulars. However, indiscipline among the guerrillas reduced their effectiveness. A nervous or trigger-happy man would fire before he was supposed to, and orders got misconstrued in the heat of battle.

By February 1958, when the combined forces of Che and Fidel attacked an army position at Pino del Agua, south of Bayamo, the war entered a more expanded phase. Although the regulars were not wiped out in this battle, the guerrillas killed eighteen to twenty-five men and captured thirty-three rifles, five machine guns, and abundant ammunition. The action was interesting as an example of Che suggesting an aggressive tactic of which Fidel disapproved. At one point Che wished to attack wooden huts occupied by the regulars with Molotov cocktails from short range. Fidel told him that though he might try this, nothing suicidal was to be attempted and, above all, he himself must not endanger his life. As a result Che, who got wounded more than once during the campaign, did not try his scheme. Following this battle, the Third Column, under Major Juan Almeida, moved toward the zone of Santiago, and the Sixth "Frank País" column, under Major Raúl Castro, crossed the eastern plains and moved on to Pinares de Mayari.

On April 9 the urban movement, which had evolved a quite different revolutionary strategy from that of Fidel and the Sierra fighters, organized a general strike. It was, however, a hopeless flop, arranged with too little preparation and support—the Communist Popular Socialist Party stood aside, for example—and what should have been a violent strike degenerated into the liquidation of many of the July 26 partisans in the cities. This, after the failure to coordinate the *Granma* landing with the Santiago rising, gave the decisive advantage in the July 26 Movement to the rural fighters, and the experience shaped Fidelista and Guevarist theories about revolution in Latin America.

But the immediate consequence was that Batista's army, which numbered about forty thousand, decided that it had to eliminate the guerrillas, who were acting as a focus for dissent throughout the island. A quarter of the army was deployed to reduce about two hundred men in the Sierra Maestra. After two and a half months' skirmishing, however, they had sustained about a thousand casualties and abandoned some six hundred weapons. Che, in his *Reminiscences,* does not dwell on the methods by which this remarkable victory was achieved; but it is clear that much of his advice in *Guerrilla Warfare* must derive from the experience of this period. Guerrilla mobility, which is used to attack a regular column in rapid blows from different directions, the decoying of regulars into ambushes, and the "minuet," in which encircled troops are constantly fired on from successive quarters, must have then come into their own.

In August 1958 Che was ordered to Las Villas province, containing the Escambray Mountains, in the strategic heart of Cuba. In addition, another column under Camilo Cienfuegos marched with him with the intention of going on to the farther end of the island at Pinar del Río; but it stayed on to operate in loose association with Che in northern Las Villas. Che's task was to cut all the east-west roads in the island and he was given plenipotentiary powers to deal with other non-Fidelista guerrilla groups and set up a military government in the area. The situation with other groups was confused, but among those Che came in contact with, and managed to establish some cooperation with, were the Second National Front of the Escambray (of which Che was critical), the Revolutionary Directorate, and the Communists.

Che's trip to the Escambray, which had been planned as a four-day journey by truck, was in fact an arduous trek on foot which took from August 31 to October 16. During this march, in which support from the local peasantry was much less forthcoming than Che had been used to in the Sierra Maestra, the columns suffered from bombing, ambushes, and hunger. However, the rural guerrillas, supported by urban sabotage, completely disrupted Batista's "elections" on November 3. Cienfuegos and Guevara operated in a whirlwind of activity, blowing up roads and bridges, including the central highway and railway, and attacking small garrisons which the Cuban army was in no position to relieve. By mid-December the island had been cut in two, and the disintegration of the dictatorship and its army was increasing rapidly. By the end of December, with all the small towns in central Cuba in rebel hands, Che organized the capture of Santa Clara, the strategic city of 150,000 to which the Cuban army had committed ten or more tanks and an armored train. In the course of four days of house-to-house fighting the city was taken. The armored train, encircled and attacked with Molotov cocktails, was a total liability in these conditions, and its defenders surrendered. Batista, realizing all was lost, fled. Camilo moved on Havana and Che occupied the capital's fortress of La Cabaña. The military phase of the revolution was over.

How good a guerrilla leader was Che in Cuba? In simple military terms he was probably no better than Fidel Castro or Camilo Cienfuegos, to name only two of the others. What distinguished him was his utter determination that every guerrilla should be a revolutionary, his ability to systematize experience for future occasions, and his enthusiasm for both the military and nonmilitary sides of guerrilla warfare. The political radicalization of a somewhat heterogeneous body of peasants and ad-

venturers, admirers of Fidel and opponents of Batista, was epitomized in Che's emphasis on cooperation with the peasants and
agrarian reform. To terrorize the peasants under the guise of a
guerrilla was possibly the worst sin in Che's book (the normal
punishment was execution), and wherever he could, he paid the
peasants for food. A definitive agrarian reform would lead directly to a dispossession of the privileged Cuban classes and a
confrontation with imperialist landholders and sugar buyers.
Guerrilla Warfare indicates in the widest context Che's ability to
evaluate his experience: in *Reminiscences* he recounts how a
clash at El Hombrito, in which an attack on the advance guard
of an enemy company led to the withdrawal of what was left of
their 140 men, came to be adopted as a standard way of halting
a column on the march.

His enthusiasm for warfare must have been infectious. Like
Fidel, he was as delighted by the capture of a new gun as a
child is by the acquisition of a new toy. The capture and preservation of weapons seemed almost more important than the
lives of the fighters. With Che's encouragement, his men were
constantly experimenting with new weapons, such as a large
catapult used for launching small bombs made of tinplate.
Che was also keen on developing simple industries in the guerrilla zone—a bakehouse, a forge for making cartridges, a leather
goods workshop, and a cigar factory were all in operation. An
electrical generator and a mimeographed paper, *El Cubano
Libre*, were other aspects of life in the Sierra. It was under Che's
auspices that regular broadcasts from a small transmitter began
in February 1958.

But when all is said and done, it seems likely that the romance
surrounding Che's life and the popularity of his guerrilla manual
may have led to some exaggeration of his role as guerrilla within
Cuba. The total military aspect of the revolution was of course
extraordinary. A victory of barely a thousand men over forty
thousand, with air support, was something remarkable. It can
only be understood in terms of the institutional weakness of existing Cuban society and the political and moral desuetude of

Batista's regime. By the end of 1958, severely battered by the guerrillas, the army and police were falling like a pack of cards. For this reason the victory at Santa Clara was less wonderful than it seemed. The commander of the armored train, for instance, fled before the fighting started, and the casualties of the battle were not heavy.

Banker and Minister of Industry

The revolution was carried out with tremendous speed and with headlong enthusiasm. Within six months of the fall of Havana there had been instituted a radical agrarian reform which in practice resulted in the setting up of state collective farms and the wholesale direction of agriculture by INRA (Instituto Nacional de Reforma Agraria), the reform institute; within two years nearly all Cuban and foreign firms had been expropriated; within thirty months the CIA-supported invasion at the Bay of Pigs had been routed; on December 2, 1961, dispelling talk that Cuba was developing any new "humanist" political philosophy, Fidel Castro declared: "I shall be a Marxist-Leninist to the end of my life." (In early 1960 Che had said, "I have never been a Communist . . . dictators always say their enemies are Communists.") By April 1962 *Pravda* had acknowledged the Marxist-Leninist character of the Cuban regime and its place in the Soviet bloc.

For most of this time the traditional Cuban Communist Party, though it tried to take advantage of the way the wind was blowing, was left gasping for breath at the radicalism of Fidel, Raúl, Che, and the small group of revolutionaries that rode the maelstrom. After Fidel had attacked the Stalinist old-guard Communists in a speech on March 13, 1962, it was clear from the new ORI secretariat—which included President Osvaldo Dorticos, the Castro brothers, Che, and one "old" Communist, Blas Roca—that the new Cuban Communist Party being built would reflect Fidelista interpretations of Marx and Lenin.

Though the Cuban Revolution was in many ways chaotic and informal, Che, driven by his opposition to North American imperialism and his determination to make a real revolution, played a critical, radical part. Soon after Fidel entered Havana Che was sent on a world tour to explain what was going on, calling at Communist capitals en route, and later in 1959 he became head of the industrial department of INRA. In the early days of the revolution the Agrarian Reform Institute was one of the agents of nationalization of firms, in addition to managing the expropriation of land and the running of shops, schools, and welfare centers. Che at this time is credited with having brought in foreign Communist experts—Chilean, Mexican, Guatemalan, Belgian and French—to advise the Institute. He was also a forceful advocate of the immediate take-over of U.S. lands in Cuba and of the no-compensation principle. In the summer Che had already been accused by an investigatory commission of the Organization of American States of organizing an abortive invasion of Nicaragua by Cuban-based rebels.

In November 1959 he was named president of the National Bank of Cuba, and in this capacity he played a leading role in the socialization of the economy and in the establishment of trading links with the Soviet bloc. The appointment of Guevara to the bank represented a victory for the pro-Communist radical elements in the revolution; it occurred at about the same time as the dismissal of such anti-Communists as Faustino Pérez and Manuel Ray, the imprisonment of the anti-Communist Huber Matos, and the disappearance of Camilo Cienfuegos. When Mikoyan visited Havana in February 1960, it was Guevara who signed the Cuban–Russian trade agreement which provided credits and oil for Cuba and a market for her sugar, and it was he who insisted that Texaco, Shell, and Esso should refine the Soviet oil. When the Western companies refused to do this, they were put under government control at the end of June, the United States simultaneously cut the Cuban sugar quota, and on October 19 the Eisenhower Administration imposed a trade embargo. (As early as March 17 Eisenhower had given the order for the organization, training, and equipping of anti-Castro militants.)

Che's versatility and energy at this period were at their highest: in April his handbook on guerrilla warfare had been published, and at the same time he was head of the "Department of Instruction" at the Armed Forces Ministry, where he was responsible for developing the 100,000-strong people's militia and for the revolutionary indoctrination of the army. The revolutionary leaders were thinking in terms of a possible U.S. invasion from soon after their take-over, and the people's militia was designed as an extra line of defense (it did, in fact, perform valiantly at the Bay of Pigs). With some of the guerrilla leaders divided on the issue of Communism, and the revolution getting more intense, it became extremely important to establish the ideological purity of the rebel army.

Che is also thought to have had a hand in setting up the secret police, the G2, whose functions became more necessary as counterrevolutionary terrorism and invasion alarms grew. In a radio broadcast published [4] in the Popular University series in June 1960 Che explained his own attitude at this time: "I can call myself a soldier. . . . I do not pretend to be an economist. I am like all the revolutionary fighters, simply in this new trench where I have been placed."

Cuba's trade partnership with the Communist countries became even closer in December 1960, when a new sugar agreement committed them to take four million tons in the following year. Che, who had spoken earlier of the "economic slavery" involved in Cuba's dependence on the U.S. market, did not seem to worry about any political dangers in the new situation. On the contrary, he argued that the Soviet bloc was one of the areas in the world in which sugar sales might be expected to rise, although in fact the Soviet Union was self-sufficient. However, he fully recognized the industrial problems created by such a fundamental switch in source of supplies from U.S. to Communist sources—even industrial measurements were different—

[4] Under the title "Political Sovereignty and Economic Independence."

and in February 1961 he was put in the front line: he became head of a new Ministry of Industries.

This post was after his own heart, for there was nothing he would rather have seen than Cuba exchanging its monocultural economy for one with a diversified industrial base. But the technical obstacles were enormous. Apart from the muddles among the foreign Communist advisers—at one stage it was thought that Cuba and Czechoslovakia had much more in common than they did—Cuban industries were hampered by the emigration of managers, the depletion of supplies of U.S. spare parts, and the sheer confusion caused by the new system of production.

In April 1961, of course, the economy was further disrupted by the mobilization necessary to defeat the Bay of Pigs invasion. One report had it that Che had been slightly wounded in the course of the affair. At the first Production Congress in August he strongly criticized the armed forces for wasting enormous amounts of money. He also admitted that none of the nationalized industries were reaching their targets, and that industrial statistics were almost nonexistent. Nevertheless this had not stopped him from making a very optimistic speech when he had addressed the Inter-American Economic and Social Council at Punta del Este earlier that month.

This conference was held to fill in the outlines of President Kennedy's Alliance for Progress, an alliance from which it was pretty obvious that Cuba was to be excluded. Che said that Cuba had already received $357 million in credits from the Socialist countries up to 1970, and that the Cuban growth rate would run at ten per cent per year. He used what proved to be one of the last chances for a Cuban leader to appear at an inter-American gathering as a guest to complain about the counterrevolutionary activities of the United States, the odd fact that it was now offering $2 billion over ten years instead of the $3 billion which it had ridiculed Fidel Castro for suggesting before, and the whole philosophy of the Alliance. He mocked the "revolution of latrines"—U.S. and OAS experts were always talking about improving water supplies instead of the nationalization of the means of production. His outing was a considerable propaganda success.

But the autumn of 1961 was a bad one both for the economy and for ordinary Cubans who fell foul of the developing terror. Bottlenecks, breakdowns, and inefficiency brought shortages, the Church was attacked, and counterrevolutionary books and newspapers became hard to obtain. In the meantime the old cadres of the Communist Party got to work, placing their men in key positions in factories and organizations and acting in a "sectarian" way. Though refugees exaggerated tales of shootings, the pressure on counterrevolutionaries became sharper.

In all this Che seems to have become a scapegoat. He was probably not against the terror; like Raúl Castro, he felt that the revolution should be on its guard against being too merciful to its enemies. But the economic failures, though in some measure the responsibility of the revolutionary leadership as a whole, were also to some extent exacerbated by his own policies. The expensive "humanistic" policy, the building of houses, clubs, and children's crèches which so attracted outsiders in the early days, had been supported by Che, as it encouraged ordinary people to identify with the revolution: "We are building thousands of houses, although we know that from a purely economic point of view it would be better to build factories," he had said in 1960. This generosity had to be paid for later. Similarly Che, who admitted the mistake in mid-1963, was being extremely ambitious in his industrializing policy: without a proper sense of priorities money was invested in the production of articles which could be more cheaply obtained from the Soviet bloc, while sugar output suffered.

In November 1961 Carlos Rafael Rodríguez, one of the old Communists, developed a new plan, and Che seemed to be eclipsed. Although he criticized the plan in March of the following year and took part in the Fidelista revival which resulted in the expulsion of the old Communist Aníbal Escalante and the reforming of the ORI, his prestige as an economist may have already suffered permanent damage. In mid-1963 Fidel formally renounced the policy of rapid industrial diversification in favor of concentration on the cane fields and cattle.

Che was naturally involved in the events leading to the Cuban missile crisis of October 1962. Early in July a Cuban delegation under the chief of the armed forces, Raúl Castro, had visited Moscow; and in August Che led another, which seems to have discussed both economic and defense matters. Apart from Khrushchev's own purposes, it is likely that the Cubans themselves had wanted the Soviet rockets as a guarantee of their security, and the Kennedy–Khrushchev dialogue over Cuba's head can have been little to Che's taste. If the rockets were being removed in return for a U.S. promise not to invade Cuba, was not the island's fate dependent on a continuance of the Soviet–U.S. entente, and ultimately on U.S. good will? This endangered not only its role as a challenge in itself to U.S. imperialism, but also its prospects of inspiring revolutions throughout Latin America. Though Castro was attempting to develop his own revolutionary path, independent of the Sino–Soviet squabble, Che resented the dependence on the Soviet Union's economic support, its own penchant for peaceful coexistence, and its determination to keep Cuba to an agricultural role in the international division of Socialist labor.

In 1964 and early 1965 the signs multiplied that Che was getting restless. In ideological journals he fought a running battle with the old Communist bureaucrats who were anxious to introduce material incentives for workers into the Cuban economy. Che, by contrast, thought this was retrograde, and concentrated on the need for moral stimulus. The revolution, he proclaimed, should evolve a new man who did not need bourgeois carrots. Simultaneously there was evidence of friction with Castro himself. In an article for the Uruguayan magazine *Marcha* he described the original myth of the July 26 Movement as "the disaster of Castro at Moncada." On other occasions he had been suitably laudatory of both Castro's military ability and the

Moncada exploit. Che may also have been favoring the Chinese line of world revolution.

On March 24, 1965, old guard Communist Blas Roca, in his column in the Communist daily *Hoy*, attacked Che as "the apple of discord in the Socialist front" and alluded to an attempt to distribute pamphlets explaining the Chinese ideological position. But Che did not stop acting as the spokesman for the Cuban revolution abroad: in March 1964 he led the Cuban delegation to the United Nations Conference on Trade and Development at Geneva, and in December he represented Cuba at the United Nations.[5] He subsequently toured Afro-Asian capitals, including Peking, and returned to Havana on March 14, 1965. After a routine interview granted to a Panamanian journalist on April 19, he disappeared.

Departure from Cuba

Che's disappearance from the public eye caused international interest. But the Cuban regime was slow to satisfy the general curiosity. Some individuals associated with him in the Ministry of Industry were moved from their posts, a new currency was introduced to replace the one with his signature, and, although his wife and daughter appeared at the May Day parade, there were no condolences later in the month when his mother died; the customary congratulations on his birthday in June did not appear in the press. But it was clear that the disappearance did not represent a repudiation.

Castro, who said that wherever Che was he would be serving the revolution, praised him in speeches, his books were on sale, and plenty of posters of him appeared on July 26. Finally, on October 3, Castro cleared up the mystery in a broadcast from Havana in which he announced that Che had resigned

---

[5] In his speech at the UN he predicted that "Colombia will become the Vietnam of America."

from the Cuban Communist Party, given up Cuban citizenship, and left the country "for new fields of battle." He read out a letter from Che, dated April 1, 1965, which was a peculiar mixture of independence and self-criticism. His only serious mistake, the letter stated, was not to have confided more in Fidel since the first moment in the Sierra Maestra and to have insufficiently understood the latter's qualities as leader and revolutionary. Che left his family to be looked after by the Cuban state as he entered new fields in the fight against imperialism: he freed Cuba of all responsibility for his actions.

After ten years devoted to the concerns of Cuba, Che was once again the stateless revolutionary he had been when he met Castro. But though the gesture of renunciation of his Cuban citizenship and party membership might have seemed quixotic, it was easy enough to understand. To what extent he was encouraged to go and to what extent he volunteered is not certain, but he had several understandable reasons for wishing to leave. As he had told the United Nations in December 1964, he wanted to see Latin American revolutions everywhere and, with Brazil just fallen to General Castello Branco by arms and Chile to Frei by ballot, and guerrillas prospering nowhere, he must have felt the need for a new push. Although Cuban patronage had not helped any other guerrillas to victory, Fidel too, from the 1962 Conference of the Latin American Peoples in Havana on, was determined that his revolution should have Latin American echoes. But while this was something on which Che and Fidel were agreed, Che cannot have liked Cuba's alliance with the USSR of peaceful coexistence and the parlous effect of the Sino-Soviet split on the cause of international revolution, itself at stake in Vietnam.

Che may also have found that personal differences with Fidel were growing. This was ironic, as he had criticized the old Communists—and even the urban wing of the July 26 Movement—for failing to appreciate the importance of Fidel's personal leadership in the days of the Sierra. In *Guerrilla Warfare* he had written that "Fidel Castro had the best attributes of a fighter and statesman. His vision made possible our landing, our fight, and our triumph." [6] But with his own reputation established as ideologist and strategist, his revolutionary purism sometimes conflicting with the compromises inevitable for a national leader, and Castro's considerable ego, personal disagreements could fester.

In particular, Che obviously distrusted the position and policies of the old Communist apparatchiks. Though he had no fear of working with the Communists in the Sierra and approved the totalitarian Marxist–Leninist evolution of the Cuban Revolution —and in his vision some bureaucratization was inevitable—he reacted quite negatively when he saw the old Communist cells move into action. The old PSP, after all, had cooperated with the Batista dictatorship in its time and it had not been quick to support Fidel after he reached the Sierra. It had been chary of the whole doctrine of armed revolution, as orthodox Communist parties in Latin America continue to be, yet its men did their best to cash in on Fidel's achievement. Che despised bureaucrats and he did not care for sectarian attitudes and pressure groups. In the circumstances his renunciation of his Cuban party membership may have had some extra significance.

In a broader sense one may ask whether his departure from the island represented any disillusion with the results of the revolution. The answer must be that it did not, though Che thought he could contribute more by starting the continental revolution than by doing a desk job in a firmly based government. In a letter to his family in Argentina at about the time he left Cuba he wrote: "Many call me an adventurer—and that I am, only one of a different sort—one of those who risks his skin to prove his platitudes."

After he was said to have left Cuba, he was reported all over the place, not only in Latin America. During the next year and a half he may have visited North Vietnam and certainly

[6] Che Guevara and Mao Tse-tung: *Guerrilla Warfare* (combined edition of their respective works), with foreword by B. H. Liddell Hart (Cassell: 1962), p. 137.

spent a period organizing guerrilla operations in the Congo; according to pro-Chinese Communists in Latin America after his death, he was forced to desist by Castro, who was himself being pressed on the issue by the Russians. Thereafter Che prepared in Cuba for his Bolivian expedition, training a carefully selected group of senior Cuban officers for the purpose. Among them were two alternate members of the Central Committee of the Cuban Communist Party, and one full member, Commandante Juan Vitalio Acuña Núñez ("Joaquín" in Che's Bolivian war diary), who had until then been director of the Cuban army's guerrilla-warfare center. On November 5, disguised as a balding Uruguayan businessman, Che—who had travelled via Czechoslovakia, West Germany, France, and Brazil —arrived at La Paz airport in Bolivia. The most ambitious undertaking of his life, the founding of a revolutionary movement that could physically extend to all the states of South America and involve the United States in several new Vietnam-type interventions, had commenced.

If he had succeeded, he would indeed have converted the Andes into the Sierra Maestra of South America, the suggestion originally made by Fidel and approved of by him. But in attempting to start a new Latin American revolution Che cannot have been under any illusions, either as to the risk he himself was running, or the risk of failure for the whole enterprise. In *Guerrilla Warfare* he made the famous assertion: "Given suitable operating terrain, land hunger, enemy injustices, etc., a hard core of thirty to fifty men is, in my opinion, enough to initiate armed revolutions in any Latin American country." [7] Revolutionary situations could be created. But even Che had recognized that where peaceful change was possible the way of armed revolution was incautious, and he fully appreciated that the Cuban experience, including his own advice to guerrillas, was being taken to heart by reactionary armies and their U.S. advisers. For fully six years, under their own leaders but with active Cuban support, guerrillas in Guatemala, Peru, Venezuela, and

[7] Guevara and Mao: *Guerrilla Warfare,* p. 147.

Colombia had tried to imitate the Cuban revolution without success.

In ideological terms, too, the triumph in Cuba had made its repetition difficult: Cuba added a third voice to the competing forms of Communism in Latin America, while the enemies of Communism, who had been unable to pinpoint Castro when he was in the Sierra, opposed his siblings as Reds. Meanwhile, as for himself, Che in his letters both to Castro and to his family in Argentina expressed his awareness that death was a possibility: he had lived too dangerously in the early days in Cuba not to appreciate this.

The Bolivian campaign

Che's Bolivian campaign was a disaster. To choose Bolivia, in the first place, as the site for a major guerrilla attempt was a doubtful option. Geographically the country was large and diverse, ranging from the jungle headwaters of the Amazon in the east and savannah land in the southeast through rugged Andean mountains to the high *altiplano* in the west. Its population density is the lowest in South America. (Che's base camp was in a particularly empty region.) Surrounded by five countries with no official sympathy for guerrillas, it meant that, though a Bolivian revolutionary regime might be able to foment disorders within its neighbors' populations, the existing military rulers could count on the interested help of other governments in repressing a menace to all. (Brazil did in fact contribute napalm for the Bolivian government, and Paraguay, whose border was nearest the affected zone, took special precautions to guard the frontier.[8]) Socially and historically Bolivia presented obstacles to a Castroite insurrection. Seventy per cent of the people were Quechua- or Aymara-speaking Indians, without a sophisticated political consciousness. The average standard of living was one of Latin America's lowest—unlike Batista's Cuba, the country

[8] Argentina and Peru also took frontier precautions.

had only a small middle class—and the growth rate from 1945 to 1965 had been only 1.3 per cent per annum. Moreover, the country's dependence on tin exports, largely purchased by the United States and the United Kingdom, rivaled that of Cuba on sugar. But the distinctive factor in recent Bolivian history was that the nation had gone through a major revolution in 1952.

Che himself must have known all about it from his own travels in the early fifties, and in his guerrilla manual he paid tribute to it for giving Cuba three "outstanding examples"—the abolition of the army, agrarian reform, and the nationalization of the tin mines. The quasi-Socialist, quasi-Fascist revolution of Paz Estenssoro and the MNR (Movimiento Nacionalista Revolucionario) had run out of radicalism and the party itself had broken up by the early sixties, but its effects were lasting.

The destruction of the regular army after fighting in 1952 meant that a new one, with a much more popular character, had been set up under MNR guidance. This was trained and equipped by the United States. It was no coincidence, therefore, that General Barrientos, who became President after a military coup in 1964, was a Quechua speaker of peasant origin. The agrarian reform, though it had resulted in inefficient *minifundios*, meant that many Indian peasants owned land for the first time and were tentatively brought into the political system. Peasant militias had been formed by the MNR. As for the tin mines (the oil fields had been nationalized as long ago as 1937)— while COMIBOL, the state enterprise in charge, wrestled with high production costs, technical backwardness, and overstaffing, the tin miners had established a strong bargaining position. They had achieved a fair measure of workers' control, and, ever since their fighting in 1952, they had arms. Altogether the status quo which Che came to upset had a considerable amount of public participation coupled with a strong institutional framework. On the other hand, it was true that widespread poverty still contrasted with surviving wealth, in some areas there were suspicions that the old landlords were recovering their position, a growing army was balanced by a decline in the miners' strength, and the United States had large influence on politics and finance.

From Che's point of view a significant fact was that there were no competing guerrillas already established in Bolivia. But otherwise the complicated and treacherous panorama of the left was unpromising. The Bolivian Communist Party was a disunited Moscow-line group, not psychologically fitted for the Havana road to Socialism and without much weight in its own purlieus. On December 31, 1966, Che had an unproductive meeting with the party's secretary general, Mario Monje. Monje insisted that he would cooperate only on the understanding that he would have over-all control, at least while the revolution was geographically restricted to Bolivia. Che, who had seen the total incomprehension of the old Cuban Communists regarding the requirements of guerrilla warfare in the hills and who had come to Bolivia to initiate a continental revolution, insisted that he would be supreme commander in the field.

The issue was not merely tactical, it was strategic: in contrast to the *Granma* venture, the new one, with its strong Cuban support in manpower and money, was inevitably international from the start, and Che's intention was to correlate guerrilla uprisings in Peru and Argentina with his own. An essential aspect, which was bound to be unacceptable to orthodox Communists, was that all those who wanted the revolution would have to forgo distinctions of nationality, political sect, and rank.

The effect of Che's rupture with Monje was far-reaching. Though individual party militants came to his aid, the Moscow machine actively prevented volunteers from joining him, and the establishment of an urban network had the most formidable obstacle. (Whether there was an extra hazard in the treachery of Guevara's principal courier and possible mistress, "Tania," may never be known.[9]) There was only one Communist splinter group which joined Che in a body, a small, heter-

[9] "Tania," identified as Haydee Tamara Bunkebider, may conceivably have been a Soviet agent deployed to keep watch over Che's Bolivian project. But evidence for this charge is slim and partial.

odox Chinese-line faction under the leadership of Moisés Guevara—who was killed in the course of the guerrilla campaign—and some of them had great difficulty in adjusting to combat conditions. The majority of Chinese-line Communists in Bolivia had not much to offer and claimed afterwards that Che had not consulted them. Finally, there was also a Trotskyist party of some importance, the Partido Obrero Revolucionario, which had a following among tin miners in particular. Although a few miners associated with Moisés Guevara were part of Che's ill-fated group, the Latin American Trotskyists had strategic and ideological differences with Havana.

In practice, a miners' rising could never be sustained for long on account of their dependence on outside supplies of food; the actual mines were some distance from each other and from La Paz, the capital, and so in a drawn-out guerrilla campaign they could really only perform at the climax. (In fact, Barrientos occupied the mines after a major strike before mopping up the guerrillas.) The absence of supportive organizations mattered because of the spread-out terrain of Bolivia and the difficulty of communications; the situation was markedly different from the Cuban experience in 1956, when the July 26 Movement already had a sound urban network and Fidel Castro, as a former *Ortodoxo* politician daring to act against an unpopular regime, could command a wide range of sympathy.

Finally, and of critical importance, no native Bolivian of stature could be found to act the charismatic part of Fidel. The obvious candidate, with whom Havana was in touch, was Juan Lechín, the enigmatic trade-union leader who had been a Vice-President in Paz Estenssoro's MNR government and had been continually opposed by the U.S. Embassy. But he proved cautious in the event, and though two Bolivian Communist brothers, Inti and Coco Peredo Leigue, became useful guerrilla commanders, the crucial point was that "Ramón," as Che described himself, was the over-all leader. Though this reflected credit on his initiative and experience and the international aims of the movement, the absence of local notables meant taking a risk with

Bolivian nationalism: if his role were made public prematurely, nothing would show more obviously the insubstantial local basis for the guerrillas or prove more simply government charges of Castroite invasion.

The guerrilla enterprise got under way efficiently enough with the training of some forty men on a remote ranch, the Casa de Calamina, which Coco Peredo had bought in the middle of 1966. Che, in his diary, recorded the arrival of nearly twenty Cubans by the end of December 1966, and his disappointment at the slow recruitment of Bolivians. The guerrillas built a jungle base near the ranch not far from the Nacahuasu River (Che's spelling—also spelled Nancahuazu) and some fifty miles north of Camiri, the oil town. This, as Murray Sayle described it in his report in the *Times* of April 11, 1967, was a remarkably permanent affair: conforming to Che's preferences, it included a slaughterhouse, a field hospital, baking ovens, and even gardens growing vegetables.

What was interesting was that Che had decided to set up such a camp so early in the insurrection. In his *Reminiscences* it was clear that he found that such a feature—which contradicted his own maxim of permanent mobility—could only be practicable after the guerrillas were strongly established in a certain area (a conclusion underlined in Régis Debray's *Revolution in the Revolution?*). But from his Bolivian diary it is obvious that he overrated the security of the ranch vicinity at the beginning, and a neighboring landowner who thought an illicit cocaine still was being established seems to have been only one of those whose suspicions were aroused.

Che did not establish any other camps on this scale, and its discovery, following a clash nearby with the Bolivian army, announced the arrival of the guerrillas to the government. This ambush, on March 23, 1967, resulted in the deaths of seven soldiers and the capture of eighteen prisoners, whom Che released. Though it has been claimed that this action gave away the guerrilla enterprise before it was ripe, and the discovery certainly played havoc with the group's nascent urban communications system, Che had earlier forecast the need for action and movement by then. Lack of security precautions by "Marcos," [1] the leader of the vanguard, may have led to the discovery of the group, and for this and habits of quarreling and insubordination Che replaced him.

In March the guerrillas also suffered from deserters, who informed the army of their supply lines, numbers, arms, and even Che's own presence. The condition of the guerrillas at this time, as described by both Debray and Che in his diary, showed that in spite of the experience of the Cuban nucleus, they were suffering from many of the faults that had beset Fidel's expedition in its infancy: ideological deficiencies and friction among the men and many desertions—Debray put them as high as seventeen. Careful choice of recruits and security of information were two of Che's hard-learned principles that were not observed. The guerrilla force seems to have been as psychologically ill prepared for operating in sparsely populated, rugged and jungle country—without as yet any real popular support—as the *Granma* group was when it first straggled up the Sierra. The camp by the Nacahuasu, containing photos of Che and lists of guerrilla medical patients by their first names, was an intelligence windfall for the Bolivian army.

Following the discovery of the camp and the capture in April of Régis Debray, which indicated the direct Castroite interest in the guerrilla movement, the Bolivian army prepared countermeasures and put pressure on the United States for help. Given the fitful radio communication with Havana, Debray's capture meant the removal of a valuable courier, although the publicity given to his case was moral encouragement for the guerrillas. By mid-May, when Che received a message from Havana which implied that the isolation of the guerrillas was total, it was obvious that the "international" aspect of the Bolivian mission had been severely weakened: the capture of Ciro

---

[1] Identified as Comandante Antonio Sánchez Díaz, a Cuban who had formerly been military governor of the Isla de Pinos and an alternate member of the Cuban Communist Party.

Roberto Bustos, the Argentine who was to have coordinated a simultaneous uprising in Argentina, had postponed the likelihood of action there, while the Peruvian "El Chino," [2] who had had plans for a simultaneous rebellion in Peru, had had to abandon them and join Che's band as an ordinary combatant instead.

By June the relatively efficient Bolivian Eighth Division, commanded by Colonel Joaquín Zenteno Anaya (a former Foreign Minister of his country) was patrolling the area between Santa Cruz and Vallegrande with the advice of U.S. counterinsurgency experts. In addition, groups of army rangers were being given special courses in antiguerrilla warfare which seem to have made a crucial difference to the quality of the Bolivian forces.

Meanwhile Che attempted to recover the initiative by rapid marches northward and the sort of guerrilla skirmishing at which he was adept. In four months the guerrillas killed or took prisoner some fifty men and nine army officers, and on July 6 they took the town of Samaipata on the main road from Santa Cruz to Cochabamba, one of the country's principal east–west communications routes.

At this stage it might have appeared that the guerrillas were making good progress; but Che's diaries show that their situation was already critical. They were suffering from an almost total breakdown of communications with the outside world— Che depended on the Bolivian government radio for his day-to-day news—compounded by ignorance of the geography of an area for which such maps as they had were hopelessly inadequate. From April until September, when the former rear guard under "Joaquín" was eliminated by the army, much of Che's marching and countermarching was in hopes of regaining contact with this separated group. Under the circumstances, it was hardly surprising that Che was unable to add recruits to his column of twenty-five and every loss was a perilous step nearer extinction. For the leader himself, the lack of medical supplies meant that his asthma gave him trouble. Little progress was made in win-

[2] Identified as Juan Pablo Chang Navarro.

ning support from the peasants, who were punished by the army where they collaborated with the guerrillas.

By August and September the tide was obviously turning against the guerrillas as the Bolivian army, pouring large numbers of men into the affected zone, began to win some successes. Troops discovered more of Che's hidden caves by the Nacahuasu with valuable documents and medicines—one of the guerrilla camps was turned into an antiguerrilla training center—and all ten of "Joaquín's" group, including "Joaquín" and the romantic "Tania," were eliminated. During the last week in September the guerrillas, whose mobility was reduced by the poor condition of their Peruvian doctor, fell into an ambush and lost three dead, including Coco Peredo.

By the first week in October the Bolivian army was confidently announcing that the guerrillas were encircled, and President Barrientos commented, "If Guevara is still in Bolivia, here he will go to his grave." By Sunday October 8, two fresh companies of Bolivian troops, probably acting on a peasant tip—the Bolivian government had put a price of 500,000 pesos (slightly less than $5,000) on Che's head—had the small guerrilla nucleus trapped in the Quebrada del Yuro. Che is said to have commented that if they got involved in a fight before 1 p.m. things would go badly, but if they could hold on until 4 p.m., it would be possible to slip away under cover of nightfall.

The obvious way to escape was down the valley and, in accordance with his normal habit of attempting to divert the enemy, he asked for volunteers for a suicide squad to stay and give covering fire. This was an old Cuban practice: to encourage competition for the work of greatest danger. He picked Inti Peredo and two other Bolivians as well as his Cuban bodyguard, "Pombo," [3] and two more Cubans for this task. But unknown to Che, the bottom of the valley was sealed off, and when—after the battle had begun at about midday, with the army using mortars and heavy fire against them—his group attempted to get away, it ran into more of the enemy. Che was wounded in the

[3] Identified as Captain Harry Villegas Tamayo.

leg. Even so, he is believed to have tried to make a break with the miner Willy, but they were surrounded by Bolivian soldiers. According to Fidel Castro, Che had been effectively disarmed, with the barrel of his automatic destroyed and no magazine for his pistol, and they seem to have surrendered without resistance. The firepower of the guerrillas in the engagement had sufficiently impressed the regulars for early reports to have suggested that the troop was about twice its actual size. The Bolivian army suffered casualties, and about ten guerrillas got away. Five days later, about twelve miles northeast of La Higuera, the surviving group killed five soldiers and a civilian guide in a fierce engagement. Again they managed to get away. Long after the thirty days of Cuban mourning for Che were over, and the extraordinary farce of Debray's trial and sentence in Camiri had disappeared from the headlines, the five surviving guerrillas were arrested in the Chilean Andean village of Todos Santos, on February 22, 1968. They had eluded their Bolivian pursuers in a trek of some 1,400 difficult miles, and their reward was a hero's welcome by the Chilean Socialist Party, and air tickets to Havana via Easter Island and Prague. But they had failed to regroup and restart the guerrilla uprising; Che's Bolivian campaign was over.[4]

In his tribute to Che, Fidel Castro quite rightly asked: "What is so strange about the fact that this master died in combat? What is stranger is that he did not die in combat on one of the innumerable occasions when he risked his life during our revolutionary struggle." In particular, the actual initiation of a guerrilla *foco* (focus for insurrection) was recognized by all to be the most hazardous part of a campaign. One may even wonder whether, if Che had been in the party that had escaped the army net at La Higuera, he might not even then have established a viable movement. But in the long reappraisal for revolutionaries that would follow Che's death, certain factors would have to be

[4] In July 1968 Inti Peredo, one of the surviving guerrillas, who had by then returned to Bolivia, published a defense of Che's strategy of continental liberation, and added that the "National Liberation Army" would return to the mountains.

considered. On the tactical level, it was obvious that his band had not observed all the tactical rules he had preached and, though he himself was famous, the expedition lacked the popular local leader which was one of the requirements laid down by *Guerrilla Warfare*.

At the strategic level, the disaster also threw doubt on the methodology of revolution in Latin America: the assumption by both Che and Havana that throughout the region the objective conditions for revolution were so promising that a spark from outside could be introduced into any country with incendiary effect. From this point of view Bolivia was as good a place to try as any. Debray, who had pointed out the limitations of action by the tin miners on their own in *Revolution in the Revolution?*, had also written that this was the South American country where the subjective and objective conditions for armed struggle were best combined. But if defeat was to be the springboard for a revolutionary that Debray supposed, the theoreticians would have to consider again whether there was such an identity of sociopolitical conditions in Latin America as to permit any free-lance revolutionary like Che to attempt action anywhere, without advanced political preparations and with equal chance of success. As for the U.S. counterinsurgency experts at Fort Bragg and elsewhere, the Bolivian experience was a reminder that the current revolutionary strategy could be forestalled by prompt military action alone: where the revolutionaries opted for a small, vulnerable *foco*, containing both the military and political leadership of a movement that had yet to strike roots in a country at large, it could be wiped out quite easily.

The guerrilla theorist

For as long as guerrilla wars are fought, Che Guevara will influence the fighters. His book on the subject has turned up in the knapsacks of NLF troops in Vietnam and is consulted by African nationalist leaders. By comparison with Mao's popular work on the same subject, it is impressively practical. Che's manual is concerned with the details of fighting as much as with the general principles. He talks about using the enemy's weapons, the use of mules and mines, the importance of footwear in the field (he himself was wearing a pair of moccasins when taken in Bolivia).

Throughout his book there runs a strong element of common sense. "What is the best age for a guerrilla? It depends on a person's background. Generally sixteen to forty years is satisfactory when the band lacks a fixed base, but twenty-five to thirty-five-year-old men are to be preferred." "The guerrilla fighter is a soldier who, like a snail, carries his home upon his shoulders, and therefore his pack must contain the smallest quantity of items of the greatest possible utility." "Arms and ammunition are extremely precious items on the battlefield, never leave a dead guerrilla behind without first recovering his gear." [5]

The attitudes inculcated are essentially humane. Discipline in the group is to be maintained by reason and conviction; no one is to be executed, except in an emergency, without a fair hearing. A guerrilla never abandons a wounded comrade to the enemy's mercy and, except for the worst enemy criminals, the guerrilla disarms prisoners and lets them go after a scolding. Radio broadcasts must stick to the truth. Guerrillas must display impeccable moral conduct and strict self-control—they must be ascetics. In particular, their attitude to the peasant population must win them support; they do not steal, and if they cannot pay for things they leave IOU's.

Che wrote his manual before the Marxist-Leninist conclusion of the Cuban Revolution had been acknowledged, but the cornerstone of his thinking was that the guerrilla must be a social reformer. It was this that distinguished him from a common bandit. In particular, the guerrilla must be an agrarian revolutionary. The principle Che enunciated, that "in the underdeveloped countries of the Americas, rural areas are the best battlefields for revolution," became the chief division between Havana

[5] *Guerrilla Warfare*, pp. 117 and 128.

and the Moscow-line Communist parties of Latin America. But the lack of a coherent ideological doctrine in the manual—one reason why it could be used by militants of different persuasions —shows through. At one point Che writes: "Men so dedicated must have an ideal, one that is plain and simple and worth dying for. The right to have their own land and the enjoyment of fair social treatment motivate farm laborers. For industrial workers it is having a job, a decent wage, and social justice. For students and professional workers, the idea is more abstract, such as freedom." Further on, he says: "Since recruits join up with fuzzy concepts of liberty, freedom of the press, etc., they need indoctrination on guerrilla aims, economic factors and motivations of national history, national heroes, behavior in face of injustice, analysis of the current situation." [6] Information for foreign news media should confine itself to facts about the war.

With the passage of time, the experiences of the existing guerrilla movements in Latin America, and the development of disputes between Havana and Moscow and the orthodox Communists in the hemisphere, Che refined, universalized, and perhaps dogmatized the lessons of *Guerrilla Warfare*. (His fascinating *Reminiscences* provide, in an anecdotal and memoir form, the historical background to the lessons of the manual; they also include his motto for a putative guerrilla: "constant movement, absolute mistrust, and eternal vigilance.") For instance, in his preface to a book by General Nguyen Giap, the North Vietnamese guerrilla leader, on "people's war" he criticized the concept of "self defense" maintained by peasants. Though useful for liberated areas, this did not have the creative revolutionary possibilities of the guerrilla *foco*.

Che became much more definite about the role of agrarianbased revolutionaries in Latin America. Leaving aside the loopholes in *Guerrilla Warfare*, he told the OSPAAAL Executive in 1967 that liberation in the Americas would be produced, in the majority of cases, by armed struggle, and would have the prop-

[6] *Guerrilla Warfare*, pp. 129 and 144.

erty of converting itself into a Socialist revolution. He became more certain that a guerrilla force, rather than any other group in a country, would be the vanguard of revolution. Its rigorous way of life and its closeness to the peasantry made it ideologically proletarian, whereas city revolutionaries remained petty bourgeois. In an original contribution, he suggested that political and military leadership of the revolution should, if possible, be united in one person.

Finally Che, in his adjuration to the Tricontinental, put the Latin American guerrillas into a world perspective. Driven by his hatred of North American imperialism, he appealed to Latin America to create the "second or third Vietnam" in order to help the NLF and divide the Yankee oppressors. He looked forward to the creation of international proletarian armies ready to launch into guerrilla struggle anywhere under the same banner of "the sacred cause of the redemption of humanity." Mao had talked of the world's countryside of Asia and Latin America surrounding and revolutionizing the United States, the world's capitalist city, but Che seemed to give the idea sharper edge.

The ideologist

Che wrote many articles on ideology in Cuban magazines. Yet he never devoted a whole book to the subject. But his general attitudes were well known, and they were utopian. He believed that revolution should purify a man, and that the postrevolutionary generation in Cuba should be like the "new men" that idealists wished for in Russia in 1917: humane, courageous, needing neither to be bribed nor bullied. He was against the bureaucracy associated with Stalinism, the bureaucracy relished by the old Communists of Cuba and the bureaucracy which had been the main contribution of Communist parties in Latin America before the Cuban Revolution came on the scene. This type of bureaucracy, Che knew only too well, was narrow-minded, self-seeking, and could all too easily become a kind of *pastiche* of a typical existing Latin American government, with its overstaffing, red tape, and avoidance of decision.

Che was against any kind of Socialist realism in the arts. He thought that Cuba should not have material incentives in its factories and that capitalist notions of market value were out of place. In his economic ideas he clashed not only with the old Cuban Communists but with governing parties in Eastern Europe which were experimenting with more elastic methods of pricing.

Democracy, the word which was to exercise the Czech Communists the year after he was killed, was not something that bothered him particularly, although he advocated that the revolutionary cadres in the Cuban PURS should be founded on the local choice of "exemplary workers." But representative democracy, of which the Czechs still had a not unhappy memory, had little inspiration for him. As operated in Latin America, it had so often been a way in which privileged groups of politicians, with small participation from the mass of the population, had ratified or exchanged their privileges to their own satisfaction. In Communist terms, he was a firm adherent of the doctrine of democratic centralism and the transmission of orders from above.

Che was extremely candid about the inefficiency, low productivity, and generally poor results achieved by the Cuban economy in its first years of revolutionary management. In April 1962 he told sugar workers that they were working "with enormous inefficiency," and in a scathing speech to trade-union officials the month before he exclaimed that "The achievements of the revolution . . . are confined to the establishment of a few small consumer-goods factories and the completion of factories started under the dictatorship." But the poor quality of so many Cuban Socialist products would not weaken his faith: "Does that sort of thing happen under capitalism? No. Why should it happen under Socialism? Because it is in the nature of Socialism? No, that is a lie, one can say anything but not that. It all happens because of our shortcomings, our lack of revolutionary awareness, insufficient control, and our lack of revolutionary vigilance." [7]

But somewhere between Che's attacks on bureaucracy, his moral exhortations to raise production (which included the use of Socialist competitions and an attempt to get a national wage scale irrespective of the profitability of any one industry), and his desire to ignite the whole Cuban population with the enhanced revolutionary will experienced by a handful of Sierra fighters there seems to have been a gap: it was as though he wanted the end but not the means, which could have been either bureaucracy plus terror as in Stalinism or the material incentives becoming popular in Eastern Europe. Che never convincingly explained how Cuba should achieve its economic targets if moral suasion failed, and talk of "insufficient control" and "lack of revolutionary vigilance" perhaps concealed a fallback into the uglier, mandatory aspects of a totalitarian democracy.[8] But though Che had not claimed much knowledge of economics at the start of the revolution, he learned fast enough to be able to stand up to the infighting of Marxist economics. Whereas when he was head of the National Bank, it had seemed to play a crucial part on the Cuban scene, in the March 1964 issue of *Cuba Socialista*, he was able with quotations from Marx to argue with the then president, Marcelo Fernández, that the Bank should have a strictly technical and subordinate role in a planned economy.

[7] Quoted by Boris Goldenberg: *The Cuban Revolution and Latin America* (George Allen & Unwin: 1965), p. 257.
[8] In the essay "Man and Socialism in Cuba" Che wrote: "The vanguard group is ideologically more advanced than the mass; the latter is acquainted with the new values, but insufficiently. While in the former a qualitative change takes place which permits them to make sacrifices as a function of their vanguard character, the latter see only by halves and must be subjected to incentives and pressures of some intensity; it is the dictatorship of the proletariat being exercised not only upon the defeated class but also individually upon the victorious class." In *Venceremos!: The Speeches and Writings of Ernesto Che Guevara*, edited by John Gerassi (Weidenfeld and Nicolson: 1968), pp. 392–3.

The most fascinating document connected with Che, shedding light on his attitudes as guerrilla leader, ideologist, and man, only emerged after his death. This was his diary of the Bolivian campaign, whose release to Havana by Antonio Arguedas, the Bolivian Minister of the Interior, came almost closer to toppling the Barrientos cabinet than the miners' turbulence or Che's military strategy the previous year. The diary meticulously records the day-to-day incidents of guerrilla life, the assaults of insects, and the bouts of hunger and jealousy among the men. Che's irritation with the lack of cooperation of the Bolivian Communists and the tactical errors of the guerrillas, as well as his disappointment at the slowness in winning peasant support, recur throughout, but his fundamental faith in the armed way of revolution did not falter. On July 14, 1967, when two of the parties supporting Barrientos left his government in one of the misleading maneuvers that apparently forecast the doom of the regime, but which scarcely harmed it, Che commented: "The government is rapidly disintegrating. It's a pity we do not have 100 men more at this moment." [9] On August 8, Che, who had been riding a little mare because of his asthma, drove a knife into her neck in his anger at her weary pace. The situation was deteriorating for the guerrillas, and he called them together in the evening, admitting the adverse outlook, his own physical weakness, and his declining self-control. In the circumstances his faith in the moral and historic value of revolutionary action became tinged with desperation:

> It is one of those moments in which big decisions have to be taken; this type of struggle gives us the opportunity to turn ourselves into revolutionaries, the highest state of the human species, but it also allows us to graduate as men; those who are unable to reach either of these two stages must say so and quit the struggle.[1]

The Bolivian narrative is sometimes dull and sometimes entertaining. It was intended as a day-to-day account by the commander of the army that would liberate the Latin American

[9] Che Guevara: *Bolivian Diary* (Cape/Lorrimer), p. 116.
[1] Ibid., p. 127.

mainland, and it was not a theoretical document. (It is believed that Che was working on a general history of ideas while he was in Bolivia.) But in this store of personal reminiscence there is little sign that Che in Bolivia changed his mind about any of his political, military, or ideological concepts.

In his farewell letter to Fidel, in 1965, Che said that he had been grateful for the opportunity to work as a "builder." But though he did not shrink from trying to run a revolution after it had been militarily successful, the overriding feature in his ideology was the primacy of the revolutionary experience itself. It was in the small, fighting, popular vanguard that Socialism and moral excellence were reared. Revolution became something mystical. But it was also in history an instant that could not be repeated for the island of Cuba, and his international vision of Cuba as the free land in the Yankee empire of the Americas, sponsoring guerrillas in all directions and in a permanent state of war with imperialism, was an effort to prolong the revolutionary experience for future generations of Cubans. In China Mao was to launch the Cultural Revolution for a similar end. The motto of the OLAS conference in 1967—"It is the duty of a revolutionary to make revolution"—spoke for its absent leader too, and it meant more than just a swipe at the nonrevolutionary Communist parties of Latin America.

The world legend

As a person Che was charming, and his frankness about Cuba's problems impressed many who met him. His prose style too was direct, without the florid adornments popular in Latin America, and his correspondence was colloquial and often humorous. When Batista announced his death, he cabled that he was in the best of health. He was a cultured man who enjoyed literature and music and retained his boyhood pleasure in mathematics. His working hours in his Havana ministry were erratic, and he sometimes stayed at his office far into the night. His asthma was partly to blame for this; periodically he had to take time off when he had a severe attack. He was a heavy cigar smoker but had no other personal vices. He lived simply in Havana after the revolution. He was fond of dogs and had a pet with him in the Sierra.

His ruthless attachment to his ideal of revolution made havoc of any family life, though he married twice. His first wife was a Peruvian leftist, Hilda Gadea, whom he seems to have married when he was in Guatemala and by whom he had a daughter. She afterwards said she had lost him to the revolution, and though she came to Cuba after the fall of Batista, they were divorced. He subsequently married a Cuban whom he had met in the Sierra, Aleida March, by whom he had more children. When he left Cuba, he abandoned this second family and, in his farewell letter to Fidel, asked the Cuban state to look after them. He kept in touch with his Argentine relations, and his mother arrived in time to see him take part in the victory celebrations in Havana in 1959.

Che's legend became magnified in Latin America and the rest of the world by his disappearance in 1965 and the tributes paid him at the OLAS gathering in 1967 and, as with another contemporary victim, President Kennedy, the manner of his death gave it new currency.

Different people got different things from Che, of course, but the group most profoundly affected were perhaps the students. Both in Latin America and Europe they could identify with his attack on imperialism and bureaucracy, and societies that fostered both, and could sympathize with his yearnings to liberate a continent and the romantic, anticonventional, and Robin Hood mystique of the guerrilla. It was striking that in the upsurge of European student militancy in 1967 and 1968 he was one of the inspirations. In West Germany the left-wing student leader Rudi Dutschke went so far as to name his son Hosea Che. His portrait appeared frequently in the May 1968 demonstrations in Paris, where it seemed that the legend of Che had arrived transmuted in the terms of Régis Debray.

This was worlds away from the Che of rural revolution, or the strong direction of the economy and collectivization of agriculture that had epitomized the Minister for Industries. The Che remembered in Paris was the man who had denied that bureaucratic Communist parties were best placed to perform the vanguard role in a revolutionary process, and the Che associated with the voluntarist, humanist aspects of the early phase of the Cuban revolution. He became an almost ideal man of action for the alienated young intellectuals of the West.

In Latin America, of course, he was a subject of great curiosity and sympathy among militants. But it remained to be seen whether his example would indeed lead masses of them to reach for their rifles in the way he had hoped. Apart from the ill success of the Bolivian mission, there were other reasons why Latin Americans could be more critical of the man and his methods. To a large extent he represented to them the imitative, if not imperialist, aspects of the Cuban Revolution. But after some nine years, in which the Cuban economy had not been an unsullied success and in which continued appeals for insurrection in the rest of Latin America had achieved little, the prestige of Havana had somewhat diminished. The idea of an Argentine, Brazilian, or even Peruvian or Paraguayan having to make revolution in theoretical or actual obedience to the Caribbean island stretched sympathy too far.

Cuba, of course, did not stop its encouragement for the armed way—there was a fresh attempt on the Haitian dictator within nine months of Che's death—but it was more likely to be in the long term that Che's legend would bear fruit. Those throughout the region who were struggling for economic and political independence of the United States and a revolutionary change in social structures had acquired an international martyr. In the past, leftists in the area had been eclectic in their programs, dependent on local leaders and the local political scene, with the exception of the Moscow Communists, even while international cooperation between Latin American governments and armed forces was growing. In the future the Che legend might provide the left with a unifying myth of Bolivarian force, and even his international proletarian armies might not seem impossible.

The Latin American revolutionary

Che is a unique figure in modern Latin America, and one has to return to the heroes of the independence struggles in the early nineteenth century to find a man like him, ready to fight anywhere in an abstract cause. He is the armed philosopher who, with Fidel Castro, symbolized most clearly the domestication of Marxism-Leninism to Latin American conditions by means of the Cuban Revolution. Fidel has admitted that when he met Che, the latter had "a greater revolutionary development, ideologically speaking, than I had." Without knowing all the intricacies of the development of personal and political relationships in the Cuban leadership, it seems clear that Che played an influential part in the process by which the leadership came to call itself Communist and Cuba developed close links with the Soviet bloc. The adaptation of Marxism-Leninism in which Che was concerned had at least three significant features: first, it adjusted Marxism to the historical Latin American tradition of personal leadership, or *caudillismo;* second, it transmuted age-old traditions of banditry, peasant risings, and militarism into a new ideology; and third, it moved to satisfy Latin America's old yearning for an original political philosophy with a high spiritual content.

The adjustment of Marxism to the old Latin idea of a *jefe máximo* was of the utmost importance. Before either Communism, or even the Cuban Revolution, there was a man—Fidel Castro—who had the boldness to challenge Batista with arms. Much of the heresy, in Muscovite eyes, of the Havana line was a consequence of this: the late involvement of the working class in the revolution, the belated construction of a totalitarian Communist Party, and even the notion that a handful of guerrillas were capable of overthrowing existing governments all over the

continent. This personalism was something rather new in orthodox Communist experience. Although Tito in Yugoslavia had
established such personal authority over the Communist Party
there that he could lead it to break with Stalin, he had been a
Communist for many years before the party became the effective government.

In Latin America too the Communists had faced the fact that
local leaders might be well endowed with charisma: Luis Carlos
Prestes in Brazil, for instance, who had not been a Communist at
the time of the long march which made him a national hero, was
a classic example. But he had become an obedient Muscovite
after his conversion, switching easily from armed revolution to
peaceful popular-front tactics after 1935 to conform with the new
Stalinist strategy.

Fidel Castro was different, uniquely himself, and the old Communists who criticized him in the Sierra for *caudillismo* had a
point. The *persona* of the armed revolutionary leader, appealing
to patriotism and not in the pocket of anyone else, was nevertheless as powerful a force of attraction in Cuba in the late 1950's
as the armed leader had been in Latin America as a whole for
over a century. Che, of course, had recognized Fidel's unusual
personal qualities when he first met him in Mexico, and had
thrown in his lot with him. He summarized the Fidelista contribution to Marxism-Leninism in Latin America when he said
that a popular leader was one of the prerequisites of a successful
revolution, and that ideally political and military leadership
should be vested in the same person. But though he admitted
that Castro was an exceptional character, he did not regard this
as making the Cuban Revolution a special case.

Another criticism by the old Communists in Cuba of the proud
guerrillas in the hills was that they were militarists, an argument
thrown back at the other Muscovites after the triumph in Havana's scornful attacks on rhetorical revolutionaries. Che had told
a Communist leader during the Sierra period: "You are capable of
creating cadres who can silently endure the most terrible tortures
in jail, but you cannot create cadres who can take a machine-gun

nest." This was true enough, and the result of dogmatizing from the Cuban experience was that the rural guerrilla and the absolute primacy of the armed way of revolution—to which Che came to commit himself completely—became the Havana line for export.

In many ways this combination touched fruitful chords in Latin American minds. Peasant revolts and banditry, often colored by the Robin Hood syndrome, were part of the history and folklore of many countries. To such memories Che and Fidel added the magic of social revolution. That a change of regime, the customary Latin *revolución*, should involve some shooting was traditional, and that a social revolution—as in Bolivia or Mexico—should involve some more was inevitable. The orthodox Communists, mouthing revolutionary slogans yet living by wage claims and the ballot box, defied this tradition; Che and the Cubans fused it with Marx. The Fidelistas had to destroy the Cuban regular army, and thereafter they made thousands of others vicarious members of the rebel army by forming the popular militia. Apart from its practical value in consolidating the revolution against armed attackers, this was undoubtedly good psychology. The image of the armed revolutionary, which Che symbolized, was creative in terms of Latin America, but it might have some of the same drawbacks as traditional militarism. Although Castro had promised in 1959 that he would not introduce compulsory military service, he did so in 1963, and it could be argued that, particularly after the missile crisis had guaranteed the survival of the regime, Cuba spent too much on defense.

Communism Havana style was also an attempt to produce an independent political philosophy for Latin America. It was Castro's achievement that in spite of the economic dependence on the Soviet Union that followed the Soviet-Cuban sugar agreement he kept himself free to determine his own line on Latin American policy.[2] The voluntarist and humanist aspects of the revolution, though they might be overshadowed in the course of

---

[2] Economic dependence may explain his policy in other matters. Cuba's was one of the few Communist parties outside the Warsaw Pact to accept the Soviet invasion of Czechoslovakia in August 1968.

time, remained attractive in the region. The emphasis on a new revolutionary morality, particularly associated with Che, made an impact in a continent whose culture was steeped in the values of Catholicism. Altogether, by showing that Communism did not need to be accompanied by slavish obeisance to Moscow and that it could be accommodated to Latin sensibilities, the Cuban leadership and Che were opening the eyes of their contemporaries to its possibilities.

It is easy enough to pick holes in Che's theory of revolution in Latin America, particularly after the end of the Bolivian adventure. Was it all just an intellectual's romance, bearing little relation to the actual attitudes of the different groups of peasants in a diverse continent, or to a changing social reality where the flight to the towns, the growing urban predominance, and the expansion of middle social strata were notable facts? Was it possible that Cuba, where for instance Sergeant Batista in the thirties had corrupted the old army after an NCO revolt, really was abnormal? Was Che wrong to commit his prestige to Bolivia, where the risks were at least as great as in the Cuban landing, and where a setback might have continental repercussions? Certainly, to the nonpartisan observer, Che's program of making a revolution with the aid of a band of fifty men in the countryside seems like the hardest way of going about it. It has yet to bring results anywhere in Latin America outside of Cuba. Had Che perhaps become a bit too dogmatic about the methodology of revolution, perhaps a little vain, and, at thirty-eight, even a little too old for the game when he launched off into the Bolivian jungle? All these things are possible, and the revolution he worshipped may not have been so excellent as to merit his human sacrifice. But in a part of the world that places much store by heroes and dreams, the career and writings of the guerrilla theoretician from Argentina, the apostle of the immaculate revolution, will not easily be forgotten.

Alfredo Stroessner

Asunción

Asunción, the capital of landlocked Paraguay, has the heat, the indolence, and the chaffering crowds of a tropical town in a story by Somerset Maugham. Competition between shoeshine boys, who seem to be seven- or eight-year-olds, is intense. Rattling old streetcars ride around the main streets, and drivers of the latest-model American cars, jostling each other in minuscule traffic jams, play Colonel Bogey as a warning on the horn. In appearance people look mestizo, the Spanish–Guaraní mix that is reflected in the existence of the two official languages. The Hotel Guaraní, a prestige building in the center of the city which was recently built with the funds of the Social Welfare Institute, stands in beleaguered modernity, its small complex of travel agents, fancy shops, and banks surrounded by women selling lace knick-knacks. In one square is a mausoleum containing the remains of the López family, the nineteenth-century dictators whose foolish war with the Triple Alliance—Argentina, Brazil, and Uruguay—impoverished the country and decimated the population. In another square is a captured British tank, a spoil of the successful Chaco War with Bolivia, 1932–5. Down by the Paraguay River and the large connecting lake is the Presidential Palace, with the barracks. Soldiers are to be seen playing games and conducting rudimentary exercises down on the flats by the river. When the flag is run down at sundown in the Plaza Constitución, the trumpets sound and any civilians round about stand at attention.

The only way in which a visitor can tell that he has come to one of the most durable and classic of South American dictatorships is by noticing a neon sign above the Plaza of Heroes which twinkles every night the message: "Peace, work, and well-being with Stroessner."

The present author met General Stroessner, who is affable with foreign journalists, when the President was fifty-five. He seemed heavy and ponderous in his movements and not at all the lively, alert figure of the peeling election posters. A taciturn man, with wary eyes, he starts work each morning at 4:30 a.m. and expects ministers, ambassadors, and the like to attend him immediately on being summoned. In the anterooms of the Presidential Palace there are always people, of all conditions, waiting to see him to present petitions. In a country of only two million, where so much power is vested at the top, any complainant feels he has the right to go to the President. Although Stroessner will sometimes sit for hours as schoolchildren file past him, just for propaganda purposes, there will always be petitioners who cannot see him. On Thursdays, for instance, he spends all the day in his capacity as Commander in Chief, signing promotions and equipment orders in the barracks. For state occasions he moves around the country with an armed guard, but frequently, particularly when he is off duty in the evenings, he drives himself in Asunción without protection. He is a perfectly familiar sight to the population, and in recent years there have been no threats to his life. But an awareness that a history of fear lies not far below the surface comes as soon as a foreigner asks for a biography of the President at any main bookshop: one is cautiously referred to the Ministry of Tourism, whose standard work is *Paraguay, Land of Lace and Legend,* and one is regarded suspiciously as an *agent provocateur.*

Early days and participation in the Chaco War

Alfredo Stroessner was born into a German Paraguayan family in Encarnación in 1912. Encarnación, situated on the Río Paraná and opposite the Argentine town of Posadas, was always a fairly important town and more open to outside influences than most

Paraguayan settlements. German immigrants had been arriving in Paraguay since the 1890's as part of a movement which had also been influencing the nearby Brazilian states of Paraná and Rio Grande do Sul. Alfredo's father, Hugo, who married a Paraguayan girl named Heriberta, was an early arrival who set up a brewery in Encarnación. At the age of sixteen-and-a-half their son joined the army, becoming a cadet at the Military School. Such a move by a teen-ager would have been well understood in most Latin American countries, particularly in the year of the Wall Street slump: not only did the army offer a secure job and reasonable promotion prospects for a young officer, but it guaranteed prestige for life and a favored participation in national affairs. Paraguay's martial history heightened the normal Latin American attractions of a military career, and Stroessner must have been aware of the possibilities of a war with Bolivia over the Chaco in the not-too-distant future.

Although Paraguay was poor and unsettled—there had been a civil war between 1921 and 1923—the Liberal governments of the twenties of Presidents Eligio Ayala and José P. Guggiari were conducting a very careful policy over the disputed Chaco territory. Army outposts in the area were instructed to give the Bolivians no cause for offense, and the temperature of the Asunción press was kept low. But at the same time, in July 1924, plans had been laid for a permanent army of four thousand men which could be expanded on mobilization into a force of twenty-four to thirty thousand, and in 1925 President Ayala approved the creation of four groups of 5,820 men each, with artillery, planes, and cavalry.

All this was costly. While Paraguay was meticulous about servicing foreign debts that dated back to the end of the War of the Triple Alliance, in 1870, these Liberal governments were spending up to sixty per cent of their budget on arms purchases and military preparations. Arms purchases amounting to $2 million were made in Europe and included seven Wibault planes and seven Potez 25's. Officers were sent to the best European military academies. From 1926 to 1930 a French military mission was responsible for instructing the infantry, revising military regulations, developing the artillery, opening schools of military and naval aviation, and giving advice on the latest systems of fortifications of the sort that had proved their worth at Verdun.

The area which gave rise to the war of 1932–5 was sparsely populated and unattractive, lying between the Rivers Pilcomayo and Paraguay, and stretching westwards to the foothills of the Andes. Except during a rainy season, water was scarce. Among the few groups to tackle the problems of agriculture in this semi-desert were some religious colonies of Canadian Mennonites who, by miracles of patience, were able to conjure wheat and other temperate crops out of the earth. They were behind the Paraguayan lines, and the army felt responsible for their protection.

There were rumors of oil in the Chaco. The territorial dispute had its roots in the breakup of the Spanish Empire, and there had been talks on several occasions between Bolivia and Paraguay; but the uninteresting nature of the area and the small amount of physical penetration by either side permitted each to maintain contradictory views on sovereignty without practical damage.

But in the twenties penetration of the patrolling and fort-building type increased. Partly this was to create a better bargaining position for negotiations, but inevitably it led to clashes. Both sides were arming, and the Bolivians, with a larger modern army under the command of the German general Hans Kundt, dismissed the military potential of the million Paraguayans. After the failure of negotiations in Buenos Aires in 1927–8 an incident at Vanguardia, where a Paraguayan major, Rafael Franco, organized the capture of a Bolivian fort without higher authorization, led to war fever on both sides. In December 1929, after Bolivian reprisals, Paraguay ordered general mobilization and Bolivia ordered a partial one. But the results were a shambles. It turned out that the Paraguayan high command had no plans for a general mobilization and the necessary arms had not yet arrived. It was such an army, with three thousand regulars and ten thousand reservists, that the young Alfredo Stroessner was joining.

The farce of failed mobilization and the fact that the Paraguayans had broken the Bolivian code and were able to announce that the Bolivians were planning an offensive in January 1930 gave a new opportunity for peace initiatives. There was a conference on a nonaggression pact, and both Washington and Latin American neutrals did their best to mediate. In 1931 the governments in both Bolivia and Paraguay changed hands. An elected President, Dr. Daniel Salamanca, took over from a junta in La Paz. But this was not a contribution to peace. He was an opposition leader with no administrative experience, who was an advocate of a strong role in the Chaco: in 1929 Bolivia had finally accepted her loss of the old Pacific coastline, and Salamanca argued that she should look eastward instead to the tributaries of the Río de la Plata. In Paraguay students and radical elements had demonstrated against the Guggiari government and, although the high command had prevented the ambitious Major Franco from adding his troops to the rebels, the withdrawal of the Colorado Party from Congress led to a crisis and the President's resignation. The new President, Dr. Eusebio Ayala, was an experienced diplomat anxious to defend Paraguay's rights in the Chaco. Mediation attempts broke down because of the intransigence of both Bolivian and Paraguayan public opinion, which would not accept the abandonment of any forts as part of a settlement. After further military incidents it was clear by July 1932 that the two countries were in fact at war.

Stroessner was a participant in the first big battle of the war as a platoon commander in a special regiment made up of cadets and instructors from the Military School under Major Arturo Bray, a brilliant commander who had fought in the British ranks in the First World War. The battle took place at Boquerón, a Paraguayan fort which the Bolivians had captured and then entrenched. The Paraguayans, whose morale was high, cut off the fort and, with a two-to-one local numerical superiority, defeated four thousand Bolivians. Each side lost about two thousand men before the Bolivians surrendered, and the scarcity of water led to great hardships. Part of the regiment in which Stroessner was serving played an important role in beating off a Bolivian relief force. This Paraguayan success caused a crisis in the Bolivian high command and indicated that the belligerents were not as disparate in strength as outsiders and Bolivians had thought.

Stroessner distinguished himself sufficiently at Boquerón to be transferred to the artillery in December 1932. He became a section commander in a battery of "75" field guns. Anything to do with artillery on the Paraguayan side in the Chaco War was a responsible post because, while it was effective, it was also expensive. The army that won at Boquerón had only fifty-nine guns. The care of each, and the accurate use of shells, were of the greatest importance to a country which was trying to win a war on a slender budget.

Throughout 1933 Stroessner saw plenty of action in the southern zone around Nanawa, which the Bolivians were trying to capture by a strategy of position and frontal assault. This was the Paraguayan First Corps area, and the Commander in Chief in the Chaco, the able Marshall Félix Estigarribia, had his headquarters nearby. Broadly his strategy was defensive, though he was able to take limited tactical offensives. But as the war progressed more and more favorably for Paraguay, the theatre of action moved gradually westward toward the Andean foothills. Stroessner received recognition for his courage and efficiency, and on April 20, 1933, the jingoistic Major Roque Samaniego, who commanded the detachment in which Stroessner ran the artillery, congratulated everyone for resisting heroically the attacks of four Bolivian regiments the day before. The Bolivians fled hurriedly, leaving their wounded and over 150 dead, and throwing away their equipment.

By the end of 1933, after the successful battle of Campo Via which resulted in the surrender of eight thousand Bolivians, Estigarribia was firmly on top. Although Paraguay, which had never had any military aircraft, could no longer afford to buy new weapons, she was able to keep going on captured arms. By then she had acquired over eight hundred machine guns and nearly thirteen thousand rifles in this way; of the 77,000 troops that

Bolivia had originally sent to the Chaco only 7,000 were left. The losses, as recorded by a U.S. military historian, Captain David H. Zook, Jr.,[1] were staggering: 10,000 Bolivians were prisoners, 14,000 had died in battle or were missing, 32,000 had been withdrawn as wounded or sick, 8,000 were immobilized by the straggling communications, and 6,000 had deserted to Argentina. Throughout 1934 the superiority of the Paraguayan leadership and the higher morale of the men—the Bolivians mutinied on several occasions during the war—continued to keep their army in command, although lengthening communications lines, shortages of suitable conscripts, exhaustion of funds, and even the problems of looking after the increasing number of prisoners were adding to the difficulties.

On December 5, Stroessner was cited for his distinguished conduct in the battle of El Carmen, one of Estigarribia's greatest victories, which, as the citation rightly said, culminated in the "total destruction" of the Bolivian Tenth Division. At the end of November the Bolivian reverses and the mutual suspicions of the higher political and military leadership had resulted in an army coup and the overthrow of President Salamanca.

In February 1935 Stroessner was made commander of a Stokes Brandt mortar group and acted as such in the unsuccessful battle of Villa Montes. Villa Montes had been a Bolivian headquarters when their troops were still stretched across the Chaco. Now it was an advance redoubt for the defense of Andean Bolivia itself. Unwisely and uncharacteristically Estigarribia permitted the Paraguayans to take heavy losses in the course of frontal attacks. While the Bolivian artillery, guided by aerial reconnaissance, caused heavy damage, the Paraguayan gunners ran out of shells. Although there were further attempts, the Paraguayans never did manage to take Villa Montes, nor the equally important town of Camiri farther north, whose oil deposits were a main objective after the capture of the Chaco. An armistice was agreed on in Buenos Aires on June 9, 1935.

[1] David H. Zook, Jr.: *The Conduct of the Chaco War* (Bookman Associates: New York; 1960).

Stroessner emerged from the war a battle-hardened young officer with a reputation for valor. Almost certainly he knew more about himself, his potential for dash and leadership, and also more about his fellow Paraguayans, their martial qualities and their ability to endure suffering. From the front lines the victory of a Paraguayan David over a Bolivian Goliath could be seen as due to superior military leadership, higher general morale—the division between the Hispanicized Bolivian command and an Andean Indian infantry forced to fight in the lowlands offered a miserable contrast—and closer cooperation between the political and military commanders.

But for Paraguay as a whole the war had been a mixed blessing. Victory had wiped out the psychological traces of defeat in 1870 but at the cost of giving renewed prestige to military men, and raising a whole new crop to dispute domestic power for another twenty years. The country was financially and socially exhausted. Whereas, by the end of the war, Bolivia could confidently set about raising a new army, the proud Paraguayan regiments that had fought with 1,600 men at Boquerón were down to 250–400 each—the total fighting force was now scarcely 15,000—and the bankrupt treasury depended utterly on Argentine good will for the continued supply of shells and gasoline. Paraguay had spent $124 million and lost 36,000 dead.

Civil war, and the overthrow of Dr. Chávez

The end of the war and the return home of the troops brought a new strain on Paraguay's always fragile political institutions. The problems of the peace negotiations and jealousies of officers sent into the reserve, some of whom complained that the monthly pension of 1,500 gold pesos for life awarded to Estigarribia was too much, made inflammatory material. Colonel Franco, the hotheaded but glamorous hero of Vanguardia, who had proved an intrepid divisional and corps commander in the war, rallied the conspirators of 1931 in a *Putsch* against the Liberal government on February 17, 1936.

The "Febreristas," as they were called, took over power for eighteen months. A curious mixture, they borrowed ideas from both national and international Socialism, though their binding force was Franco's personality. But the Chaco peace negotiations, whose alleged generosity to Bolivia had been used by the Febrerista conspirators as an issue, rebounded against them in power. Military irritation with an accord of May 1937 which was to lead to a full peace conference in September enabled Colonel Ramón Paredes, commander of the Chaco forces, to depose Franco in August. The Liberals were restored to power. In 1939, running as a Liberal, the war hero Estigarribia, who had subsequently served as Ambassador in Washington, was elected President. In the following February he dissolved Congress. With the help of a plebiscite he imposed a new constitution on the country which was to go unquestioned until the mid-sixties, when President Stroessner had his own reasons for altering it.

This document gave great powers to the executive and only small ones to the legislature, and reflected the views of both modern Paraguayan officers and many world political leaders of 1940. Some of its articles offered apparent protection for political and individual liberties, but their effect could be negated by a strong interpretation of Articles 32, 35, 37, and 52. Article 32 provided that the state should supervise and regulate the organization, functioning, and activities of groups or bodies of a public nature; Article 35 said that the guaranteed liberties were all of a social nature and that public order required that their exercise be limited by law—to foster hate or class struggle among Paraguayans was not permitted; Article 37 said that anyone joining the country's enemies, giving them aid, or in any way threatening the independence or security of Paraguay, committed treason; while Article 52 permitted the President to declare a state of emergency whenever the functioning of the constitution was threatened and enabled him to arrest suspected persons. Estigarribia's personal rule was cut short by his death in September in an air crash. He was succeeded by his chief army ally, General Higinio Morinigo, who proceeded to install his own dictatorship.

At elections in 1943 General Morinigo was the only presidential candidate. His rule was tough, and he managed to be friendly at the same time with both the Farrell–Perón régime in Argentina and the U.S. Embassy, which gave him some aid. He improved health services and communications, but political opposition was grimly suppressed. Then, in mid-1946, the regime changed suddenly, and Morinigo expelled the Nazi and Peronist sympathizers from his government and the top army command, invited Colorados and Febreristas to join the cabinet, and spoke of free elections in the near future. Almost overnight politics returned to Paraguay, exiles returned from Uruguay and Argentina, and a new trade-union movement grew rapidly in which Febreristas and Communists vied for control.

But so much activity frightened Morinigo. The antagonism between Febreristas and Colorados within the cabinet and the burgeoning trade unions caused a conservative reaction in early 1947. Morinigo sacked the Febreristas and formed a new cabinet of army officers and Colorados. The prospect of congressional elections was allowed to fade into the background. Then in March a rebellion began in the army garrison of Concepción, in the north of Paraguay, which started a large-scale civil war and came near to overthrowing Morinigo. On one side was a heterogeneous mixture of Febreristas, Liberals, and Communists with Rafael Franco as the outstanding military leader. They were backed by at least half the army, much of the diminutive air force, and, after a mutiny in Argentine waters, the two patrol boats of the Paraguayan navy. With Morinigo on the other side were the Colorados and the remainder of the army, which included the First ("General Bruguez") Artillery Regiment and its commandant, Alfredo Stroessner.

Stroessner had stayed in the artillery after the end of the Chaco War and settled down to the routine life of the barracks with its professional courses, garrison reviews, and the rest. Official reports on his progress stressed his initiative, his industry, and his capacity for command. In 1938, his teacher in one of his courses, Major Stephan Vysokolan, said that he was the best at mathematics in a class of twenty-five, with a great capacity for independent work, and that he would be good in command of antiaircraft guns. In 1940 he attended an artillery course in Brazil, where his physical strength, as well as his other qualities, drew attention. The Brazilians in their report said that he arrived "with a weak understanding of the technique of shooting and topography"—which, considering that, unlike them, he had fought in a war for national survival, might be dismissed as national prejudice. But of course it is a reminder that in military lore, as in other matters, Paraguay tended to follow some way behind her larger neighbors.

In the peace talks it had been suggested that the armies of both Bolivia and Paraguay should be reduced in size to five thousand men. Stroessner then was part of a small professional army in which every officer must have known every other and in which the maneuvering for power within army and state and any other plots against the regime had big repercussions. In these cross-currents Stroessner seems to have stayed fairly loyal to the Morinigo régime. As early as September 1943 he was being cited as a brigadier in the category of regimental commanders for his "correct attitude" in a minor Chaco rising of that year. But it was not for another two years that he was promoted to the post of commandant of the "General Bruguez" Artillery Regiment. Under the army artillery commandant this made him the most important gunner in Paraguay and gave him a crucial role in the 1947 civil war.

It is impossible now to be certain why Stroessner sided with Morinigo then, though one may be reasonably sure that it was not for partisan political motives. The two traditional political factions were the Liberals, with their strength in the urban professional class and their friendship for Argentina, and the Colorados, based on the countryside and looking to Brazil. Both were fairly authoritarian in spirit, and Stroessner's choice of the latter was unlikely to have been swayed by their somewhat sterile rivalries. As a man of conservative temper, however, the place of the Communists among the opposition may have dissuaded him from joining it, and he may well have had personal differences with the bouncy General Franco. On a careerist view he may have decided that there was more to be gained by staying with Morinigo, having already got a senior position, while if Franco succeeded, the latter's long-standing clique would have priority for the top army jobs.

The uprising, which started in Concepción and among the Chaco garrisons, had a phony air at first. Morinigo kept control of Asunción and, short of regulars, sent levies to the front. For at least four weeks government troops were camped on the Ypane River while a Brazilian mediation mission, led by the redoubtable Negrão de Lima, attempted the impossible task of achieving a compromise. While a few rebel planes made raids on Asunción, dropping ten-pound bombs by hand, the total casualties of the first four months were estimated by an American journalist[2] at no more than one thousand. The rebels retreated when they could have resisted, and the government commanders unconvincingly offered a rebel spoiling sortie at Tacuatí as a reason for postponing their conclusive offensive. In fact, each side was hoping that the other would fall apart as a result of intrigue, defection, or the work of mediators, and thus make it unnecessary to shed the blood of former friends and colleagues. This was true to a hallowed Latin American tradition.

But the character of the war changed suddenly when General Franco, in one of the lightning moves that had been a trademark in the Chaco War, put all his troops onto riverboats and came downstream to invest Asunción, leaving Concepción open to capture in the meantime. This put Morinigo in a desperate position. Differing reports said that he had to go into hiding in a foreign embassy, that his government had to withdraw from the city, and that the capital was defended by only 2,200 loyal troops from a force of 8,000. At the cost, however, of arming the Colorado partisans and fierce street fighting in the city suburbs,

[2] Mac R. Johnson, New York *Herald Tribune*, July 1, 1947.

Morinigo not only resisted successfully but, aided by government troops from elsewhere and the arrival of a cargo of Argentine ammunition, routed the rebels. It was at this time that one of the rebel chiefs was supposed to have said: "The finest noise that we could hear would be the sound of Stroessner's guns." Stroessner's guns, however, were part of the loyal relief column which helped to rout the rebels in mid-August. Some 1,650 rebels were killed, the rest surrendered, and General Franco fled to Argentina.

The aftermath of the war, which established a Colorado ascendancy that was to last at least twenty years, was filled with partisan reprisals. Asunción's jails were crammed with suspected or actual rebels, torture was commonplace, and citizens were not safe to wander the streets without wearing a touch of red, the Colorado color. An indeterminate number fled to Argentina, some by swimming the Paraguay River, and joined the thousands who had gone to find work there for nonpolitical reasons. Personal differences split the Colorado victors, and for a chaotic period of about two years governments were constantly being changed by coup d'état. After the seventh in fourteen months Dr. Federico Chávez became President in 1950.

Stroessner, who had been caught on the wrong foot at least once in the helter-skelter political confusion—he was known as "Colonel Boot" for a while after being driven to the Brazilian Embassy concealed in the back of a car subsequent to a failed coup in 1948—rose fast under the dictatorial Chávez. In September he became commander of the artillery and in the course of 1951 he became Commander in Chief of the Armed Forces. It was from this position of strength that he was able to ensure that the fall of Chávez, in May 1954, should lead to an interim government composed of his own friends and to his own election as President in July in a balloting in which he was the only candidate.

If Stroessner did not in fact engineer the whole plot against Chávez, he very quickly took advantage of it. What appears to have happened was that Chávez tried to arrest a cavalry regimental commander suspected of wanting to restore to power a group of men which included the former Minister of the Interior, Tomás Romero Pereira, who as head of the Colorado Party was to prove one of Stroessner's closest collaborators. While Colonel Nestor Ferreira, commander of the First Cavalry Division at the big Campo Grande barracks outside Asunción, supported Chávez, Stroessner displaced him and told the President that he was infringing on military dignity. The cloudy doctrine of "military dignity" has been frequently cited in Latin America, normally to protect the armed forces from civilian authority.

On this occasion the coup was not bloodless—the Asunción Chief of Police, Roberto Petit, was killed after cavalrymen attacked the police station—but it was quickly apparent that Stroessner could restore order among the cavalry and it was he who ordered shops to reopen. Within less than three days the Chávez cabinet, which had fruitlessly sought refuge in the War College, and there been surrounded by Stroessner's troops, resigned. Observers were surprised that Stroessner did not take a ministry himself, but the provisional President was Pereira, the other new ministers were the Commander in Chief's friends, and within a week everything became clearer when Pereira announced that there would be elections on July 11, 1954, and that Stroessner would be the Colorado candidate.

On the whole, the coup makes most sense in terms of personalities, but other issues may have been involved to some degree. Fears that Chávez was trying to build up the strength of the police as a paramilitary organization may have motivated both the rebellious cavalry and Stroessner. In the perennial juggling of Argentina and Brazil in Paraguay's foreign relations the Chávez government's heavy commitment to Perón's Argentina may have counted against it. Perón had set up ATLAS (Agrupación de Trabajadores Latino-Americanos Sindicalistas), his hemispheric labor body, in Asunción in 1952, and as a result of his first state visit to Paraguay in October 1953 the latter signed a treaty of economic union with Argentina. The anti-Chávez coup occurred a few days before a second state visit by Perón was due. On the other hand, a mixed group of landowners and businessmen—which had included the provisional President, Pereira —had been urging that a $5 million international loan be used to improve road communications with Brazil so that new coffee lands and other resources in the frontier region could be developed. Stroessner, though his relations with Perón were to prove pragmatic, could have been expected to work for friendlier links with Brazil.

Political life under the dictator

Stroessner was elected President with a quarter of a million votes for a term lasting until 1958. Like President Morinigo, but unlike his immediate predecessors, he also remained Commander in Chief of the Armed Forces, so that his apparent strength was formidable. But in fact his power tended to grow only as his durability was proven; at first, observers noted that he consulted army and Colorado leaders frequently, and they argued that perhaps he was not the strong man he looked.

During the fifties opposition politics in Paraguay was effectively outlawed and the most likely way in which the régime might be removed would be through a successful military coup. Attempted coups, halted at various stages before fruition, were a regular feature of this period. Given recent Paraguayan history, both the government and the different groups of plotters knew that every attempt had to be taken seriously, and Stroessner used the prevailing uncertainty as an excuse for continuing to rule Paraguay in a state of siege, with Colorado strong-arm men ready to appear on the streets at short notice.

Throughout Latin America military coup-making has always been in essence simple, and the small scale of the Paraguayan armed forces, and the fact that a large proportion of the population lives within a hundred miles of Asunción, make it even easier. Just a small handful of officers, stationed in Asunción and able to lead their troops into the streets and public buildings, may, acting in concert and with surprise, change the government. To offset these advantages, Stroessner could rely on the loyalty and informal intelligence system of the Colorado Party. Though there might not always be perfect harmony between the two, and though it was clear that Stroessner was more a *caudillo* whom circumstances had thrown with the Colorados rather than a good party man, the two had a strong interest in mutual support. Any coup which brought back the Liberals or Febreristas would deprive the Colorados of all their dubiously won privileges and lay them open to the sufferings they had inflicted on their enemies.

Stroessner had also to rely on his own diligence in knowing the individuals and general mood within the services, and ensuring that all those in a position to cause trouble were personally loyal. As a career officer in a small army, of course, he knew many of the officers well anyway, and he made sure that their rights and their requirements for equipment were cared for. The armed forces took a high quota of the national budget and, from the new American cars of the senior officers down to the money that a conscript was able to send home to a peasant family, they appeared as a fount of riches and welfare.

The fall of General Perón in 1955, who escaped from Argentina via Asunción, inevitably set off shock waves in Paraguay, where the governing Colorados had been generally friendly to the Argentine régime. Just before Christmas there was an attempted coup by part of the cavalry division and artillery elements, in which a key role was played by Méndez Fleitas, the president of the Central Bank, who had also had a shadowy part in the cavalry disaffection which paved the way for Stroessner's Presidency. Fleitas resigned from the Central Bank on December 29. Tension continued in early 1956. It was generally considered that the new anti-Peronist government of Argentina was supporting Stroessner's opponents; economic pressures were reflected in a fall in the currency, and the New York *Herald Tribune*[3] reported that a clandestine anti-Stroessner radio could be heard in Paraguay.

[3] On February 13, 1956.

Military commands were changed in February, the national university was closed in April to prevent a student strike against the regime, and Stroessner made changes in his cabinet in May. While the President was trying to remove vestiges of Peronist influence from the regime, sympathy for the fallen dictator among the Colorados could still be an embarrassment. Party toughs aided by the police broke up meetings when an anti-Peronist Argentine student delegation came to Asunción, and they forced it to return.

In November 1956, while countries elsewhere in the world were preoccupied with the effects of events in Hungary and Suez, the major news in Paraguay was that Rafael Franco had been met by an estimated eight thousand people on his arrival in Asunción. The government at once deported him on the ground that he was implicated in a plot. This may or may not have been provable, but an indication of the current state of political insecurity was given at the end of that month, when Stroessner gave safe conduct to forty-six opposition politicians who had taken refuge in foreign embassies in Asunción. In May 1957 the government announced the discovery of a Liberal plot to overthrow it, and twenty-four persons were arrested.

Toward the end of the year the Colorados announced that Stroessner would be their presidential candidate again in 1958 and, significantly, Edgar Insfran, the Minister of the Interior and one of the abler men in the cabinet, resigned to manage the election campaign. Once more Stroessner was the only candidate.

The regime gradually evolved in the course of Stroessner's second term of office in response to both domestic and international changes. Domestically the major fact was the national awareness that Stroessner was an abler and more durable ruler than the previous run of aspirant dictators. But at the same time, in the context of the Americas, the replacement of Batista by Castro in Cuba and the United States's response in the Alliance for Progress made him look rather more of an anachronism. While it was increasingly in General Stroessner's interest to make himself more respectable in inter-American eyes, and in particular to pay some lip service to the U.S. passion for democracy, internal conditions were making it easier for him.

In 1959 the Febreristas and the traditional Liberals signed a joint manifesto proclaiming La Unión Nacional Paraguaya, in which they were to work together for constitutional government and against tyranny. This pact did not disavow violence—though it was possible that the involvement of the two groups together might simplify the tasks of Stroessner's intelligence—but the withering of partisanship was a stage toward peaceful participation in Paraguayan politics. In 1960 a new Christian Democrat movement was founded, taking its inspiration from the growth of the Chilean movement, and attracted some able young supporters. Its significance was that it was the first group to rule out the possibility of coming to power by a military coup.

Around 1962–3 Stroessner succeeded in persuading some of the Liberals, led by Dr. Carlos Levi Ruffinelli, to contest the presidential election of the latter year and to occupy a block of seats in Congress (twenty out of sixty) as a loyal opposition. Dr. Levi Ruffinelli explained to the author that this participation was agreed on at a Liberal conference held in exile in 1962 on the grounds that continuing violent opposition was proving sterile. However, a large faction in the party doubted whether anything more could be achieved in a situation in which the government would continue to hold all real power and was angry at being asked to accept Stroessner's terms. The party therefore definitively split.

In the sixties the Febreristas were also evolving in a way in which they could begin to experiment with electoral politics. After a probationary period they were accepted as a member party in the Socialist International, and in Paraguay it was believed that they were receiving financial support from German Social Democratic sympathizers. General Franco himself was living peacefully in Asunción, no doubt with the tacit understanding that he would indulge in no provocative activities, by mid-1967.

Benignity did not overtake public life suddenly, however, and guerrillas crossed into Paraguay in 1960—the May 14 Plot—and again later, but were always mopped up. Among plots of the sixties was one organized by a Colorado splinter group, the Movimiento Popular Colorado, at Caacupe in 1964. But while Colorados continued to monopolize political patronage, so that it was very difficult for a lawyer who was an active opponent of the government, for instance, to make a living, it was also true by the mid-sixties that terror had become a much less obvious feature of political life.

The culmination of the more pacific turn of the regime was achieved in elections to a constitutional convention in May 1967. In Asunción itself observers considered that they were conducted reasonably fairly, and that it was due to disorganization and lack of experience by the opposition parties more than to anything else that opposition tellers and ballot papers were not available at every polling place. In the countryside, however, where voting was much more subject to the influence of local Colorado bosses, the results were certainly defective. All the main parties participated in the elections and, while the Colorados inevitably were awarded the majority of seats, the Liberal Radicals (the traditional Liberals), the Levi Ruffinelli Liberals, and the Febreristas were given small representations, in that order.

The constitutional convention formally recognized the longevity of Stroessner's rule. The Estigarribia constitution of 1940, while it had created a strong executive in deference to the historic predilections of Paraguayans, had also offered one or two sops to the Liberal penchant for constitutional government, and one of its articles forbade a President to serve more than two consecutive terms. Stroessner had already stretched this by running again in 1963, when it was explained on his behalf that from 1954 to 1958 he had merely been using up the unexpired part of Chávez's time. But in order to be elected again in 1968, as he felt it his patriotic duty to be, it became necessary to alter the constitution. The opposition parties took the opportunity to press for an end to imprisonment without trial and the long-standing state of emergency. But, secure in the backing of the

Colorados, Stroessner did not need to give anything away. After the adoption of the new constitution he ran for a further term in February 1968, against candidates of the three other parties, and won by an overwhelming majority.

By then Stroessner had been in office so long that political opponents could say, and a large number of ordinary Paraguayans probably felt, that he was a better ruler than any obvious alternative. He himself insisted frequently on the peace and stability which he had created, however dubious these might have been. For students of Paraguay there were two possible conclusions at this point: either the optimistic one that Western-style democratic party politics was taking root under the shadow of the regime, offering the country a more hopeful future than the violence and coups of the past; or the pessimistic one that dictatorships spawn only dictatorships, that the regime was still keeping political opposition on a tight rein, and that little had happened to make political conflict more peaceful in the future. Only time, abetted by events in the rest of Latin America, would give the answer.

Civil liberties and a police state

The regime has claimed that Paraguay possesses a free press, but this is not true. The main daily of Asunción, *La Tribuna*, with a sale of about thirty thousand copies, contains no political commentary. Of the other available morning papers, *La Patria* is the official Colorado paper and *El País* is government-controlled, and the Asunción evening *La Tarde* is also a government paper.

Broadly speaking, dissent is kept to the small-circulation weekly press—and all the main political groupings, including the Catholics but of course excluding the Communists, have journals—and even then discussion of certain topics brings reprisals. While the Febrerista and Liberal journals may print outspoken criticism of the government and the opposition prints the names of political prisoners, criticism of the personal life of the

President or on sensitive foreign policy issues is taboo. Journalists find themselves imprisoned and paper-sellers risk being beaten up. The real limits on press freedom were shown in 1967, when a member of the opposition wished to start a paper with the offensive title *Prensa Libre* (Free Press). Government permission is essential for a new publishing venture, and it was not granted. Stroessner's own views on the press were given in a speech on August 12, 1955, when he said:

> I am against the classification of the Press as a bad or a good one, because I feel that the written and spoken word should not have any other aim but good. If a bad Press exists, it should not be called Press, because if we believe in God and therefore believe ourselves to be servants of God, we must always abstain from sowing the seed of evil in the spiritual furrows of the people and of humanity.

The scope of the press in Paraguay, where less than half the adult population can read, was necessarily narrower than the possibilities for television, which was set up in Stroessner's era. On the inter-American commercial pattern, it might occasionally show international films, but its opportunities for elucidating Paraguayan problems—at least where the regime was involved—were almost nil. An example of the close interest the President took in even the advertisements was shown by the case of a commercial that used a clock time of 9 a.m. for transmission at various times in the day. After seeing it a few times, he called up the TV station and said that it could only be allowed to continue if the clock told the actual time, as otherwise simple viewers might be confused.

In spite of international objections and, recently, pressure from the Catholic hierarchy in Paraguay, the Stroessner regime has been perfunctory in its attitude to the rule of law. An Amnesty International report of 1966[4] gave damning examples as well as casting a strong light on the tortures and discomforts

---

[4] Compiler: Amnesty International, *Prison Conditions in Paraguay* (August 1966).

that a political prisoner risks. General Stroessner had inherited a "state of emergency" under Article 52 of the constitution, with its widespread powers of arrest and control of movement, but made no effort to regulate this in a special law, as the article also prescribed. Although the courts had ruled that Article 26— which provides for arrest only by warrant and for detention for no more than twenty-four hours without a court hearing of *habeas corpus*—overruled Article 52, neither warrants nor *habeas corpus* were allowed, and when courts freed someone, he was often rearrested under Article 52. Except for electoral purposes on two occasions, the "state of emergency" lasted until the constitutional change of 1967, and the practice has continued since.

The repressive powers of the executive were considerably strengthened by Stroessner with the proclamation of a law "For the Defense of Democracy" in October 1955 whose first two articles are as follows:

ARTICLE 1. Those who rise up with armed force against the constituted authority partially or totally to supplant the democratic, republican organization of the Nation, by the Communist system or any other totalitarian regime, shall suffer the sentence of five years to ten years imprisonment. Proposition, conspiracy, and formal instigation to commit this offense shall be punishable, when they are accompanied by preparatory acts, by half the aforesaid term.

ARTICLE 2. The following will be subject to a sentence of six months to five years imprisonment: (1) Those who spread the Communist doctrine or any doctrines or systems whatsoever, which propose to destroy or change the democratic, republican organization of the Nation by violence. (2) Those who organize, constitute, or direct associations or entities which have as their objective, either openly or clandestinely, to commit the offense set out in the preceding clause.

This law, whose penalties could be stretched to cover almost any form of opposition to the regime, was challenged by a Christian Democratic high-court judge, who ordered the release of the first prisoner brought to trial under it. The order was ignored by the police. Although Paraguay has no secret police—

the paramilitary police force is commanded by an army officer
—the Amnesty report stated that torture had taken place in the
presence of General Duarte Vera, the long-time Chief of Police
under Stroessner.

The Central Department of Investigation at Asunción Police
Headquarters pursues political opponents. Individuals have often
died from torture, and their bodies have been thrown into the
Paraná or the Paraguay River. In 1965 six young men, all but
one members of a Communist youth group, were tortured to
death in a police station in Asunción. The Amnesty delegate,
Anthony Freire Marreco, reported that in 1966 there were perhaps only 150 political prisoners, though he doubted whether
many would fit the Amnesty definition of prisoners of conscience.
Some had genuinely plotted or taken part in acts of violence,
others might just be victims of the personal enmity of someone
within the regime, and possibly connected with rackets in which
regime members were involved. The delegate concluded that all
the concentration camps which had been holding anti-Stroessner
guerrillas had been closed, with the possible exception of Peña
Hermosa, an island prison in the Paraguay River.

Under Stroessner the worst sufferers were the Communists,
including the wives of party activists, even though the party had
never achieved much standing in the country. But the regime
defined "Communism" as it chose and this was one justification
it used for repression of the trade-union movement. In August
1958 there was a general strike by the Confederación Paraguaya de Trabajadores which, after several arrests of union
leaders, issued in a final collapse after eleven days. After this
the Government took over the CPT and a new executive committee was imposed, a majority of whom were Colorado members.

For a country with a tradition of toughness and an unsophisticated social structure, it is possible to argue that much of
the "police state" aspect of the regime—not just the arrests but
the telephone tapping and trivial harassment of opponents—
passed over the bulk of the population to strike only at an

elite. But the effect was to perpetuate obsolete political and social structures and to isolate Paraguay from the processes of questioning and innovation that were altering the rest of the continent.

Foreign policy—Brazil, Argentina, U.S.A.

Paraguay, sharing its borders with three neighbors, has always been aware of the exigencies of foreign policy and has been particularly involved in the interplay between Brazil and Argentina. But though Brazil had long wished for influence in Asunción, Paraguay's heavy dependence on river traffic between Asunción and the Río de la Plata her main trading outlet inevitably gave Argentine relations a special importance. For reasons of sentiment and policy Stroessner began his term with rather more amiability for Brazil than Argentina, though by the sixties he was on equally friendly terms with each. The fall of Perón helped to sour Argentine–Paraguay relations for a while. At the same time President Kubitschek of Brazil was befriending Stroessner with military and police instructors, weapons, and money. A highway was built from Asunción to the Brazilian frontier at the Iguassú Falls, where a bridge was thrown across the Paraná River. This gave overland access to the Brazilian port of Paranaguá with shorter shipping times to Europe and the East Coast of North America than was possible from the Río de la Plata ports. The Castello Branco regime in Brazil is also thought to have given financial aid to Stroessner.

But by then a new cause for friction had arisen between the two countries—a border dispute over the Guaíra Falls, upstream from the spectacular Iguassú Falls. The dispute arose over interpretation of the 1872 treaty which ended the war with the Triple Alliance and was activated because of Brazil's desire for more hydroelectric power for the states of Mato Grosso and Paraná. Brazil effectively annexed the falls, whose production capacity was estimated at twenty million kilowatts, and there was a strong suspicion within Paraguay that the government was not fighting on the issue as it should. When students of the National University in Asunción demonstrated against a hand-over of the falls in 1966, several were briefly imprisoned.

Although the Stroessner regime has always been unpopular in left-wing circles in both Argentina and Brazil, relations at the official level have usually been smooth, if not warm. The armed forces of both countries have had their own links with Paraguay, ranging from training missions to the exchange of visits by Chiefs of Staff, and their view of Stroessner has usually been friendlier than their compatriots'. This, of course, had renewed importance when first Brazil, under Castello Branco, and then Argentina under Onganía, came under military governments again in the mid-sixties. By then, when his own mild liberalization had started, Stroessner was able to boast a new kind of respectability in the Americas.

Despite memories of the Chaco War, Paraguay and Bolivia have been on good terms in the Stroessner period. Official speeches on both sides have talked of the war as an error, promoted by foreigners, which interrupted the harmony of two sister peoples. The Paraguayans have shown no conceit, and the Bolivians, at least as far as the great majority are concerned, have not been eager to even the score. When Bolivia faced the guerrilla outbreak of 1967, Paraguay increased its vigilance in the Chaco in cooperation with the Bolivian authorities.

Chile and Uruguay, two small countries with perhaps the keenest democratic outlook in South America, have been the most firmly disposed against the Paraguayan general. Many political exiles have congregated in Montevideo. Even so, Stroessner has visited both countries. Apart from its rabid anti-Communism —which meant that in the sixties Paraguay was still paying close attention to the need for amicable relations with places like Formosa and South Korea—the Stroessner dictatorship is weak on ideology. But as a dictatorship it has tended to be polite to others of the same breed, and in 1957 the President paid a state visit to the Venezuela of the notoriously tough General Pérez Jiménez.

Throughout Stroessner's rule there have been rumors of Nazi war criminals living in Paraguay. The most popular candidates have been Dr. Mengele, the concentration-camp doctor, and Martin Bormann. The assumption has been that Paraguay, with its dictatorship, its German colony, and its poor communications is a natural haven for wanted men. In 1960 the West German Ambassador is said to have been told by Stroessner to desist when he inquired whether anything was known about Mengele. Even for normal criminals Paraguay has had a reputation as a country which rarely extradites offenders.

In international affairs, Paraguay's most important policy is one of unswerving friendship for the United States. In contrast to most Latin American states, which either from principle or expediency criticize the United States from time to time, Stroessner has maintained a consistent public attitude of loyalty. He once said that he regarded the U.S. Ambassador like an extra member of his cabinet, and Paraguay's vote at the United Nations and in the Organization of American States has regularly been cast in favor of U.S. policy.

But from the American point of view such faithfulness has not been an unmixed blessing. In the early fifties the State Department under President Eisenhower was not too anxious about the details of Latin governments so long as they were stable and anti-Communist, and permitted foreign private investment. Such a line was a Republican restatement of Franklin Roosevelt's "Good Neighbor" style of nonintervention; but even under the Eisenhower Administration this line was being attacked inside and outside the State Department by those who wanted a more active and democratic Latin American strategy. This was reflected in Vice-President Nixon's ill-received tour of 1958. In the course of it he made a brief visit to Paraguay and urged Congress and President Stroessner, in a speech which was largely censored, to operate a more democratic system of government.

When the activist policy reached fruition in the Kennedy Administration's Alliance for Progress, with its specific commitments to democratic government, land reform, and the like, Paraguay and the small number of other dictatorships raised a problem. On grounds of backwardness their needs were usually greater than those of the other Latin countries and, in Paraguay's case, for instance, their anti-Communism and friendship for the United States were proven. The result was some tension in government-to-government relations, illustrated forcefully in a speech by Adlai Stevenson at Stroessner Airport, Asunción, in June 1961, in which he told the Paraguayan regime that the United States expected changes in the political atmosphere in return for the help that was to be given.

Nonetheless, the regime did get the money—possibly equal to two-fifths of the country's own annual revenue in the first five years—and though Alliance workers might be disappointed in their Paraguayan missions, there was not much the United States could do about it. It was committed to the Alliance as a cooperative hemispheric project, and so most of the money was disbursed by multilateral agencies to which the biggest contributor was unwilling to dictate. The Alliance was supposed to be all-inclusive, and the Latin American members, understanding the tendency to military rule in the area, were less willing to blackball Paraguay because of General Stroessner. But an interesting sidelight on American attitudes to the General was given by the democratic purists of the Peace Corps. Not until 1967, years after the Alliance was operational in Asunción, could the Peace Corps be reconciled to working there. The transfer of the American Presidency from Kennedy to Johnson, Paraguay's valued support for the U.S. intervention in Santo Domingo, and the installation of new military regimes in Brazil and Argentina all conduced to a warmer climate between Washington and Asunción.

Stroessner, of course, has always maintained that Paraguay was enjoying perfect democracy, and an inkling of the way in which he approached the United States was given in a speech to the diplomatic corps in May 1956. Paraguay's policy, he said, was one of "complete adhesion to the policy of the United States, the great nation which for its culture, for its strength, for its moral and material progress has earned the distinction of being First Soldier and First Arsenal of Democracies." The ties of the U.S. Defense Department, through military aid and professional training, were often closer to military governments in Latin America than the State Department would have liked and produced an equally curious language of eulogy. Arthur Schlesinger, Jr.[5] records that in January 1961, just before the Kennedy inaugural, General Lemnitzer, the U.S. Army Chief of staff, wrote an extravagant letter of thanks to Stroessner for a Christmas present of a tablecloth, and went out of his way to praise the General's "Christian qualities."

The regime exploited its U.S. connections for domestic purposes, though it had to be careful that patriotic feeling was not offended at any hint that the country had become a sort of North American satellite. The jejune propaganda that could result was illustrated by an exhibition in a Ministry window in Asunción in mid-1967: U.S. space feats were celebrated with photos of the Paraguayan Chaco taken from a Gemini capsule and with the minute Paraguayan flag which had gone around the world in space.

Economic progress under Stroessner

The country has made some economic progress under Stroessner, though it is hardly dynamic. Roads are built and schools—at an average of one a week, the President said in 1963—cattle-raising and coffee-growing have been encouraged and, apart from one devaluation relatively early in his term, the value of the guaraní stays enviably stable by comparison with most South American currencies. Though incomes are very low even by Latin Ameri-

[5] Arthur M. Schlesinger, Jr.: A *Thousand Days* (André Deutsch: 1965), p. 180.

can standards, the average diet, thanks to the ready availability of meat and fruit, is one of the best in the area.

But despite efforts to expand industry, the economy remains in a primitive state, overwhelmingly committed to the production of primary agricultural products. Rumors of oil finds have failed to materialize into a cheap native source of power. Nearly all manufactures are imported, many (including cars) from the United States rather than from the more expensive but nearer industrial producers of Latin America. This free-trading bias to the economy, and its backwardness, are reasons why—although the Stroessner regime was prepared to cooperate in the Latin American Free Trade Area and regional integration plans—it has emphasized that special arrangements would for a long time be necessary for Paraguay.

The worst feature of the country, though not susceptible to a simple solution, is the lack of jobs in relation to the growth of population. This shows up in several ways, ranging from outright unemployment—about which trustworthy figures are hard to find—through widespread underemployment to emigration. Estimates suggested that anything up to a fifth of the Paraguayan labor force was working outside the country by the mid-sixties. Most of these workers found jobs in Argentina as unskilled manual laborers—men working on building sites, women as housemaids. But included among the emigrants was a small number of able and well-educated persons, a "brain drain" caused by the lack of advanced training and careers in a backward agricultural economy. In this significant group political grievances against the regime were also a motive for departure. The Colorado government had no ideological objection to economic planning or public ownership—indeed, it nationalized the British-owned railways—but lack of infrastructure or much of an entrepreneurial class made results slow in coming.

The regime's high spending on the armed forces and militarized police, at least a quarter of the annual budget, reduces its opportunities in other directions. Conscription for two years is the norm. Looked at as a welfare and employment agency, of course, the army serves a purpose, but its funds are not a directly productive investment. The employment situation and the simplicity of the economy have not been propitious for the development of successful trade unionism. In addition, independent trade unionism was an obvious political target for the regime, afraid of both its hostility and its potential power. The circumstances of the government's absorption, in 1958, of the Confederación Paraguaya de Trabajadores after the failed general strike give some idea of the way in which the workers' group suffered from the regime's manipulation. Nineteen fifty-eight had been a bad year for inflation, and there had been official acknowledgment of the need for salary raises of up to 149 per cent. Yet when the CPT asked for a raise of twenty-nine per cent, which was recommended for acceptance by an arbitration commission with both government and employers' representatives on it, the regime claimed that the CPT was encouraging subversion and arrested the entire executive committee.

Stroessner himself is probably not much interested in the economy except where changes could have direct political effects. He avoids grandiose projects and once admitted that little had been done, though that was much compared with what had been done before. In conformity with the Alliance for Progress, Paraguay nominally began a land-reform program. As in other Latin American countries, there were a small number of large landowners, including expatriate companies, but the regime seemed in no hurry to dispossess them. Instead, it seemed more likely that reform might largely mean the settlement of hitherto unoccupied lands.

Personal habits, family, and friends

General Stroessner is married to a quiet schoolteacher, Eligia Mora Delgado, from Villa Hayes, a town near Asunción named after an American President of the nineteenth century who arbitrated in favor of Paraguay after its defeat by the Triple

Alliance. The couple have three grown children: Gustavo Adolfo, in the Air Force, Graciela Concepción, a teacher, and Hugo Alfredo, who accompanies his father on some of his official business. But in no sense has the family as a whole taken over the running of the country as was true of the Somozas in Nicaragua or the Trujillos in the Dominican Republic. In fact, the ordinariness of the Stroessners' position is shown by an incident recounted of the younger Alfredo, a lively, humorous fellow. When his chauffeur jumped a traffic crossing, the policeman on duty took aim and shot him, in accordance with local custom but without respect for the great man's son.

The General himself, in the brief leisure time he allows himself, is supposed to be a good family man, although Asunción gossip maintains that at least one potholed road in the capital has been repaired because the President got fed up with being bounced about each time he was visiting a girl friend. His relaxations include chess, fishing, and flying. The chess club in Asunción stands in a dilapidated building, but there, late at night, one may see the President and Commander in Chief playing to his heart's content with any club member who drops by. With all her rivers, Paraguay is rich in good fishing, and Stroessner often flies to islands in the Paraná River, where Liebigs the meat company has ranches, for a fishing weekend. He is sometimes accompanied by a friend who is head of a brewery. The President also loves flying—an art which his eldest son had learned by the age of thirteen—and even the most isolated township cannot rule out the possibility of his dropping in, piloting himself, out of the blue.

Stroessner is most industrious. The climate dictates that people start work in the capital soon after 7 a.m., but the President may already have held a cabinet meeting by then. In the middle of the night he may still phone the various army commands to make sure that all is well. One may fancy that this unusual application is a tribute to his German parentage, but the result is that he is exceedingly well informed about what is going on inside Paraguay, and especially within the armed forces.

It is hard to say whether he is vain. His name has been liberally splashed around the country—the Asunción airport is an example of the sort of object baptized—but he seems too hard-headed to have decreed this himself. Electoral posters of him say, "One will, one people, one hope"; but, unlike Trujillo, he has not styled himself "The Benefactor" or anything of the sort. But the personalist tradition in Latin America, magnified in a military dictator who emerges after much turbulence, makes for sycophancy among underlings. Among the Colorado Party hacks and the most dependent army henchmen there are plenty such.

The army was Stroessner's first love, and it probably remains his first interest. Within it he has retained his power by juggling commands—the tiresome may easily be banished to the Chaco or an embassy abroad—and a judicious use of rewards and sanctions. No man, apart from the Commander in Chief, may think himself too powerful, and the latter's inspections are encyclopedic. His own reputation for courage and *machismo,* a peculiarly Latin mixture of gallantry and bravado, is a basis for his power over the military. A typical example of this, related in Asunción, dates from the confused politics of the 1940's. He was suddenly sacked from a garrison artillery command and sent to prison in an upset of the period. The new commander made the mistake of inviting ministers and army leaders down to see him installed, but by the time they arrived, the man who came out to welcome them was none other than Alfredo Stroessner. He had succeeded in staging a mini-coup, talking his way out of prison and fixing the garrison, before the authorities had learned what was afoot.

In the government, and with the Colorado Party, President Stroessner is supreme. Some of his associates—like Tomás Romero Pereira, the Colorado leader—have worked alongside him for years, and some ministers have been in the cabinet for a decade. But he does not let any of them get so strong that they are a threat to himself. When Edgar Insfran, the former Minister of the Interior and campaign manager, appeared to look like an heir apparent in 1966, he was summarily dropped from the government. Under the constitution, if Stroessner were to die, the head of the Supreme Court would take over and order fresh elections. But in practice things might not be so simple, with power in both the army and state suddenly up for grabs and no defined Stroessner succession.

The President is known as a friend to his friends, and nobody doubts that the regime is corrupt. He does not live ostentatiously, and on the whole his cronies do not either. But the whole mixture of authoritarianism and backwardness which is the reality of political and social Paraguay is an invitation to bribery. If anyone wishes to set up a new factory, for instance, he needs the permission of the government and it is desirable to grease the necessary palms. Abuses in the expenditure of Alliance for Progress money are alleged.

One of the biggest rackets is in contraband, and although the regime sometimes makes gestures against it, lucrative connivance describes the official attitude better. The value of the contraband trade may be anything up to U.S. $5 million a month. Much of the frontier is scarcely populated, and smuggling is a simple operation. Periodically a major scandal occurs, giving some insight into the kind of malfeasance lurking in the background.

In May 1966 two German bank clerks who had got away with one million marks from a Frankfurt bank were traced to Paraguay by Interpol. The Chief of Police, General Duarte Vera, and the head of the investigation department, Alberto Planas, called on the men at their Asunción hotel in the middle of the night and told them that they would put them across the border into Brazil in a police plane if they gave them the money (which they had given to the management in an envelope for sakekeeping). But the Gran Hotel del Paraguay, where they were staying, has a German management, and the woman at the desk saw what was going on when she was asked to extract the money from the safe, and phoned the West German Ambassador later. In the morning the Ambassador complained to Stroessner, who put the two policemen in prison temporarily.

Though on this occasion the President showed his displeasure, one suspects that it had more to do with the importance of the German business community locally than with any serious drive to root out fiscal misconduct.

The soldier as ruler

The narrow patriotism which has been an enduring feature of Latin American countries since independence approaches mania in Paraguay, and it is impossible to judge General Stroessner as a Latin American figure without remembering this. The 1930's saw the rehabilitation of the dictatorial López family, which had been responsible for Paraguay's near-annihilation in 1864-70— celebrations of this heroic national calamity are still continuing —and the martial virtues are ones to which almost every citizen would still subscribe. Hence the country is psychologically adjusted to rule by a *caudillo* in 1969, long after such figures are little more than a barbaric nineteenth-century memory elsewhere.

The liberalization of later years aside, Stroessner is essentially a tough personality, able to conquer other armed men by force of character, quick thinking, and the sort of courage that appeals to soldiers, and able to impose his will on the rest of the country by guns. This is to simplify both the man and the situation; but it is obvious that in Paraguay one is dealing with an army general quite different from Perón in Argentina, or the "Nasserist" officers of Peru, or the modern big-country rulers like General Onganía in Argentina or Marshal Costa e Silva in Brazil. Stroessner is something more archetypal altogether, not interested in the military as an engine for social change or bourgeois "modernization," nor, in spite of image-building by subordinates, in himself as a mass-media political superman.

Only a country whose civil politics were still dominated by two such nineteenth-century parties as the Colorados and Liberals, lacking both a genuine ideology and a fundamental democratic basis, could have thrown up a military dictator so lacking in political ideas in the 1950's. Stroessner's social ideas were of a simple conservatism. ("The fatherland is founded on the cement of the home. Policy which strengthens the moral and material factors which make homes firm is patriotic policy which fortifies the Nation," he stated once). Most of the activities of his government seem to reflect nothing but opportunism. This too is archetypal: his purpose in ruling is to maintain power, guided only by a vague sense of patriotism.

The military *caudillo* in the nineteenth century responded to the need for a personal leader who could provide protection against violence in turbulent conditions, and Stroessner's emergence in the fifties had the same origin. The continuance of the tradition in Paraguay illustrates the essential sterility of a political system in which army officers are politicians carrying rifles, and dictatorship and the transfer of power by violence are usual. Dictatorship, in this tradition, does not provide generalized protection for the whole community, as can be seen from the Paraguayan example. The only people basically who are looked after are the adherents of the strong man, and even then there is nothing to stop the god from devouring his votaries. For in its purest South American form a dictatorship corresponds to the ancient definition of tyranny—a condition in which the leader is not accountable to the populace, which holds no rights except at his pleasure.

Stroessner, of course, is not a typical Latin American military ruler today because the isolation, smallness, belligerence, and backwardness of Paraguay are unique. But even in the most sophisticated army and society in the region a military ruler cannot escape the common tradition that he represents, including the limited transferability of a chieftain's power and its continuous vulnerability to rival coups from the barracks. In other countries the quotient of personal toughness and courage under fire need not be so high, and the "chaos" from which the strong man "rescues" them may be the less tangible violence of monetary collapse or social unrest. There, too, there are frequently countervailing forces to balance the military—political parties or trade unions of greater strength than in Paraguay—which draw the army boss more irrevocably into civilian politics and controversy over policies and administration. Yet in his claim to offer national leadership more patriotically disinterested than could be provided by any civilian politician, Stroessner's approach is common to most Latin military men who aspire to lead their country. The claim rests on the idea of the military as an independent, patriotic force—one of the few accepted far-reaching national institutions in a Latin American country—peculiarly charged with maintaining the state's continued existence and, by virtue of its discipline and weapons, peculiarly effective for this purpose. Though the defects of this doctrine are sadly apparent in Latin America, with armies ridden by highly interested political factions and civilians coerced by arms, it is still widely popular among Latin American officers.

But if it is fair to describe Stroessner as a survivor from the age of *caudillos*, he himself is not a total political primitive nor an unintelligent man. But for his skill and industry, he would have been just another passing Paraguayan plotter. In order to flourish, he has had to proclaim that his country is a democracy, and to do something to make the contrary appearances less deceptive. He has had to agree in principle to theses of agrarian reform, economic development, and regional cooperation which, if they ever came about, would probably make his kind of personal rule much harder, if not impossible. Though it has not placed limits on his power, he has nevertheless carried out a partial liberalization and cut down on the use of physical coercion in dealing with the government's opponents. Perhaps if Batista in Cuba or Trujillo in the Dominican Republic had managed even this, they might have staved off both their departure and the ensuing revolutions. Stroessner's departure, of course, is a matter for himself to decide, unless he suddenly loses control in the army. The Colorado Party has proved willing enough to support him in office as long as the spoils of office are shared with its members. He has proved invulnerable to critics outside Paraguay, and time has made him respectable. Yet for as long as he remains President of Paraguay, he will be a reminder to Latin Americans that their hemisphere has not yet outlived the romantic but pernicious attraction of the soldier leader— "the man on horseback."

Eduardo Frei Montalva

Frei in London, 1965

"It is appropriate that President Eduardo Frei of Chile should now pay a State visit to Britain," rumbled *The Times* leading article,

> for he is the most significant political figure in Latin America today. This is not just because of the progressive policies at home which have made him the prototype of the radical, non-communist Latin American leader. No less important is his range. This can be seen geographically in his desire that Chile and her neighbours should draw sustenance, political as well as economic, from Europe in addition to the United States.

The President's European tour in July 1965, in which he saw nine heads of state including Queen Elizabeth in twenty-four days, was the high-water mark of his reputation overseas. Many others, besides *The Times*'s leader-writer, wanted to see in him "the most significant political figure in Latin America today," because he had apparently saved Chile for democracy by defeating the Socialists' and Communists' Presidential candidate, Allende, the year before, because he offered hope that the social injustices of Latin America could be removed without an unpleasant Castro-style revolution; and because he had this unexpected faith in the saving grace of Europe. He came as the spokesman for a wonderful new "revolution in liberty."

He arrived in Britain on July 13, having been treated to the unusual privilege of three private exchanges with his previous host, President de Gaulle. He was put through the traditional mill of a State Visit—the drive through Whitehall in open landaus, the state banquet in Buckingham Palace, a look at Stevenage New

Town and the Atomic Energy Authority. Driving in the fifth carriage down Whitehall, and not likely to have been recognized by sightseers, was the British architect of Frei's visit, Sir David Scott Fox, the then ambassador in Santiago, who was subsequently moved to Helsinki. Sir David—concerned to rebuild an Anglo-Chilean connection which went back to the days when Valparaíso was called the most British city outside the Empire, and the Prince of Wales (later Edward VIII) had opened a British club on the outskirts of Santiago—had been the first European ambassador to extend such an invitation to Frei after his electoral victory.

It is not often that state visitors to Britain are welcomed with enormous popular enthusiasm—the Queen's visit to Chile three years later offered a warmhearted contrast—and the first South American President so honored was no exception. But his visit to Britain, as his trip to Europe as a whole, helped put the new Chilean government, which had recently been criticizing the U.S. intervention in Santo Domingo, on the map of international politics. Sanguine observers in Britain might even compare the reforming zeal of the Christian Democrats with the still fresh fervor of a local Labour government. Frei, who had the Queen to lunch with him in Claridges and invited her to pay a visit to Chile (eventually occurring in November 1968) had said before coming that he was not looking for great financial help from Europe. But Foreign Minister Gabriel Valdés, who accompanied him, was able to announce that Britain would be training more Chilean students, engineers, and technicians and would send her own technical experts to Chile.

Frei had a virus which forced him to cancel a visit to Cambridge, but he seemed to have enjoyed himself. His farewell message to the Queen was delicately phrased:

> Your people's welcome everywhere has been spontaneously friendly. . . . May God bless Your Majesty, His Royal Highness and all your House, and long preserve the greatness and influence of the United Kingdom so necessary to this troubled world.

Background, education, and editorship

Eduardo Frei Montalva was born in Santiago, the Chilean capital, on January 16, 1911. His father was a Swiss immigrant from Zurich who had an undistinguished job as a bookkeeper on a small farm in Lontué, a locality south of Santiago. Here the young Eduardo first went to school. But if there was not much money in the family, there was plenty of encouragement for hard work and an Old-World respect for learning, so that when Eduardo finished primary school at the top of his class, he went to Santiago for secondary schooling at the Institute of Humanities. After his father's death he did private tutoring to pay for his own education and support the rest of the family, and entered the Law School at the Catholic University. Frei was a good Catholic, and even in Lontué he had been struck by the vast gap in living standards between the rich and the peasantry; he had concluded, with an adolescent's idealism, that this was an un-Christian state of affairs.

At the time of Frei's arrival in the university Chile was enduring the rigors of the Great Depression. With her heavy dependence on the export of nitrates and copper, destitution was widespread. In spite of the country's long-standing democratic tradition, which was unusual in Latin America, it had succumbed to the stresses of the times, and to a dictatorship under an army man, ex-War Minister General Carlos Ibañez. Political parties were suppressed, and university students were supposed to get on with their studies, but in the Catholic University a group of able students started to exchange ideas on the state of society under the aegis of the National Association of Catholic Students. Among them were Bernardo Leighton, Rafael Agustín Gumucio, Radomiro Tomic, and, not least, Eduardo Frei himself.

These young men felt their first allegiance was to the Conservative Party, the historic clerical party in Chile, but at the same time they were impatient with its social conservatism, which seemed particularly inapposite during the Depression. It was as though the older clerics were so busy defending the privileges of the rich that they had forgotten to love their neglected neighbors.

In 1933 Frei was elected president of the National Association, and the same year he became president of the Chilean Catholic Action Youth. The following year he represented Chile at a congress of university youth in Rome and took the chance to travel widely, attending lectures in Paris of Jacques Maritain, whose ideas of revitalizing Catholicism as an agent of social change were strongly influencing the clique of Catholic students in Chile.

Frei's interest in social problems was demonstrated by the thesis he chose at the university. Although in the faculty of law, he wrote about the salary structure in Chile and ways in which it might be changed: he wanted to end the practice of an annual adjustment of salaries and introduce methods of co-ownership. On graduation, following his return from Europe, he became manager of a daily paper, *El Tarapaca*, in Iquique, the nitrate town in the arid north of Chile. By then he was married to a girl from an old Chilean family, María Ruiz Tagle. The fact that such a young man had such a responsible position may only, perhaps, be explained by his prominence in the ranks of the Conservative youth and the powerful contacts this must have given him. But his maturing views of social Catholicism must have made him uncomfortable, as *El Tarapaca* was owned by nitrate interests.

Nitrates, as mentioned, had hit bad times during the Depression. Although Chile was the only producer of natural nitrate, used for both fertilizer and munitions, the invention of a process for making it artificially by a German, Dr. Fritz Haber, in the First World War had destroyed the monopoly. From Iquique Frei tried to proselytize the nitrate workers, maintaining the superiority of social Catholicism to Marxism, Fascism, or the traditional Chilean parties—Liberals, Conservatives, and Radicals. In the process he attacked traditional capitalism, somewhat to the annoyance of his paper's proprietors. During this period he wrote his first book, *Chile Desconocido* (*Unknown Chile*), which was an appeal to young people to participate in politics and to bring the alienated poor into society. He described the underdevelopment of Chile in the following terms:

Of 665,225 children of school age only 460,110 are being educated, that is to say 205,115 remain illiterate. Of every thousand births 125.2 are illegitimate. Of every thousand babies 235 die before they are one year old. In Norway 4.9 per cent die.

While in Iquique, Frei twice ran for Congress. Although he received the highest vote in the province of Tarapaca in 1937, the fact that the Falange, the new party that he and other young Conservatives had formed, had failed to get a sufficient vote over the nation as a whole to qualify for the minimum number of seats required meant that he was not returned. In the middle of the year he returned to Santiago, leaving his post at *El Tarapaca* to Radomiro Tomic, his friend and election-campaign manager. In Santiago he would be able to develop a law practice, and Rafael Gumucio, the Conservative Senator whose son was in the social Catholic circle and who himself supported their point of view for a while in Congress, made it possible for him to gain entrée to *El Diario Ilustrado*.

The Falange and the 1930's

Chilean politics in the thirties was highly complicated, but stimulating. Carlos Ibáñez had controlled the government from 1925 to 1931 (he had actually been popularly elected President in 1927), but although his rule was a disguised dictatorship, the collapse of copper and nitrate prices and widespread resistance by students and white-collar workers brought him down. Then followed a period of rapidly changing governments—including a short-lived Socialist Republic under a colorful adventurer of Irish extraction called Marmaduque Grove—until Arturo Alessandri won the presidential elections in 1932. Though a Radical who had acquired a reforming reputation as President in the twenties, he was now tired, and his second term was distinguished by cautious government and conservative fiscal policies.

Nonetheless, under this prosaic government, in the interstices of a multiparty system (one center party was called the Partido Democrática, another the Partido Democrático) a great deal of thought about the country's needs, as well as sheer political maneuvering, was going on. Parties at the extremes were also active: although the Communist Party had only been founded in 1921, it was by the mid-thirties already strong in the unions and a pillar of political demonstrations; while a Movimiento Nacional Socialista founded by the half-German Jorge González von Marees, whose bands of grayshirts were subsequently called the Popular Socialist Vanguard, was also a force to be reckoned with.

The evolution of the Conservative Youth into a separate party, distinct from the Conservatives as such, was complete after the 1937 elections, which produced six congressional deputies for them. By then the young men were known as the Falange, a denomination that was to cause considerable embarrassment then and in later years. The explanation given for this was that with the increasing violence at political meetings some form of protection was necessary for the young Conservative leaders. Bernardo Leighton was beaten up at a gathering in Talca, and the extreme left broke up a young Conservative meeting in Antofagasta. At this stage Manuel Garreton, the group's chief in the Chamber of Deputies, decided a militia must be set up, the Falange, and its name spread to the politicians as such. The Falange took as its symbol a red arrow crossing two horizontal parallel bars, which was said to indicate the revolution of Christian youth conquering the extremisms of right and left (the insignia of Von Marees's movement was a crooked bolt of lightning). Under Maritain's influence, the Falange was anti-Franco and anti-Nazi, but there was no doubt in Chile that there was an element of Fascist thinking in the Falange Nacional. Manuel Garreton had come back from Europe in 1934, affected by Mussolini's corporativism and Gil Robles's love of constitutional order, and it is probable that he borrowed the term "Falange" from Antonio Primo de Rivera.

That the Chilean Falange should have had this connection was hardly surprising, given the wave of thought in progressive Catholic circles on how to avoid the class warfare postulated by Marxists. The Chilean group loathed the excesses of capitalism, the weaknesses of liberal economics, and the creation of an outcast, proletarian nation subsisting in the same country beside privileged landholders. On the other hand, they loathed equally the inhumanity, the lack of respect for individual personality, the atheism, and the social warfare they saw in Marx. For them Christianity was the unique revolution in history, though it had been betrayed by clericalism and self-interest. But while they talked from the start of the need for some Christian revolution, they also wanted social harmony and the reconciliation of classes, and it was never clear how both could be achieved at once.

Nevertheless, given this mixture of views, it was remarkable that they did not support Franco or turn against democracy. The main reasons, perhaps, were that Franco, a military man supported by the clerics and the privileged, was too obviously stamping out social reform and that they, like most of the Chilean elite, were too addicted to democracy. The experience of Ibañez, occurring just when they were at the university, intensified their dislike of dictators.

The Falange, benefiting from the coalitions inevitable in a system of multiparty proportional representation, briefly had a minister in the Alessandri cabinet. Bernardo Leighton, in his twenties, was Minister of Labor until he resigned over the closing of a satirical magazine, *Topaze,* and Conservative plans to push the Finance Minister, Gustavo Ross, as the presidential candidate in 1938. Ross's narrow defeat by a Popular Front candidate, Aguirre Cerda, supported by a wide range of parties including the Falange, was a decisive factor in its move away from the right. Aguirre Cerda set up the Chilean Development Corporation (Corporación de Fomento de la Producción) to give the state its own economic leverage and to help Chile break her dependence on primary products which were largely exploited by foreign interests to meet the needs of industrialized countries. At the same time he wanted to do something about education, health, and the intractable land problem; but the lack of a congressional majority and the outbreak of war in Europe before his death in 1941 limited his opportunities.

The making of a President

Throughout the forties the Falange was still only a very small party, but Frei's importance in it became more marked. From 1940 to 1945 he was professor of labor law at his old university, the Catholic University in Santiago. In 1941 he was elected president of the Falange for two years, and he was re-elected twice in succession. But the loneliness of the party's position, detested by the Conservatives and Right and resented and distrusted by the Left, was illustrated by his book of 1942, *Aun es Tiempo* (*There's Still Time*), in which he wrote:

> In every historic catastrophe, in the decay of any nation, there have existed minorities which were there at the time and were not heard; great newspapers closed their doors to them; the great parties mocked them; their great enthusiasms were ironically observed and their solutions, the only ones possible, were ridiculed as impractical.

The progress of the Second World War and the relative popularity and progressiveness of the Aguirre Cerda government brought Frei and the Communists onto the same platforms. In October 1944 Frei appeared at a Communist-organized rally in a Santiago theater and said that, as in France and Italy, it was necessary for social Christians to work with Communists. Chile was poor and could not afford to have the forces of progress split, particularly when the Fascist GOU regime was ruling Argentina. In 1945 Frei became Minister of Roads and Public Works for nine months.

President Juan Antonio Ríos, who had succeeded Aguirre Cerda and had widened further the center–left coalition, predicted that his Falangist minister would be President himself one day. But Frei resigned the following year after a crowd was fired on at a political demonstration in Santiago. His term of office was not without memorials. He was responsible for the remaking of the Avenida Bulnes, one of the central thoroughfares in the capital, and also for paving a road from Santiago to La Serena, the next President's home town, whose beautification became a government priority.

More significant was a Frei plan for a national fund for irrigation which never actually materialized. But the scheme had the twin aims of increasing the irrigated area of the country by nearly a half over twenty-five years and of financing a measure of agrarian reform by which seventy per cent of the newly irrigated land was handed to small farmers. In its ingenuity and expansionism, and its willingness to use state intervention to effect a reform while simultaneously preserving property rights, this plan was a forerunner of many Christian Democrat proposals in the fifties and sixties.

Although Frei's period of office was so brief, he made a good impression, and his stature in the Falange was communicated to Chileans in general. When the party was being formed, Bernardo Leighton, Manuel Garreton, and the Rafael Gumucios, father and son, were perhaps better known, but by 1946 Frei was, if not *the* leader, at least one of the most significant two or three.

Following President Juan Antonio Ríos's death another Radical, González Videla, was elected President in 1946. The next year, with Cold War fever growing elsewhere, the Falange, under pressure from Archbishop Caro of Santiago, stopped cooperating with the Communists. In elections in 1949 for the Chamber of Deputies in which fifteen parties took part (the Communists had been outlawed the year before) the Falange came out fifth with 20,000 votes, a long way behind the big old parties: the Liberals, with 65,000, the Radicals with 90,000 and the Conservatives with 100,000. By this time the differences between Liberals and Conservatives, the traditional anticlerical and clerical parties, had softened considerably; in economic outlook they were both conservative. The Radicals, a more modern party of the urban bourgeoisie, had something in common with their namesakes of the French Fourth Republic—they aspired to become the governing party, yet retained periodic fits of radical conscience. In 1949 Frei was elected Senator for the northern region of Atacama and Coquimbo. The following year he served as Chilean delegate to the United Nations.

The breakthrough for Frei and his party occurred in the dull Presidency of the former strong man Carlos Ibáñez, who was elected in 1952 with a broom as his symbol. The seventy-four-year-old Ibáñez ran with the support of his Agrarian Labor Party and his appeal was a personalist mixture of Socialism and anti-corruption. But in fact his administration was conservative, the end of the Korean War hurt the prices of primary products, and a disillusioned electorate was willing to listen to new voices. In 1954 there was a curious episode when Ibáñez, who was always changing his cabinets, offered Frei full power to institute an anti-inflationary program. For a week it was a sensational possibility canvassed by the political world; but nothing came of it.

Throughout the fifties Frei's personal reputation for probity, good sense, and concern for development became a more well-known asset, and congressional reporters regarded him as one of the most promising speakers. Whereas in 1953 the Falange had only three per cent of the national vote, in 1957, when Frei was elected Senator for Santiago with a large majority, it had thirteen per cent.

That year the Falange, which had amalgamated with a similar social Christian party, changed its name and became the Christian Democratic Party. (The Partido Social Conservador was led by a presidential runner-up, Eduardo Cruz-Coke, and in about 1950 had seemed as popular as the Falange.) In this way the party emphasized that it stood beside the governing parties of Italy and West Germany as part of an international political phenomenon. But while the Chilean Christian Democrats were quite happy to identify with the social concern evinced by Pope John XXIII, they emphasized in their domestic propaganda that theirs was not a confessional party. In 1958 Congress, over President Ibáñez's veto and with Christian Democratic support, revoked the Defense of Democracy Law which had made the Communists illegal. The same year Frei, head and shoulders above the other Christian Democrats, was the party's candidate for the Presidency and came in a most respectable third. The final figures were: Alessandri, the candidate of the Liberals and Conservatives, 387,-207; Allende, the candidate of the Socialists and Communists, 352,915; Frei 255,168; and Bossay, the candidate of the Radicals, 190,832.

1964 election campaign

Frei never really stopped running for the Presidency from 1958 on. Although the 1960 municipal elections were a victory for the Liberal-Conservative coalition and the Radical Party, the administration of Jorge Alessandri was ineffectual and it became increasingly clear that the trio of traditional parties was unable to put up a presidential candidate in 1964 who could win. In these circumstances Frei had one issue which both his underlings and the foreign press advertised strongly: if Frei was not elected, Salvador Allende, the Popular Front candidate so narrowly beaten in 1958, certainly would be. However, this did not stop Frei from running as candidate of the "Democratic Left"—part of Ibáñez's Agrarian Labor Party and a body called the "New Democratic Left" backed the Christian Democrats—but there was always a certain incompatibility between the aim of defeating the Communists with the aid of conservative voters and achieving the revolution in liberty of party propaganda. At the time of the 1964 election, of course, the Alliance for Progress had made it fashionable to imagine that democratic reform was a viable prospect in Latin America, and Christian Democracy, with its apparent appeal to Hispanic tradition, seemed from the outside to be a heaven-sent alternative to Fidel Castro. In Chile, the newspaper reports went, the wave of the future for Latin America was rising. The Christian Democrat campaign was organized with great care. There were congresses of women, professional people, and *pobladores*—the inhabitants of the shanty suburbs of Santiago and other cities—to develop ideas and consolidate support for Frei. Positions in the trade-union and student movements had been built up. In June an estimated 250,000 young people gathered in the Parque Cousino in the capital to hear the candidate speak after a march from all parts of the country described as "The March of the Young Country." Highly detailed policy statements were distributed. There would be 360,000 new houses built over the next six years, 100,000 new proprietors would be planted on the land. "In the last ten years with what has been paid abroad for food which we ought to produce, we could have totally reformed agriculture, doubled industrial capacity, or set up mining industries capable of exporting more than $200 million worth a year," Frei told a gathering of professional people. Saving would be encouraged, juridical recognition given to the neighborhood associations in the shanty towns; the civil service would be reorganized, the integration of Latin America fostered. Kennedy-like appeals to break Chilean stagnation were a constant theme.

For copper, the country's most valuable export, Frei was faced with the need to counter Dr. Allende's promise of nationalization. In 1958 he had defended the foreign investment in the industry and contented himself with urging the need to increase output—a common-enough remedy in political circles. For 1964 something more was needed, and this was "Chileanization," a scheme for partial nationalization that was agreed on with U.S. interests for the purposes of the campaign.

In spite of their political differences, Frei was a personal friend of Dr. Allende's, and this helped to restrain electoral bitterness. In March 1964 a FRAP candidate had won a by-election at Curicó, causing general alarm, and from then on there was little risk of a Conservative–Liberal candidate. The third candidate who did enter, Durán, a Radical, tended to hamper the strength of Allende. But Frei's success in September was unexpectedly complete: he won fifty-six per cent of the votes cast.

Political evolution of the Presidency

The general pattern of Frei's Presidency was one of great expectations and early achievements followed by slowdown, extensive battles with political opponents, and a creeping disillusion. To begin with, the enthusiasm was tremendous. "My sole objective is to proceed to the fundamental transformations of which Chile has need. My government will give itself to the poor, the peasants, those who suffer, and those who have the right to hope for better days," Frei told a crowd in Avenida Bernardo O'Higgins as he stood on a balcony after his victory.

Following his presidential success, he proposed several bills on agrarian reform, Chileanization of copper, and so on, but they got nowhere in a Congress in which Christian Democrats were in a minority. However, the congressional elections of March 1965, in an unusual vote of confidence in a President, gave the Christian Democrats a majority in the Chamber of Deputies. But in the Senate, where only a portion of places were renewed, the party remained a minority. The result, though impressive, meant that in the Senate the Christian Democrats would need to make *ad hoc* alliances, with Radicals, Unión Nacional (former Liberals and Conservatives combined) or with Communists or Socialists to get their bills passed. The belief that the victory of the Christian Democrats had polarized politics sufficiently to put an end to the interparty deals that had given a Fourth Republic air to Chilean politics for so long was not vindicated. Chileanization of copper was followed by a long-drawn-out copper strike; Promoción Popular, the Christian Democratic self-help scheme, lacked statutory support; and by late 1967 it was clear that the government's housing and agrarian reform programs were a long way behind schedule.

Of growing seriousness, too, was the battle against inflation, which, after being apparently curtailed in 1965 and 1966, showed signs of getting quite out of control in 1967. Within a short period the President changed his economic minister twice. In 1965, the year of Frei's European tour and of the U.S. intervention in Santo Domingo which was opposed by Chile, his foreign policy got off to a mixed start. Chile continued to press for the most rapid possible advance toward regional integration at all meetings of ministers and officials of the Latin American republics. But here disappointment with the slow progress of the Latin American Free Trade Area was responsible for an independent integration initiative with the more equally sized Andean countries. The Presidents' adoption of economic integration as an urgent priority at the Punta del Este conference in 1967 was something of a vindication for Frei's thinking.

But if things were not easy for Frei, his domestic opponents were quarreling at the same time. The Marxist Socialist Party was trying to outbid the Communists on the left by adopting a Cuban revolutionary line—although most of its leaders made it clear that they proposed a democratic road to Socialism within Chile itself—and a moderate splinter group separated in the process. The Communists were legalists and strongly anti-Cuban. What might have been a quite abstract ideological dispute became a roaring chasm between the two parties in 1967, the year of the guerrilla attempt in neighboring Bolivia, and Dr. Salvador Allende, the Socialist veteran, organized a hero's welcome for the surviving guerrillas when they escaped to Chile in 1968.

The Christian Democrats themselves were not immune from strains. Among the older party members there were conservatives who felt that Frei should not attempt to go too fast; when there were setbacks, they used them as an excuse for delay. The students, on the other hand, advocated an alliance with the Communists in order to mobilize all progressives for the "fundamental transformations." In early 1968 Frei routed the left at a special party conference which supported his austerity program, but in March 1969 the Christian Democrats lost their majority in the lower house in elections which saw a resurgence of the Partido Nacional and modest gains on the left.

Inflation and austerity

Frei's economic policy was bedeviled from the start by conflicting expectations. The *pobladores* in the shanty towns and the Christian Democrat trade unionists who supported him did so in the belief that the revolution in liberty would involve a transfer in spending power to the underprivileged. Many of the party programs, from land reform to the crash education expansion, were going to be expensive. At the same time, in all classes there was a hope that the arrival of Frei would mean a sharp reduction in inflation. In 1964 the cost of living rose by thirty-nine per cent, and although Frei wanted the rise kept to twenty-five per cent in 1965, it had already reached sixteen per cent by the end of the first six months.

In both 1965 and 1966 wages, over which the government had little direct control, went up faster than the technocrats had programmed. But because industry was working at such a small percentage of capacity (as low as forty per cent in some sectors) at the end of the Alessandri Administration, quite startling rises in productivity could be achieved by the Christian Democrats. In addition, low import prices contributed to a genuine brake on inflation in Frei's first two years. But even then it was clear that some of the government's nostrums were inflationary. The government itself raised the controlled price of milk by forty per cent to help break the stagnation in agricultural output. The cost-of-living index, used as a guide when wage demands were formulated, came in for sustained opposition attack on the grounds that it was underestimating the true rise in prices. This campaign was so successful as to have largely discredited the index within three years.

In 1967, forecast as the year of the elimination of inflation, the dam against inflation broke. Several big unions, including the steelworkers, won wage rises of thirty per cent at the start of the year and, in a maneuver of the Socialist and Communist groups in Congress, workers all over the country were encouraged to look on this as the norm. In late 1967 Sergio Molina, the Finance Minister, presented a stiff austerity program which included the suspension of the right to strike for a year and a system of compulsory saving by which, instead of all workers obtaining a twenty per cent cost-of-living adjustment at the start of 1968, they were to receive only fifteen per cent in cash and the rest in savings certificates issued by a capitalization fund. Employers would be required to pay an equivalent amount into the fund, which would be used to finance Chilean development.

The row caused by these proposals was tremendous. The Communist- and Socialist-controlled Trades Union Congress organized a twenty-four-hour strike in November 1967, in which five people were shot and some two hundred arrested in the working-class districts of Santiago. At the same time businessmen were complaining at having to contribute to the fund, and the Christian Democratic national executive, which had swung to the left in the middle of the year, said that it would propose a counter-measure reducing workers' contributions and increasing employers' payments. The wide range of the opposition to the proposals harried the government continuously, but in April 1968, two Finance Ministers later, and with the wage adjustment bill driven up in cost from some 400 million escudos[1] to about one billion (about $160 million), the bill finally became law. In the end the proposal for a ban on strikes was killed in return for Communist help, and the national fund seemed to have died.

The setback that this economic defeat represented in political terms can scarcely be exaggerated. It showed that the Christian Democrats were no more capable than anyone else of restraining inflation, the bane of Chile as of so many other Latin American countries. (The U.S. dollar, worth thirty-two pesos[1] in 1945, was

[1] The escudo, equal in value to one thousand old pesos, became the unit of currency in 1960.

worth approximately a thousand times as much twenty years later.) It showed that they were just as ready as previous governments—such as that of President Juan Antonio Ríos—to resort to force in answer to social problems they had failed to resolve. It showed up, also, the political weakness of the revolution in liberty: in order to succeed, it needed the support of the other "revolutionary" parties, the Socialists and Communists, who had their own reasons for wishing to discredit it. The wage-adjustment law had only passed in the Senate with the aid of the Communists and the abstention of the Right. A predictable consequence of the Christian Democrats' electoral victories had been that the party's strong trade-union wing had lost ground, and the Communists, in particular, exploited their union and congressional strength in a pincer attack on the austerity measures.

The political disillusion that resulted from these economic failures (the GNP grew by only 2.5 per cent in 1967, compared with 5.9 per cent in 1966) was reflected in a senatorial by-election in southern Chile in December 1967, where the Radicals and Communists joined forces to defeat the Christian Democrats. Though the Christian Democratic vote had grown by comparison with municipal election results in the same area, the party had lost one of its precious thirteen Senate seats, and the Partido Nacional, which had appeared to be waning rapidly, showed signs of revival. As part of the price of abstaining on the wage-adjustment bill the Partido Nacional strongly implied that the government should delay the agrarian reform.

Although the government had been slow to adopt wage and price controls, and in fact did not institute the legislative regulation of wages that the British Labour government developed after 1964, the respective policies of the two countries had certain things in common. Both governments were trying to impose restrictions on wage rises by means of statutory limitations on collective bargaining. But both found it almost impossible in practice to curtail the ability of employers and unions to negotiate as they saw fit when the governments concerned were ultimately dependent on electoral approval. Under the circumstances, the

British government achieved much more than Frei, whose administration was also much more beset by strikes.

As part of its enthusiastic start the Frei government tightened up Chilean taxation procedures, which contributed to a rise in public revenue of nearly a third in 1966. The first two years also saw a considerable improvement in the nation's balance of payments, and between December 1965 and December 1966 its international reserves improved by U.S. $116.8 million. The government was keen to diversify and expand exports, but this improvement was chiefly owing to the high prices for copper, which still provided over sixty per cent of the country's exports.

Internally Chile was also trying to industrialize. Frei, in his third presidential message in May 1967, said that the growth in population required an extra seventy thousand jobs annually. But although the government claimed that in 1966 unemployment was only 6.2 per cent—compared with the best figure of 6.7 per cent under the Alessandri Administration—the FRAP[2] parties were dubious of these statistics and Frei was continually pressed on this issue.

Chileanization of copper

The "Chileanization" of copper was an electoral gimmick designed to trump the FRAP proposal for full nationalization in 1964. There is some evidence that it was produced in haste and cleared by the prospective Christian Democratic Foreign Minister, Gabriel Valdés, with the State Department and New York banking leaders rather than with the Braden and other companies concerned.[3] The agreement, passed in 1965, provided for the

---

[2] Frente de Acción Popular, an alliance of the (Marxist) Socialist Party and the Communist Party formed in 1958 to support the presidential candidacy of Dr. Allende. Its existence did not curtail major divisions on policy or mutual competition between the two parties.

[3] Information supplied to the author verbally in Santiago in June 1967 by an authoritative source in the nationalized iron and steel industry.

Chilean state to own fifty-one per cent of the shares in the biggest mine, Braden's El Teniente. Frei argued that the agreement's terms were justified, as Chile would thereby be able to ensure a more rapid expansion and more of the refining and ancillary operations would be conducted at home. But the financial provisions suggested that as a short-term investment the "Chileanization" policy was not advantageous: the Braden company loaned Chile almost $84 million to finance the purchase of its own shares, and in return the taxation of the copper companies' profits was reduced from eighty-five per cent to fifty per cent (at which point they still provided about twelve per cent of Chilean revenues). Much of the new investment in the mines would come from the government. Explanations to North American shareholders by the companies—which, of course, stressed the benefits they were receiving—did not help Frei, and bonus and benefit clauses in the copper bill were the cause of a long drawn out clash with the mineworkers.

From January to March 1966 the miners at El Teniente, under Socialist leadership, were on a strike which the government declared unconstitutional. There were sympathy strikes elsewhere, the government arrested or dismissed union leaders, and at another mine, El Salvador, clashes between troops and workers in mid-March resulted in several deaths and wounded. In June 1969 President Frei announced that Chile would buy out the large U.S.-owned Anaconda copper mines by 1972.

Christian Democratic policy, though its aim was to escape from dependence on copper and nitrate exports, recognized that in the short run, to acquire the capital goods necessary to establish local industries, it might be necessary to emphasize this dependence. Considerable thought was given to ways in which the profits from copper might be maximized and secured. Chile took the initiative in seeking talks in Lusaka with Zambia and other producers in an effort to harmonize plans.

Alejandro Hales, Minister for Mines, told the author in mid-1967 that Chile was concerned to obtain long-term agreements with consumers in which mutually satisfactory prices would not be at the mercy of the volatile London Metal Exchange.[4] Whereas consumption per capita was eleven pounds in industrialized countries, it was only one pound per capita in the developing world, he said, so the market for expansion was almost unlimited. In fact, for a variety of factors, which included the Vietnam War, uncertainties surrounding Zambian supplies following Rhodesia's unilateral declaration of independence, and the backlog of demand caused by the Chilean strikes, copper prices rose high in 1966 and 1967—so high that users in developed countries publicly warned that they were examining their applications of copper to see where cheaper metals might be adopted.

Although copper prices were falling again in early 1968 with peace-feelers in Vietnam, the threat remained that research and development might at any time demolish the traditional copper market as effectively as Dr. Haber hurt Chile's nitrates, putting the investment in Chileanization into question. As it was, the high prices in 1966 may not have been an unmixed blessing. Although President Frei announced that Chile—which had received exceptional U.S. aid during Alessandri's term of office—would not be requiring any more U.S. loans and presented this as a move toward independence, well-informed persons in Santiago believed that the United States, anxious to reduce its foreign aid, had decided not to augment the sudden prosperity from copper.

The Christian Democrats attempted to expand the production of minerals of all sorts—nitrates, iron, molybdenum, and manganese, among others—as well as their energy supplies of hydroelectricity and natural gas. The principle of Chileanization was also tried elsewhere, by the purchase of forty-nine per cent of the shares of the North American telephone company and the buying out of North American interests in electricity. Foreign investors were encouraged to go into partnership with the state. But the government remained suspect on the nationalization principle, and in August 1967 Radical congressmen tabled a bill to

[4] Between February and April 1968, for example, the price of a ton of copper fell from £815 to £474 on the London Metal Exchange.

nationalize the steel industry—which had become effectively de-
nationalized—as a means of embarrassing the Christian Democrats. Following the latter party's leftward move in that year,
Frei was urged to adopt a party group's report which recommended a noncapitalist road of development for Chile. Radomiro
Tomic, who was the presumed successor to Frei until he tried to
withdraw in 1969, was known to be warmer to nationalization
than the President, but the issue was a source of division in
Christian Democracy.

Agrarian reform

In agriculture Frei inherited a dismal situation. Food production
per capita was expected to be lower in 1965 than it had been in
1952, the increase in population had tended to outstrip the growth
in output ever since the 1930's, and ownership of productive land
was one of the most concentrated on the continent, with approximately four-fifths in large units. Though by comparison with
other Latin American countries, Chile had a high percentage of
her population off the land—68.2 per cent in urban areas in
1960—this did not reflect any dynamism in the rural sector. In
fact, the emigration of twenty-nine per cent of the rural population to urban areas in the decade from 1950 to 1960 almost took
on the appearance of a rout. In 1967 Frei was saying that unless
something drastic was done, a country which had in the past
been a food exporter would be spending $270 million a year on
food imports by 1970.

The problem, both in terms of agricultural production and
social backwardness, was well understood by the time Frei came
to power, not least because of the work of a plethora of international experts. The Christian Democrats arrived with a battery of
policies for the countryside which they advertised as constituting
an agrarian reform. These included incentives to increase output,
the unionization of rural labor, special help for the 100,000
families on small farms, and the regulated transfer of ownership

in the case of some, but not necessarily all, the big estates. By means of the last, Frei promised, about 100,000 peasants would become proprietors by 1970. But legislative delays, shortage of finance, doubts among the Christian Democrats themselves, and the absence of an unequivocal lead from the President himself made it unlikely that this promise would be honored. By mid-1968 only ten thousand families had gotten land.

In 1962 Chile had passed an agrarian reform law reminiscent of the suave suggestion of the Minister of Roads and Public Works in 1945. This law had empowered CORA, the agrarian reform corporation, to expropriate abandoned or badly cultivated lands and up to half the land served by federal irrigation systems. The terms of compensation were generous: a fifth of the value was to be paid in cash and the remainder over five years. However, the new government began by assuming that the compensation terms were too generous and the scope of the old law insufficiently far-reaching. Late in 1966 the constitution was amended to facilitate changes in tenure, and it was explicitly stated that property must fulfill a social function and could be expropriated as required for the public benefit by the legislature.

By the middle of 1967 the new reform law was passed. This gave the landowners ten per cent of the value they had admitted in tax returns in cash, with the rest in bonds over twenty-five years. But the value of the bonds could only be adjusted by seventy per cent of the annual rate of inflation; so, unless Chile achieved unprecedented monetary stability, CORA and the new peasant owners, who would get their title within three years, would be getting the properties cheap. The minimum size of the holdings that could be expropriated would vary according to the type of land—in some places it was two hundred hectares—but it was well above the area that could be farmed by one family without help. With the threat of the new law CORA had expropriated a hundred estates in the two and a half years before it passed Congress, but by 1968 shortage of funds overshadowed the project. In rural areas it was being said that Christian Democratic landowners had a better chance of avoiding expropriation than members of the Partido Nacional and, though it was true that most big estates could probably be criticized on the grounds of poor management, it seemed doubtful whether CORA had the strength to take over a property that was patently well run.

The normal practice was to change a reformed estate into an *asentamiento*,[5] a collective body of peasants with an elected committee assisted by CORA experts. On some of these reformed estates morale was high, the members worked hard on communal projects like building meeting halls as well as on their strictly agricultural tasks, and discipline was good. But this was by no means always the case. In some areas the government's political opponents of both right and left tried to hamper the reform. By comparison with Peru and other countries that had tried a land reform, CORA accorded a high degree of responsibility to the peasants. This, it was said, was due partly to the fact that one of the first estates taken over, in the Choapa valley, had been strongly organized by the left, and CORA had had to permit a large measure of autonomy in order to succeed at all.

Farm management on the *asentamientos* varied. In some, all the work was shared collectively, in others sharecropping continued, elsewhere families were restricted to separate small holdings and collective arrangements were few. That the change in tenure was socially desirable few could doubt; yet its other purpose, to increase output, was harder to serve. In some of the first estates taken over, where land had gone out of cultivation and all CORA's resources could be concentrated on the improvements, output doubled. But the gains from increasing the cultivated lands could not be repeated, and as CORA became more extended, it was not likely that the benefits would continue to be so spectacular. In particular, farm mechanization could not proceed rapidly, both because the equipment was expensive and because any threat of unemployment could endanger the social structure of the *asentamientos*.

While the transfer of tenure went cautiously, the Frei regime

[5] Literally, "asentamiento" means a "settlement."

achieved considerable successes in its unionization policy in increasing the wages of agricultural workers, in breaking the "inquilinato" system of a land-bound peasantry, and also in its fiscal incentives for agriculture. UN officials in Santiago in 1967 told the author that they estimated that the effect of this complex of measures was a rise in total peasant income by about seventy per cent during the first two years of the Frei regime. This restored the purchasing power of the peasantry to about what it had been in 1950.

To assist the benighted class of small peasant proprietors, the Christian Democrats used another institution, INDAP (Instituto de Desarrollo Agropecuario). Its task was similar to that of Promoción Popular in the towns—to create self-help committees among marginal groups in the population. The rural committees were encouraged to attend to electrification problems, local prenatal health services, and the like; but INDAP was divided in its hopes for the small peasant proprietors as agriculturalists. One school of thought wanted the peasants to develop cooperatives, parallel to the management systems being evolved by CORA on the reformed estates, while another wished to subsidize the most efficient small farmers with the intention that these might eventually take over their fellow farmers' land. Clearly this represented a fundamental ideological division, and the issues raised—efficiency versus equity, private property versus cooperative operations—haunted Christian Democratic policy in other fields. In the meantime INDAP, handing out small loans of thirty to fifty dollars' worth of seeds to subsistence farmers, strove to postpone their collapse as a social class.

Communitarianism

INDAP and Promoción Popular were perhaps the most explicit aspects of the Christian Democratic doctrine of "communitarianism," an almost mystical notion that had little in common with the Christian Democracy of Italy or Germany. "Communitarianism" went with "integral humanism" in Chilean Christian Democratic literature. What these terms conveyed was a disgust with the inhuman and exploitative aspects of bourgeois capitalism and an equal dissociation from the totalitarian aspects of Communism. Clearly the philosophy, which was not coherent, owed something to Marxism, to the social Catholicism of Maritain and Mounier and the Second Vatican Council, to the social disparities within Chile and to uneasy dependence on a few primary products, and to the general yearning of the Third World for something more attractive than either Wall Street or Stalin. Frei himself helped to popularize the idea of capital as a social asset, whose deployment must follow human priorities. The deliberate rejection of materialism, of a sort that would appear unusual in either the Soviet Union or Western Europe, was illustrated in an article President Frei wrote in *International Affairs* in July 1966:

> In so far as Chile is concerned, mere economic development is not in itself the only aim of the present Government. Increased production of goods and services and greater technical efficiency are only a part of our goal. The political and social implications of such developments are fundamental and it is for this reason that we consider progress as legitimate only when it reinforces rather than undermines freedom and democracy.

Promoción Popular was designed to translate communitarianism into something concrete in the urban areas. Its object was to set up a whole gamut of democratically run groups covering anything from mothers to sports groups, shanty dwellers to the occupants of well-built suburbs which lacked organizations to complain about bus services. But the general emphasis was on giving socially deprived groups their own institutions which would be able to build houses or dig drains for themselves and, at the same time, act as a two-way pressure group and link with the traditional ministries and municipal authorities.

The idea of mobilizing wasted human resources against poverty in this way was not original, even in contemporary Latin

America. President Belaúnde Terry, in Peru, was trying simultaneously to encourage something much like it. The common
distress of Latin American cities, which had burst beyond the
scope of the services of civilized urban living, was everywhere
apparent. But where the Christian Democrats in Chile were
unusual was that they had done their best to develop neighbor-
hood committees—*juntas de vecinos*—in opposition, and their
remarkable electoral advance in the late fifties owed a lot to
the response to these initiatives. Frei appointed some of the
ablest party idealists to Promoción Popular and, though it
struggled in a precarious institutional existence subordinate to
the Ministry of Housing with a budget of only $1 million a
year, local groups proliferated as a result of its activities. These
flexible groups were used for a variety of social purposes, including the spreading of information about health precautions or the
latest trend in foodstuff prices.

At the grass roots the *juntas de vecinos* and similar groups
were not exclusively Christian Democratic; but the Socialists
and Communists were understandably suspicious. Under the
auspices of Promoción Popular, for instance, young trade unionists were sent off on leadership courses. While the Christian
Democrats saw this as ideologically essential, in order to prevent
social strife and set up multiple autonomous democratic cells to
inhibit the growth of any totalitarian cancer, the Socialists and
Communists could see only a new patronage system and electoral
machine in their own areas. But the Christian Democrats, at any
rate at the beginning of Frei's term of office, acted as though
from strength and attacked their opponents in Congress for
holding up the juridical recognition of *juntas de vecinos* and
other Promoción Popular legislation. The electoral importance
of Promoción Popular was as real as the ideological: a senior
Christian Democrat estimated privately in 1967 that the whole
program could be worth 400,000 votes to his party.

Communitarianism covered a multitude of subjects including
the desire of the younger and more leftist Christian Democrats
to extend the area of nationalized industries. In theory many

such party members were attached to the idea of workers' control. Frei himself was aware that the mere change of ownership from private to public control made no necessary alteration in a worker's condition. But the practical objection to workers' control, especially for the more conservative party members, was that it would just hand another lever of power to the Socialists and Communists in the unions. Communitarianism, it was said, would enable Chile to jump beyond the feudal and capitalist stages of society at a leap. For the radicals in the party the sight of youthful African countries like Tanzania and Zambia, cheerfully nationalizing entrenched foreign subsidiaries without terrible international consequences, was a call to more drastic action.

But though Frei may have sympathized with this outlook, the apparent priorities of short-term Chilean economics seem to have made him cautious. As in Britain, with the Wilson Labour government, the ruling party's left complained that the government was abandoning its ideals little by little in the face of economic adversity. Part of the trouble was the vagueness of communitarianism as a philosophy, rapidly elevated from being the plaything of a small party in a multiparty system to being the guiding idea of a ruling majority. But it was unreasonable to assume that the conservative voters who switched to Frei in 1964, recoiling from the Communist shadow behind Allende, had necessarily adopted much of it.

Social policy

In the social-services field the Frei Administration had mixed success. Perhaps its greatest triumph lay in education, where students, the military, and teachers themselves were all involved in expanding the number of students in primary, secondary, and technical education from just over 1,800,000 in 1964 to 2,300,000 in 1966. In his election speeches Frei had complained about the half million children between the ages of seven and fourteen who neither worked nor studied, and it was probable that most of them were rescued in the crash expansion. As with other programs special help was concentrated on the marginal urban and rural areas. In two years over two thousand new schools were built, a huge increase over the Alessandri record, and over 6,500 new teachers were recruited. The school-meals service trebled its activity. As part of the expansion policy improved salaries and conditions were granted to teachers. Nevertheless they were not enamored of the government's austerity measures of 1967-8, any more than other sectional interests, and a strike by teachers for pay increases and against the backsliding from the "teachers' charter" was a feature of the campaign against austerity in early 1968. Universities too increased their admissions, which rose from 35,000 in 1964 to 48,700 in 1966.

Housing, where the Christian Democrats had promised to build 360,000 units in six years aside from making good the losses caused by earthquakes and floods, was a disappointment. Not only did the party fall well short of its own target, but by 1966, when only 28,736 new houses had been started, it seemed to be falling below the achievements of the Alessandri era. Frei blamed the copper legislation, which would have created an extra eight thousand starts in 1966, for part of the setback, but part of the trouble was probably due to the inefficiency of the official and semiofficial organs—the Corporación de la Vivienda and the Fundación de Viviendas y Asistencia Social—on which the country relied for two thirds of its building. In this and other areas the Christian Democrats seem to have failed to carry out the bureaucratic reforms which could have made the realization of their promises possible.

Still, total financial aid for housing in real terms was double in 1966 what it had been in 1964. Though it was only able to contribute a few thousand housing units to begin with, the Christian Democrats were proud of their schemes for "autoconstruction," by which individuals built their own houses with advice from the official bodies. This program, too, was aimed at the marginal urban and rural areas.

Health, roads, and pensions were other fields in which the

Christian Democrats sought to make improvements. But by the middle of Frei's term the shortage of funds, the continued pull of inflation, and the sheer loss of impetus of the genuine reformers in the administration was beginning to bring disillusionment. The social policies of the government, though they concentrated on deprived groups in the population, showed little sense of priorities otherwise. Everything was to be done at once, as could only happen in a genuine revolution—and perhaps not even then. In practice, the revolution in liberty was constrained both by the Chilean constitution and the desire to please friends and creditors in the outside world. The constitutional limitation, given that the Christian Democrats were in a minority in the Senate, was a continuing brake. Though sometimes the party talked of constitutional revisions to endow the Presidency with emergency powers, nothing came of it.

Foreign policy, regional integration

Foreign policy under the Christian Democrats was, in Chilean terms, fairly dynamic. Undoubtedly this reflected their feeling that they were part of a worldwide political movement and a harbinger of further Christian Democratic triumphs in Latin America. The most urgent priority was the development of economic integration in Latin America, which meant breaking the straitjacket of local nationalisms that had enfeebled the continent since the age of independence. Then, in general, the Christian Democrats wished to remain friendly with the United States, but to have a friendship with dignity, something different from satellite status. They also wished to redevelop the traditional links with Western Europe, to build their own bridges to the established Communist regimes in Eastern Europe, and to play a more active role in the United Nations. The only country for long omitted from their benevolence was Cuba, though in 1968 the Chilean government began to suggest that Cuba's membership of the OAS could be reactivated.

Chile had been in the forefront of the movement to greater regional cooperation from the beginning, partly by the accident that the seminal United Nations Economic Commission for Latin America was based in Santiago, and partly because it was one of the four countries, with Argentina, Brazil, and Uruguay, promoting the Treaty of Montevideo of February 1960 which brought the Latin American Free Trade Area into force in June 1961. This treaty was signed by seven members to start with, and subsequently by two more, and by the time Frei became President in Chile the initial hostility of the United States and the International Monetary Fund had largely disappeared. But although intra-Latin American trade had almost doubled between 1961 and 1964, the shortcomings of LAFTA, which had been adopted in preference to a more ambitious ECLA proposal for a Latin regional common market, had become more obvious by then.

Among the drawbacks were institutional weakness in the LAFTA secretariat and the treaty's concentration on providing for those products which were already traded between member nations rather than on stimulating the local manufacture and exchange of the numerous articles imported from outside the region. Agreements on tariff cuts took too long to reach and it was irritating to find that subsidiaries of North American or European firms were quicker to seize on free trading opportunities than the Latin American ones.

Frei and his government did all they could to remedy the deficiencies of LAFTA, to press for the creation of an effective common market instead, and to use all opportunities of political and specialist conferences to spread the gospel. One of Frei's first initiatives was to commission a report from four of Latin America's best-known economists—Felipe Herrera, José Antonio Mayobre, Raúl Prebisch, and Carlos Sanz de Santa María—who recommended in April 1965 that there should be automatic tariff reductions instead of the arduous annual negotiations, the creation of a Council of Ministers to give LAFTA political leadership and a more powerful executive board.

But progress was slow, the tremendous urgency that Chile attached to the speeding-up of LAFTA was not shared by all her partners, and early in 1966 Frei flew to Bogotá to meet the representatives of four other countries—Venezuela, Colombia, Peru, and Ecuador. It was agreed to set up a subregional grouping. These five comprised about sixty million people, were more comparable in size than the LAFTA members, and shared a relatively high national income of about $550 per capita. Another distinction of the "Five of Bogotá" was that, although Ecuador had been ruled by a military junta recently, the other countries all had civil regimes.[6] Within a short time the Five had signed agreements covering the automobile, petrochemical, and electronics industries, and the prospects for integration seemed much more promising than they had through LAFTA after the meeting of November 1965 at which the Chilean proposal for a supranational commission on EEC lines was defeated.

But, though promising in its smaller field, the Chileans did not let the prospects for the Five blind them to the object to which they were increasingly attracted: a full-scale Latin American common market. In setting their hearts on this, the Chilean Christian Democrats had to surmount all the obstacles of differing size and levels of economic development which retarded LAFTA, plus some others. The derogation of sovereignty involved in the setting-up of supranational politico-economic institutions was one for which many Latin Americans were not ready: this was as true of small, passionately patriotic countries like Paraguay as it was of large countries, proud of their resources, like Brazil. Also, in the United States, although the official position might be mildly favorable, business interests might still regard a Latin American Common Market as a threat, and siren voices from time to time put forward the idea of a Western Hemisphere Common Market—from Alaska to Cape Horn—which could only have killed all the Latin American industries.

[6] A common factor which ceased to apply after October 3, 1968, when General Juan Velasco, head of a revolutionary military junta, ousted President Belaúnde Terry of Peru.

Nevertheless, the enthusiasm of the Chileans, supported by like minds elsewhere, was responsible for committing the meeting of Presidents at Punta del Este in 1967 to agree to the setting up of a Latin American Common Market beginning in 1970. This was a tremendous step forward, but only time would tell whether this deadline could be met.

For Chile itself, a relatively small and isolated economy which could never hope to develop the sort of internal market possible for Argentina or Brazil, the advantages of a Common Market were clear enough. On her own the consequences of economic particularism—too many car plants producing too few cars too expensively—were obvious, and the Chilean elites were more amenable than most in Latin America to the idea of building supranational institutions. But even in Chile there were some industries, such as textiles, which might collapse in a common market, and though the government and enlightened firms were pushing for the scheme, it was uncertain in 1967, for instance, that even all Chileans shared their commitment.

In foreign affairs generally Chile followed a pro-Western, pro-American policy under the Christian Democrats, spiced with small gestures of independence. Frei's trip to Europe in 1965 was productive of good will and also some financial assistance. Friendly relations were maintained with the Soviet Union, whose benevolence for bourgeois Latin American governments was strongly criticized in Havana.

One gesture of independence from United States leadership concerned the question of recognition of Communist China at the United Nations. At the first debate on the subject at the UN after Frei's election, Chile, in an unusual move for a Latin American state, actually abstained. But this heterodoxy was not repeated in the vote the subsequent year. U.S.-Chilean relations were helped along by the fact that Ralph Dungan, the U.S. ambassador in Santiago until 1967, was a Kennedy man sympathetic to Frei while the Chilean ambassador in Washington, Radomiro Tomic, though not totally pro-American, was perhaps Frei's closest associate.

Nevertheless, the U.S. link did come under strain when U.S. forces were sent to the Dominican Republic. Chile hotly opposed the intervention in meetings of the Organization of American States and helped to bury the proposal by the United States and Brazil that the OAS should have a permanent "peacekeeping force," ready to intervene anywhere that a left-wing revolution threatened. At about the same time the existence of "Camelot," a misguided Pentagon attempt to evaluate sociological factors in Chile that could be harnessed to suppress revolutionary unrest, was exposed by FRAP to the embarrassment of the Christian Democrats and the U.S. State Department, which had never been told. But the differences between the two governments were made up surprisingly quickly after the U.S. troops withdrew.

One factor that may have contributed to this, apart from the explicitly pro-Western orientation of Chilean policy, was the continuing dependence on the United States for the bulk of Chile's aid and a large part of her export earnings, in spite of the attempts to diversify both. The evolution of Cuban support for guerrillas and the Chilean Socialists' support for both Castro and the revolutionaries tended to put Frei into a more conservative posture in terms of the continent. The Chilean Socialist Party set up a Santiago bureau for OLAS, the Latin American organization designed to foment armed revolution which held a conference in Havana in 1967. Frei made plain that he would not allow the Socialists or OLAS to use Chile as a base from which to subvert constitutional governments in the region. After the collapse of Guevara's guerrillas in Bolivia, a country which had had no relations with Chile after the Bolivians had revived their border grievances, the Christian Democrats diplomatically permitted the guerrilla survivors to fly to Havana via Easter Island, Moscow, and Prague, hence avoiding the risk that any anti-Castro regimes on the direct route might intern them.

As for Chile's most powerful immediate neighbor, Argentina, there was a period of high tension after a border clash in a poorly demarcated sector of the Andes. But the tension dropped when the two parties resorted to British arbitration by the terms of their old treaty, adopted when the British Empire represented justice and law enforcement around the globe. In spite of the appearance of another military regime in Argentina, Chile, though it tried to cut down on the import of Argentine beef, pursued the improvement of communications and economic and other relations. The Christian Democrats were also keen to use the United Nations and improve their standing there. The results were not always flattering: a Chilean representative was a member of the United Nations team humiliated by South Africa when it attempted to assert UN control in South West Africa in 1968.

Frei and Christian Democracy

Frei is a shy, scholarly man, who likes to go for solitary walks unrecognized. He is not a backslapping, handshaking politician in either the North or South American styles. Nor is he gifted as a manipulator of personalities and interests. His family life—he has seven children—is a model of bourgeois discretion. He lives in a modest way in a Santiago suburb and his personal life could not attract malicious gossip. He is a man who relaxes with books and ideas, and intellectual interests and ability distinguish a number of the leading Christian Democrats. Among the corps of able men at the top of the party are Gabriel Valdés Subercaseaux, the Foreign Minister; Radomiro Tomic; Raul Troncoso, the government's Secretary General; and Sergio Ossa, who is largely responsible for Promoción Popular. In the background of Frei's entourage and suspect to anticlericals was, at one time, Father Roger Vekemans, s.j., as a result of whose influence several medium-level Christian Democrats went to Louvain to study sociology.

Though links with the nascent Christian Democracy of Europe date back to before the Second World War, it is plain that the modern party in Chile is predominantly a native growth. The Christian Democrats who came to power in Italy and West Germany and who were also influential in France after 1945 were not concerned to work any revolution in liberty: they were concerned to replace the defeated figures of Mussolini, Hitler, and Pétain with some form of secure, representative democracy, to reconstruct their stricken economies and avoid a slump, to provide a structure of welfare benefits that would incorporate workers and peasants into the rebuilt society, and to keep the Communists from taking over. These essentially conservative aims, understandable in relatively affluent European conditions, were light-years away from the propaganda of the victorious Chilean party in the early sixties.

The Chileans might share anti-Communism or a belief in the virtues of regional integration, but their confused calls for a revolution derived from distinctive emotions. The dispossession of the big landowners, and the inclusion into modern society of the fifth of the population that was illiterate, would alone, done completely and simultaneously, have amounted to a social revolution in Chile. Although they might not have known where they were going, the Chilean Christian Democrats who wanted "communitarian" institutions, workers' control, or more nationalization, were often rejecting consciously the notions of free-enterprise capitalism which European counterparts would broadly affirm. Normally conservative voters in Chile were attracted away from the traditional conservative parties because it seemed that something new and different—even perhaps a "revolution"—was necessary if the country was ever to achieve economic development. To put an end to the worst Chilean poverty and to extend normal bourgeois liberties to the whole population could only be done by a degree of state intervention, and hostility to foreign and native capitalism, that many would call Socialist.

Outsiders, who did not appreciate that the Falange had existed for over twenty years before it became known as the Christian Democratic Party in Chile, were eager to assume in the sixties that it was on the point of taking the whole of Latin America in the same direction. Chilean Christian Democrats were not so sanguine, though they did their best to help like-minded groups in Peru, Venezuela, and elsewhere. Chile, with its relative affluence and its established democracy, was too much of a special case. Other countries, of course, were interested by the Christian Democrats' success at the polls, and were somewhat less interested as the revolution in liberty faltered in performance, but in any case most had parties claiming to occupy the field as reformist democrats. COPEI, the Venezuelan Christian Democrats, were always regarded as to the right of Acción Democrática.

Perhaps none of the Christian Democrats' specific proposals in Chile was genuinely original in the region; what would have been unique would have been the realization of the whole program in one country within the six-year term of one President. This was not to be. But the common experience of underdevelopment, the common desire to draw on Latin America's Catholic heritage and institutions for bettering human life, the common wish to evolve a local philosophy distinct from the shopworn models of Washington, Moscow, or Havana, and even the common approval for Christian Democracy from the United States and the Vatican, made it likely that this would be one strain in the evolution of Latin American politics, even if not a predominant one.

Within Chile itself Christian Democrats claimed, in the excitement of 1964, that they would stay in office for thirty years at least. Halfway through Frei's Presidency nothing could have seemed more implausible. The party's sudden surge forward in the late fifties and early sixties had particular origins: The Radicals had been discredited in the forties; the Socialists had scarcely recovered from Ibáñez's personalist comeback in the fifties; the Communists, still regarded as a threat by many, had only recently been legalized. And Alessandri's lack of achievement tested Chilean loyalties to the Liberals and Conservatives. In domestic electoral terms, ignoring the value to Eduardo Frei of the Cuban Revolution, Pope John, and Kennedy's New Frontier, the Christian Democrats were the only promising faces with an untarnished reputation. By the time President Frei had been in office for three years, it was impossible to say with certainty that his party's candidate to succeed him would get elected.[7]

If the Christian Democrats became a lasting feature of the Chilean scene, much of the credit would be due to Frei. Yet he was better as a prophet than as an executive, and the performance of his government was bound to be compared unfavorably with his promises. Essentially his view of a revolution in liberty did not allow for the rapid change—for example, in land tenure —that expectant believers in the slogan had been led to anticipate. Though Frei's Senate minority made him vulnerable, it remained true that he was in a stronger position than almost any previous Chilean President, and his failures may be traced to deficiencies of doctrine and of administrative and tactical skill.

In office he was criticized for losing touch with his party and with the masses; but he showed, by his vigorous defense of his policy which led to the defeat of the left-wing executive at the special conference in January 1968, that he was determined to keep control of the party. Though natural calamities, earthquakes early in his term, and a drought in 1968 did not help him, he achieved some success in his policies. His misfortune was to have aroused hopes that he was unable, even if he was entirely willing, to satisfy.

Frei's integrity, his anxiety to build the party on both sound intellectual and electoral foundations, contributed to the advance of the Christian Democrats and made it possible for them to survive the disappointments of administration. Some of his enthusiasms, such as his devotion to regional integration—particularly understandable in view of Chile's tenuous geography and regional variations—might pay large dividends after he had left the Presidency. His belief in the importance of capturing an intellectual elite in the country—the poetess Gabriela Mistral was

---

[7] As in other Latin American countries distrustful of personalism, the Chilean constitution does not permit a President to serve for two successive terms. A person may stand for the Presidency later, and in living memory both Arturo Alessandri and Carlos Ibáñez have each been President on two occasions.

an early convert—provided the Christian Democrats with an ideological base scarcely equaled by any other party except the Communists. Christian Democracy in Chile was more than Frei's personal appeal, and this was partly his work.

As a Latin American politician Frei had two familiar traits: he was the son of recent immigrants who had made good by his own ability, and he was a university professor who had gone into politics. His gravity and earnestness, so ordinary in a Swiss bourgeois, represented an image of middle-class maturity somewhat unusual in Latin America and not universally sought. If the practice of Christian Democracy has had shortcomings, it cannot undo the contribution he and his friends have made to the theory of politics in Latin America: by working on the traditional material of Roman Catholicism, they have produced a framework within which it is possible for conservative forces to embrace some socially progressive views. In the Anglo-Saxon tradition such paradoxical conservatism is accepted and has an acknowledged role in making social change peaceful. Without it Latin America has been condemned in the past to a petrified social order periodically interrupted by violent efforts at change.

Juscelino Kubitschek

The inauguration of Brasília

All through the night of April 21, 1960, the birthday of Tiradentes, the dentist father of Brazilian independence, the ball went on in the Palácio Planalto, Brasília. Outside thousands of people from all corners of the country danced and sang in the cool air of the plateau. Lights picked out the long line of functional ministries, the elegant saucer and dome of Congress, the crown of thorns of a cathedral in embryo, and, never far from the completed shapes, the red dust of a solitary spot in the Brazilian interior which had been endlessly churned from earth to mud to dust again in less than four frantic years of construction. In the middle of the ball the Governor of Bahia came up and handed President Juscelino Kubitschek a tie, acknowledging that he had lost his bet that the capital could not be transferred from Rio de Janeiro by the appointed date. The President himself, tired out by two days of celebrations which had started with a tearful farewell to the staff of the Catete Palace in Rio, left the party at about 2 a.m., at the same time as the Papal Legate. But the dancing went on.

With worldwide admiration, and considerable national enthusiasm, the President could look on Brasília as the symbol of his development policy and its inauguration as the high point of his term of office. Long enshrined in the constitution but never acted on, the change of capital also symbolized that unusual adherence to constitutional forms which was another of his fondest boasts. Above all, a Brazilian plan with Brazilian architecture set up in double-quick time by Brazilian laborers and engineers, it seemed the clear and longed-for proof that Brazil, with its strange racial mixture and its poverty and its disappointed hopes, could make it.

The return of October 1965

Five and a half years later the hero of Brasília, reviled for corruption and indecent dealings with the Brazilian Communist Party, deprived of his political rights and encouraged into exile by a military revolution, came home to a sad simulacrum of his former triumphant progresses. He arrived at Galeão, Rio's international airport, early on the first Monday morning in October. He had embarked at Paris, where he had disposed of his flat. Votes were being counted in eleven states in which governorships were at stake in the first almost-free elections that the military regime of Marshal Castello Branco had allowed. In Minas Gerais, Kubitschek's home state, and in Guanabara, the city state of Rio de Janeiro, which were the two most important contests, allies of the ex-President were strongly expected to win. But no results had been declared yet and the country, not knowing how the soldiers would take an electoral defeat, was tense.

At the airport, set on a humid island in Guanabara Bay, a small and, on the whole, well-heeled crowd included Negrão de Lima, the Guanabara candidate who had been Foreign Minister under Kubitschek; Lucas Lopes, a Minister of Finance; and other old associates. After a short pause, during which he was told that he must submit himself to inquiries by the regime's military police, the former President came out to a tumultuous welcome—waving of silk handkerchiefs, flashbulbs popping, and the chant, taken up on car horns, of "JoKaKa Sessent'e Seis" (JK for '66). Down the Avenida Rio Branco in the center of Rio crowds cheered and confetti was thrown and there were more crowds at his smart seaside apartment in Ipanema. He was carried on loyal shoulders into his main reception room containing the signed photos of heads of state, invaded for the occasion by a mass of journalists and indiscriminate hangers-on.

Yet within weeks he was in exile again, suffering from high blood pressure brought on by excessive military questioning. In a demonstration of strength Marshal Castello Branco had had passed a second Institutional Act which added to the many powers already assumed by the executive, made sure of federal control of the security forces of the states, and made it almost certain that his own successor in two years' time would be chosen by manipulation of the government's majority in Congress. For Kubitschek, in his mid-sixties, this was the end of his dreams of a return to the Palácio Planalto.

Upbringing and education

Juscelino Kubitschek de Oliveira was born on September 12, 1902, in the town of Diamantina, Minas Gerais. Minas Gerais —"general mines"—was then a poor inland state, although its mineral wealth was known and its gold had embellished the beautiful city of Ouro Preto when Brazil was still a colony. Much of it, including the part round Diamantina, the former diamond town, is hilly and its small hill villages are reminiscent of Italy. Parts are also fertile, its cheese is famous, and up to 1930, when it began to alternate with São Paulo in providing the country's Presidents, it was known as the milk in Brazil's "coffee with milk" politics. Its own politics were largely conducted by rural bosses known as "colonels," and its people had a reputation for thrift and wiliness.

Juscelino's father died when he was very young. Some say that he was only one, although he has written that he remembers his father's illness and watching the funeral cortège from a window with his elder sister. Hence he was brought up by his mother, a schoolteacher, and it is by her Czech maiden name that he is known. The original Jan Nepomuscky Kubitschek, a carpenter, had emigrated to Diamantina in 1830, and his children did well for themselves. One of them, João Nepomunceno, founded a development bank, the Companhia Popular de Diamantina, was a reforming director of public instruction in Minas Gerais, and ended up as a Vice-President of the state. Another, Augusto Elias, Juscelino's grandfather, had a small farm where his daughter and grandchildren came when they could manage a holiday. He helped to steep the boy in a love of politics and that network of friendships and enmities by which *mineiros* (inhabitants of the state were called "miners") understood it. He was "so devoted to liberty and justice that he could be and was, in a certain violent municipal election, the sole voter for a candidate of the opposition." [1]

Life was hard for Dona Julia and her two children on a schoolteacher's earnings. Her school was six miles away at one time, and she had to walk, sometimes carrying her son too. By the time he was eight, the lively slender boy was running messages between shops and offices, and his whole education until he graduated as a doctor was a simultaneous effort to study and pay for it. The Episcopal Seminary was persuaded to accept him. As a teen-ager he swapped books all around Diamantina in order to quench his thirst for reading. He has written since that his decision to study medicine, which he did at the state university in Belo Horizonte, was caused by the family frustration over his father's fatal illness and lack of medical help even to cure a minor defect in one of his own feet. Certainly his mother was a driving force behind him, no doubt because she also knew that the profession was secure and well paid. For eight years until he qualified he financed his studies by working as a telegraph operator at night.

At twenty-five he was qualified, but he wanted to go on to be a surgeon. He worked long hours in hospitals and his own clinic and shared a consultancy with his brother-in-law, Julio Soares, who from that time on became his financial adviser too. It was probably with financial help from Soares that he was able to make an expensive ten-month trip to Europe in 1930. He studied

[1] Juscelino Kubitschek: *A Marcha do Amanhecer* (Bestseller: São Paulo; 1962), p. 19. Author's translation.

briefly at Paris, Vienna, and Berlin and also traveled widely—to Greece, Egypt, Syria, Lebanon, Turkey, Czechoslovakia, Belgium, England, Italy, Spain, and Portugal. His was a social and artistic grand tour, but he saw at first hand the economic tensions, the raging arguments about democracy and dictatorship, then preoccupying Europe. He returned convinced that Brazil had it in her own power to break out of economic poverty. By the time he was back, Getúlio Vargas, alleging that he had been fraudulently defeated for the Presidency, had come to rule at the head of a military rebellion which destroyed the outworn oligarchic structure of the old Republic. To strengthen his professional position, Kubitschek took the prestigious but unremunerative post of surgeon to the Minas Gerais Military Police, and two years later, in this capacity, he was sucked into politics.

Early political career

The occasion was São Paulo's two-month revolt against Vargas and his slowness in giving Brazil a new constitution—a revolt which but for the President's astuteness could have led to bloodshed throughout the country. As it was, the Mineiro–São Paulo border saw some fighting, and Benedito Valadares, one of the rising men in Vargas's machine in Minas, appointed Kubitschek to run the medical services for the government troops. There he saw a thousand casualties, acquired a strong dislike of civil wars, and made such a good impression on his patron by his efficiency in the chaotic conditions that when Valadares took over the government of Minas shortly after, he asked the surgeon to join his secretariat.

Valadares was one of several able politicians thrown up with Vargas's rise, skillful at compromise and with an unerring sense of where power lies, a good tutor in the political game, and a tower of strength for Kubitschek's subsequent career. The latter, involved in the keen struggles for the distribution of state patronage, recalls that the low priority given to the public interest in these was distasteful. However, he had swallowed his distaste sufficiently to get elected from Minas as a federal deputy in 1934. Vargas's declaration of a Fascist-style *Estado Novo* (New State) in 1937—of which he says he disapproved—put an end to Congress, but he was sufficiently popular among the Vargistas, particularly in Minas, to be appointed to the desirable job of Prefeito (Mayor) of Belo Horizonte in 1940.

As head of the administration of the relatively new city of Belo Horizonte Juscelino had ample scope for his initiative and drive. In addition to more prosaic tasks, he threw himself heart and soul into the scheme for beautifying Pampulha, a residential district of the city created around a hydroelectric reservoir. He wanted it to be a showpiece of contemporary architecture, something that tourists would come to see which would lift Belo out of the drab ranks of provincial cities. It was then that he met Oscar Niemeyer, a barely qualified young architect, and a partnership began which was to find its consummation in Brasília. Needless to say, not everyone liked the modern designs, and Niemeyer's best-known building in Pampulha, a church, was not used for worship for more than a decade after its construction because of the opposition of the hierarchy.

The Prefeito also launched social security programs in the city and showed his sympathy for the Allies at a critical stage of the war by accepting the presidency of the Cultura Ingles society locally. The British government showed its appreciation for this gesture by sending him a cross made of fragments of the bombs that had fallen on London. Brazil's adhesion to the Allies in 1942 rendered the Estado Novo increasingly obsolete, and in October 1945 Vargas was peacefully deposed by the army.

Minas, with its libertarian tradition, was an early focus for the wartime opposition to the dictator, but Kubitschek, whatever his own views on the Estado Novo, was inevitably tarred with the Vargista brush. When parties were formed to contest the presidential and congressional elections of December 1945, Kubitschek, Valadares, and the principal figures of the Vargas machine in Minas joined the Partido Social Democrático. This party, amorphous and opportunistic in its principles and sharing some of the traits of the French Radical Party or the British Whigs, was to be the basis of Kubitschek's political strength up to the 1964 revolution. Its leadership tended to come from among the landowners and rich businessmen, its votes from the negotiable local bosses in the countryside. Its social attitudes were conservative.

At the same time two other parties sprang up: the Partido Trabalhista Brasileiro, also blessed by Vargas, aimed at urban workers and with regional power bases in Rio de Janeiro and Rio Grande do Sul, and the União Democrática Nacional, a largely middle-class party which crystallized the liberal opposition to Vargas. Partly, no doubt, because of Kubitschek's reputation for tackling urban and working-class problems in Minas, the PTB never made much headway there.

The PSD did well in the 1945 elections. It succeeded in electing the President, General Dutra, and a majority in both the Senate and the Chamber of Deputies. Kubitschek himself participated in this success, for he was a federal deputy from 1946 to 1950. At the time this may have looked less like a step forward for him than the only way open of continuing his career, for the post-Vargas caretaker government had suspended all Prefeitos until the December 1945 elections were over, and if the PSD had lost, he could not have expected reinstatement.

The ensuing period in his life is relatively obscure. During the time he was a federal deputy the Cold War began to affect Brazil, causing the cautious Dutra to outlaw the Communist Party and break relations with the Soviet Union. But Kubitschek made no distinctive impact on the national scene; he concentrated his ambitions on the state of Minas Gerais instead.

By now he not only had a proven record as an administrator and political manager but he was also a proven vote-getter, and it was with this reputation that he won the PSD candidacy to the governorship of Minas in early 1950. In sixty days of campaigning he made 207 speeches and visited 168 municipalities, a whistle-stop approach to politics that was new to gubernatorial elections. His speeches were not just set pieces: the audiences asked questions and made suggestions, and the candidate's program was debated and modified. His theme was chiefly the need to improve transportation and increase electric power, and his promises, more than his predecessors', were quite specific. He promised to double the 200,000 kilowatts which was all that Minas possessed in 1950 and to build two thousand kilometers of first-class roads. "What I start I finish" was his slogan, and he pointed to his dynamic record of five years as Prefeito for the proof. His targets would be achieved with the help of private enterprise.

Kubitschek had no trouble getting elected. In national politics 1950 was the year of Vargas's comeback, when he was freely elected President by a coalition based on the PTB. The PSD put up a weak opponent to Vargas, and there was actually some sympathy for his return in the party. Although Kubitschek's state campaign was separate, there can be no doubt that he benefited from the Vargista tide. He was installed in office in 1951 and, with the same team that had helped him as Prefeito, he tore into the problems of Minas's backwardness. By the end of 1954 he had opened over three thousand kilometers of new roads, and the installed electrical capacity had risen to 605,000 kilowatts.

The day after taking office he had authorized the setting up of mixed companies, with state and private enterprise, to develop generating and hydroelectric capacity. The first set up was CEMIG, Centrais Eletricas de Minas Gerais SA, but there were four others whose initials were to become equally familiar. The state government nearly doubled the number of places for children in primary schools, encouraged the development of phosphate deposits at Araxá and a new refrigeration industry, and created 160 more health posts. The greater availability of roads and electricity gave private industry a parallel shot in the arm. In the light of subsequent criticism of his Presidency the most ironic claim of his state administration was to have reduced the deficits of the budget.

The 1955 presidential campaign

As early as October 1954 he had started campaigning for the presidential election of October 3, 1955. From his point of view the path was strewn with obstacles. It was not just that another candidate might win more votes than he but that the President, João Café Filho, who had succeeded after Vargas's suicide in 1954, was unfriendly, large sectors of the armed forces looked on the Kubitschek candidacy with suspicion, and there were constant rumors that the election would never take place. In the circumstances the candidate was lucky, adroit, and calm.

The atmosphere was largely colored by the circumstances of Vargas's suicide, the wave of middle-class horror of corruption and gangsterdom at the attempt on Carlos Lacerda's life beforehand, and the countervailing working-class and nationalistic wave which resulted from the former dictator's death and testament. Kubitschek, who was one of the few state governors to praise the deceased fulsomely, went into alliance with João Goulart, Vargas's heir in the PTB, who ran for Vice-President on his ticket. It was, said their opponents, a campaign on behalf of a corpse. Kubitschek, who could rely on the *mineiro* votes but was less known in the rest of the country, was well balanced by Goulart, who, as Vargas's Labor Minister, had union electoral support in most states and was particularly strong in his home state of Rio Grande do Sul. On the other hand, Goulart's known admiration for Juan Perón and his extravagant support for trade-union wage claims had earned him violent hostility in the army, which had forced his resignation from the Ministry of Labor.

About Christmas 1954 a wide-ranging group of senior officers, acting with the sympathy of Café Filho, produced a memorandum urging a civilian candidate of national unity. Obviously Kubitschek was not the civilian in question and, fortunately for him, the scheme broke down over the conflicting ambitions of those favored by the military. By early 1955 the prospects had changed with the appearance of several other candidates: Adhemar de Barros, Etelvino Lins of the UDN, Plínio Salgado, the leader of Brazil's Fascist Party up to the Estado Novo, and—most crucial for Kubitschek—Juarez Távora. Távora, head of the Presidential Casa Militar, who had had a large hand in the "national unity" manifesto, was a general of great prestige and integrity. Too honest or stupid to make a good candidate himself, he was still the very best guarantee that elections would be held and that they would be reasonably fair. Twelve years later Távora admitted to the author that he had never expected to win but that the man most responsible for persuading him to run was Jânio Quadros, the new Governor of São Paulo, who felt the time was not yet ripe for him to try himself but who was desperately anxious to prevent his Paulista enemy, Adhemar de Barros, from becoming President. In due course Etelvino Lins retired and the UDN threw its weight behind Távora, who thereby became the "official" candidate.

Throughout 1955, despite propagandist threats from his opponents and even the President himself that his candidacy carried the risk of civil war, Kubitschek fought his campaign at high pressure. After an emotional send-off from Diamantina he traipsed the length and breadth of his huge constituency preaching constitutionalism, national sovereignty, and, above all, development. Sticking to his Minas practice, he promised to achieve specific goals, thirty in all, which took in the principal industries and agriculture as well as his old favorites, power and transport. In the course of public discussion the goals were slightly modified, but they undoubtedly excited Brazilians by being only just attainable in five years, measurable, and apparently decisive.

At the small town of Jatai, Goiás, a questioner asked Kubitschek if he would carry out the article of the constitution which provided for the removal of the capital to the Goian plateau, and he stumbled on the synthesizing element of his development program. Although some aerial survey work had been done in the fifties in looking for a site, Kubitschek's rapid and controversial adoptation of Brasília gave his campaign a new twist. Brasília was tangible, optimistic, constitutional, and it appealed perfectly to the candidate's sense of showmanship.

But while he was dashing around the country by plane, his handsome smile lighting up backwoods towns, his nicknames "Jusce," "Nono," "JK" on many new lips and his campaign song, "O Peixe Vivo" ringing in new ears, his able staff was arranging as much concrete support as possible. It is almost beyond doubt that they bought the help of the underground Brazilian Communist Party, which, when it was legal ten years earlier, had mustered over half a million votes, or nearly a tenth of the total, behind a lackluster presidential candidate. The UDN also believed that they had paid Salgado, who was likely to draw off some Távora votes, to continue in the race. In the press they bought the help of Rio's *Jornal de Comércio* and the nationwide Diários Associados chain. It was widely assumed too that several of the big industrial firms which had developed recently in Minas were behind Kubitschek's candidacy. The whole Brasília project, with attractions throughout the country and particularly for Goiás, was above all a vote-catcher in Minas, whose state capital would be the nearest big city to the capital, whose contractors could reasonably claim to be in the forefront of its development, and whose geographical situation, astride future communications lines between the old and new federal centers, would give it new significance.

The results, which as usual took more than a fortnight after polling day before they were complete, gave Kubitschek 3,077,411 votes, 35.63 per cent; Távora 2,610,462, 30.26 per cent; Adhemar 2,222,735, 25.77 per cent; and Salgado 714,379, 8.28 per cent. Although Kubitschek was the leader, his percentage poll was much less convincing than either Dutra's or Vargas's or than Quadros's was to prove five years later. Nearly a quarter of his total vote came from Minas, where the PSD candidate in the concurrent gubernatorial election also won a smashing victory; but in the city of Rio he came some way second to Adhemar and in the state of São Paulo, Adhemar's own fief, he came a poor third after Távora. The Northeast, where Távora was the favorite son, supported its own strongly, but Kubitschek and the PSD machine picked up most of the other states as well as the federal territories. It was noteworthy that Kubitschek had only a slim lead in Rio Grande do Sul, whereas João Goulart did relatively better throughout the country in the vice-presidential voting and triumphed in three states which his running mate had failed to take.

Tension rose in the course of the long-drawn-out count. The 1946 constitution stated that where no candidate had an over-all majority the winner had to be confirmed by Congress. The UDN attacked Kubitschek's presumed deal with the Communists and queried the large PSD vote from Minas. Carlos Lacerda's paper made much of an interview with Admiral Pena Boto in which this conservative figure had emphasized that neither Juscelino nor Adhemar had "the moral requirements for the Presidency." The situation was further complicated by the fact that on November 8, Carlos Luz, the president of the Chamber of Deputies, had temporarily taken over the Presidency from Café Filho, who had had a heart attack. Luz, an anti-Kubitschek PSD man, was widely supposed to be in league with Lacerda and the young officers who wanted to make a coup d'état to prevent the winners from taking office.

In this critical atmosphere Luz, on November 10, attempted to dismiss Café's Minister of War, General Henrique Lott. General Lott was a military disciplinarian who liked to see laws observed in both the state and the services. Less than a week after the election he had promised a peaceful inauguration for the victorious Kubitschek–Goulart team. The issue on which the acting President sought to dismiss the War Minister was of central political relevance: the latter wished to punish an officer who had made a violent speech against the "victory of the minority" at the funeral of an anti-Vargas general.

Lott's first reaction to his dismissal was pique. But by nightfall he had been persuaded by General Odilio Denys and others that the preservation of discipline in the army required him to take action against the acting President. At the head of a loosely organized Movimento Militar Constitucionalista he staged an efficient coup d'état in the early hours of the following morning.[2] While Luz with some of his cabinet and Lacerda boarded the cruiser *Tamandaré* in Rio harbor and sailed to Santos in an abortive effort to organize resistance, Lott duly installed his constitutional successor, the vice-president of the Senate, who was conveniently a PSD man, as caretaker President. When Café Filho attempted to resume his post after his illness, on November 21, Lott prevented him. Kubitschek and Goulart came into office on January 31, 1956, under the firm guardianship of Lott, after the President-elect had made a twenty-day tour of the United States and Europe in which he had welcomed foreign capital in a partnership to achieve Brazil's Fifty Years' Progress in Five.

The politics of the Presidency

As a minority President, inheriting some bitter opponents who stretched into the ranks of the services, his entry to office was hardly auspicious. Yet he was to serve his term peacefully, hand over the government in an orderly way to Jânio Quadros, and withdraw with real achievements and lasting popularity. The success was not instantaneous and the Presidency had its reverses. Yet one of the secrets lay in Lott's unusually strict control of the military and Kubitschek's cultivation of them. Within the first fortnight of his term there was a revolt of right-wing air force officers at the remote Amazon air base of Jacareacanga. He wisely extended an amnesty not only to them but to all charged with revolutionary acts since November. The navy, confused by the *Tamandaré* incident, he made special efforts to conciliate. He went for a cruise in the *Barroso,* the *Tamandaré's* sister ship, and authorized the purchase of an obsolete British aircraft carrier which was expensively refurbished and renamed the *Minas Gerais.* He also paid close attention to service pay, an issue which had helped to precipitate the doom of the Vargas government in

[2] A further account of Lott's coup and the *Tamandaré* incident occurs on pp. 224–5, in the chapter on Carlos Lacerda.

1954 and which was bound to arise again with increasing inflation.

On the awkward question of his debt to Lott, accused by the opposition of throwing his weight around and treating the new President as a puppet, he seized the initiative early. Lott's daughter was a left-wing nationalist, and it seemed that the War Minister might respond to overtures from the November Front, a left-wing nationalist outfit which presented him with a "golden sword." Kubitschek proceeded to close the Front for six months as subversive—closing at the same time Carlos Lacerda's inflammatory right-wing Lantern Club—and Lott then retired into his constitutional background. The question arose again at the end of Kubitschek's term, when Lott became candidate of the PSD–PTB coalition to succeed him. The situation then was affected by Quadros's suspected electoral strength, the President's expectations for 1965, and Goulart's unwillingness to run for the Presidency either because he thought he would be beaten or because he thought the army was not yet ready to accept him. In the event, Kubitschek only gave Lott his reluctant endorsement.

Kubitschek's term is chiefly remembered for its economic achievements and for its inflation, although the second was to be dwarfed later. From 1957 to 1961 the country's real rate of growth was seven per cent a year and it was nearly four per cent per capita. Between 1955 and 1961 industrial production grew by eighty per cent, in constant prices, steel production doubled, and the output of other industries grew even faster. This rate of growth was the highest in Latin America and one of the highest in the world. It was encouraged by the President's infectious enthusiasm and his policy of targets, evolved by an able team of economists.

Striking advances were made in electric power, with the building of great new hydroelectric power complexes at Furnas and Tres Marias. An automobile industry, set up almost from scratch, was producing over a hundred thousand units a year by the end of Kubitschek's term. Not all the targets were achieved—for example, there was a shortfall in coal output, and in some cases, as in oil, which was exploited by the state monopoly Petrobras set up by Vargas, achievement of an ambitious production target still fell short of national requirements.

Although some of the targets, such as the production of fertilizer and the building of more freezing plants, were of benefit to agriculture, the whole emphasis on industrialization was sometimes criticized as neglecting that sector. Agrarian reform, an issue that began to make itself heard particularly in the backward Northeast, was not touched during the term. But the President did give a new impetus to the correction of the regional defects of the Northeast and in 1959 sent a law to Congress creating SUDENE (Superintendência do Desenvolvimento do Nordeste), a new regional authority under the well-known economist Celso Furtado.

The inflation, which only became serious in mid-1958, resulted from a collision between the development policy and an adverse turn in the terms of trade, a heavy load of short-term debt, and limited international credit. While foreign private investors could be persuaded by Brazil's future to spend heavily on the setting up of automobile, shipbuilding, and other industries, the international institutions were mindful of the country's unhappy credit history and were anxious to apply the same financial medicine to Brazil that they believed beneficial in developed economies. In 1957 the balance of payments showed a deficit of $286 million, and it increased thereafter. The coffee growers, on whom the country still depended for about half its export earnings, became restive.

By June 1958 the economic problems were becoming more acute, and the Finance Minister resigned to be replaced by Lucas Lopes, who persuaded the President that he must follow an anti-inflation policy. But Kubitschek was hesitant. He put off action until congressional elections had shown little alteration in party strengths. He did not wish to compromise public expenditure on his targets program. By December 1958 the president of the Bank of Brazil was getting away with defiance of Lopes's orders to restrict industrial credit.

There is no reason to suppose that Kubitschek was unaware of the social tensions that would be released with uncontrolled inflation. But he was no economist, and his advisers were divided over inflation, several believing that a rate of twenty per cent a year, about what was expected in Rio in 1958, was tolerable and necessary for an industrializing society. The anti-inflation policy also became a nationalist issue which in the pre-electoral feeling of 1959 inflamed the Goulart PTB wing of his supporters into outright criticism.

The government was being very obviously encouraged in an anti-inflationary policy by the International Monetary Fund, and the U.S. government had informed Brazil that its request for a $300 million loan depended on its cooperation with the IMF. The controversy over the anti-inflation policy and the U.S. loan, coupled with notable pressure on prices and incomes by early 1959 and the strains brought on by the financing of Brasília, threatened to destroy that consensus for development that had been so fruitful in the first two years of Kubitschek's Presidency.

There is little doubt that if Kubitschek had seriously enforced the IMF package, he would have had to abandon in large part his targets program. Politically this would have been self-destructive. Effecting an unpopular stabilization at the behest of overseas interests would have made it unlikely that anyone connected with Kubitschek could succeed him, or that he could succeed his successor in 1965. His own reputation as a doer would suffer while his successor would reap the economic benefit and also some of the credit for a postponed Brasília.

In June 1959 he instructed the Brazilian team in Washington to break off negotiations with the IMF and made a dramatic appeal to domestic opinion. The country must make sacrifices to establish its economic independence. "Brazil has come of age. We are no longer poor relatives obliged to stay in the kitchen and forbidden to enter the living-room," he told the Military Club. Lopes and the others who had planned the stabilization were fired and for the remaining seventeen months of the administration inflation soared. Nineteen sixty saw a record payments deficit, and by early the following year there was three times the amount of cruzeiro money in circulation that there had been at the end of 1955. Nevertheless the President, whose use of statistics was becoming suspect, was still claiming to the National Economic Council in January 1961 that the average annual expansion of paper money during his rule was of "basically the same order" as in the first years of the decade.

In internal politics the Kubitschek years represented a lull between the traumas of Vargas's suicide and Quadros's renunciation. Partly this responded to a national need for recuperation and partly this was the result of the President's own approach. His emphasis on development distracted energies from old feuds and at the same time gave him a store of patronage to use to influence different politicians and their clients. By instinct he was a consensus politician in the Brazilian tradition, eschewing divisive measures, anxious to maintain good relations with as many groups as possible, and willing to go part of the way toward each of them. He cooperated with Quadros, then Governor of São Paulo, though the latter was constantly being cast as his deadly enemy. He was also prepared to take firm measures to promote quiet. In June 1956 he ordered the closing of the Dock Workers' Union of Rio and the National Emancipation League, both Communist-run, and two months later he had *Tribuna da Imprensa* seized when it published a manifesto against Communists and traitors in the government by Carlos Lacerda who, by happy accident, was spending much of the President's first year in self-exile.

Most important, in view of the Vice-President's status as a liability among many officers and conservatives, he managed both to tame and have good working relations with João Goulart. Although Goulart was given control of the Ministry of Labor, he had to join the President in stating publicly that he was against Communism and in May 1956 he visited the United States, where he did his best to explain that he was a good democrat. The Vice-President was bound to encourage the tendency of the PSD–PTB majority in Congress to vote higher expenditure and wage settlements than Kubitschek always wanted, and there was occasional friction. In September 1959 the President denounced an illegal strike movement and the next day had to add that this was in no way criticism of his "loyal friend and sincere ally, Dr. João Goulart." The inner history of the PTB and the Brazilian Communist party at this period is unclear. But it seems that under Goulart's protection Communists achieved a stronger position in the unions. Goulart himself was attacked from within the PTB for weakness and relying too heavily on the Vargas myth and after 1958, when his cousin Leonel Brizola was elected Governor of Rio Grande do Sul, he had to reckon with the fact that a tougher, more nationalistic demagogue had risen to claim the attention of the labor movement.

Kubitschek's foreign policy was cautious. Its main stand, as was usual for Latin American governments, was friendship for the United States. This became less profitable as his term proceeded, though it was left to Jânio Quadros to try to construct an "independent" foreign policy with as good relations with the Soviet bloc as with the United States. To begin with, Kubitschek's government made an unprecedented public-relations effort in the United States, designed to win the support of private investment for Brazil's development. In 1957, after a year's acrimonious debate and against the strong opposition of left-wing nationalists, the administration gave the United States permission to build and operate for five years a missile-tracking station on the island of Fernando de Noronha off the northeastern coast of Brazil.

In May 1958 the President made his most dramatic foreign policy move when, while the United States was still stung by the adverse reception for Vice-President Nixon on his Latin American tour, he wrote to President Eisenhower suggesting "Operation Pan America." Kubitschek did not have a detailed program; but the essence of his appeal was that hemispheric diplomacy, with its sterile juridical traditions and rigmarole of largely meaningless conferences, should be revived by a multilateral assault on poverty and underdevelopment. U.S. finance and skills would be crucial to the success of OPA, but the President saw it as a genuinely cooperative effort that could enlist the idealism of Latin Americans too. The timing of the appeal fitted in with a growing realization of the size of the development task in Latin America and an awareness of the economic resurgence of Europe, including countries that had fought the United States, which was put down largely by the Latin Americans to the unstinting generosity of Marshall Plan aid.

Eisenhower's reply to Kubitschek was friendly, and John Foster Dulles visited Brazil in August. The reception among Latin American countries was good, and the idea was applauded at a Foreign Ministers' meeting in September. Kubitschek's remark, in the course of a speech at the Catholic University, Rio de Janeiro, that "We desire to live at the side of the West, but we don't want to be its proletariat," caught the mood exactly. But OPA was transferred to the rarefied consideration of a commission of twenty-one and, although a limited multilateral aid scheme was launched in 1960, Eisenhower's Washington was not disposed to take the diplomatic opportunity. This negative reaction disappointed Kubitschek and contributed to the general souring of relations which came to a head in the break with the International Monetary Fund. Later it was generally admitted that President Kennedy's Alliance for Progress owed a lot to the conception of OPA. But Kubitschek regarded it as only part of the answer.

In other respects his policy had followed old patterns. Brazil maintained a close friendship with Portugal despite the nature of the Salazar regime. It also was careful in its approach to the Castro revolution in Cuba, upholding the principle of self-determination but voting in the Organization of American States to condemn Communist intervention there. Brazil accepted some Cuban refugees as she had also taken Hungarian and Middle Eastern Jewish refugees after 1956.

The building of Brasília

The most obvious public memorial to the Kubitschek years, Brasília, was, as has been seen, a product of electioneering. To its opponents it always remained a gimmick and suspect in that they regarded it as a wasteful diversion of funds which gave an additional fillip to the inflation and corruption of which they disapproved. The President gladly used it as a tool of salesmanship, to demonstrate to the world and Brazilians themselves the country's possibilities, but he always stoutly denied the "Pharaonic ambition" attributed to him.

The proposal to transfer the national capital to the interior had been first mooted in 1789 and was put forward in the constitutions of 1891, 1934, and 1946. A foundation stone had actually been laid in 1922. From its first mention in his electoral campaign Juscelino made it peculiarly his own, visiting the site nearly three hundred times during the forty-one months of construction, and throwing the whole resources of his administration into the job of completing an irrevocable city within his own term.

Soon after taking office, he set up NOVACAP, a new authority charged with the construction under a *mineiro* engineer, Israel Pinheiro. Congress, somewhat to its own amazement, voted in favor, and an international panel under Sir William (now Lord) Holford chose the celebrated "airplane" design, one of the least detailed in the competition, by the well-known Brazilian urbanist Lucio Costa as the pilot plan for the city. Oscar Niemeyer, who had worked with Costa before, was given the job of designing the main public buildings. It is probably fair to say that the city plan was more controversial than the Niemeyer buildings. The plan provided for a strict zonal segregation of functions and an uncompromising adherence to the ideal of a bureaucratic city in which industry must have little place. The "Cidade Livre," the allegedly temporary shanty town for the building workers, and the satellite cities in which hundreds of thousands of the capital's workers would be expected to live, were left to fend for themselves. While Niemeyer's palaces, for Congress, the judiciary, and the President, won much admiration as peaks of a distinguished wave of modern Brazilian architecture, his apartment blocks for civil servants (the *"superquadros"*) were criticized as uninteresting and impractical.

Given the political opposition that developed to the scheme, particularly in Rio, which was to be deprived of its advantages as the federal capital, there were strong political and psychological motives for haste. The astonishing drive, by comparison with the ordinary slowness of Brazilian administration, was propelled by the focusing of nationalism and a New World sense of futurity on a single object. For this the President was largely responsible. The conquest of the vast, sparsely populated interior to which the Brasília movement looked forward was a Brazilian reflection of that desire for development and national control of resources which was currently rippling through the Third World. In the messianic New World context it bore a striking resemblance to the visionary rhetoric of Canada's Mr. Diefenbaker with his "roads to resources" program and, before Kubitschek's term was out, the same spirit was to be evoked in a more sophisticated form by the New Frontier.

Kubitschek's case for Brasília was that it would break the stranglehold of the early-colonized coastal strip on the country's development, and that it would unlock the resources of the surrounding plateau and the west-central portion of Brazil. He also believed that it would promote the unity of the country—its first population came from all over—and by removing government from the sectional interests and lethargic atmosphere of highly political Rio, it would improve the quality of administration. Rio was also becoming too overcrowded and too deficient in urban services to be a worthy capital. A new system of communications, including roads from Belém to Brasília and Fortaleza to Brasília which were finished within Kubitschek's term, as well as plans for links with Manaus in the center of Amazonia and Lima, Peru, went with the new capital. Agriculture and horticulture in the environs of the new Federal District had a fillip. Otherwise, apart from the fact of the new city's existence, its benefits as a center for development would emerge with the passage of time.

The building of the "City of Hope" (the President's home would be the "palace of the dawn") was conducted with maximum publicity. On October 2, 1956, Juscelino visited the site, marked with a cross of brazilwood, and promised to pass on his mandate there. The next month work began. The Church decided that the new city should have "Nossa Senhora Aparecida," Brazil's patroness, as its own, and by October 1957 the first school was open. At the end of January 1960 a "caravan of national integration" from all parts of the country met in Brasília, and the next month President Eisenhower visited it in the wake of other international well-wishers. In April there were three days of junketings when the city was inaugurated with a Mass, the legislature and judiciary made a symbolic start, and the first act of the executive was to propose to Congress the setting up of a University of Brasília on novel lines.

It cannot be said, however, that Kubitschek left President Quadros a working capital. The immediate consequences were a duplication of ministries and delays due to breakdowns in communications between Rio and Brasília offices. Though Quadros, Congress, and the Supreme Court used the place for business, many kept homes in Rio, where there was more entertainment. Without enough housing for civil servants it was impractical to move ministries bodily, and without a Foreign Ministry building the diplomatic corps was bound to stay in Rio. Not until three lukewarm Presidents had come and gone, during which time Brasília grew at a slower, more organic pace, was there a prospect, under the enthusiastic President Costa e Silva, of the city becoming the true seat of government.

Attacks on Kubitschek's dream revolved around the cost. He claimed that it would largely pay for itself as NOVACAP auctioned the building lots. By May 20, 1958, he claimed that 960 lots had been sold for 626 million cruzeiros (about $4.8 million). The year before he had rejected an accusation that the project would cost 130 billion cruzeiros (close to $1.8 billion), saying that NOVACAP would only build public buildings and works and the rest would be done by private enterprise. By August 1958 he was saying that the projected cost would largely be covered by the sale of eighty thousand lots which would repay a capital of 24 billion cruzeiros (close to $190 million). In an auction in April 1960, thirty-two lots went for 94 million cruzeiros (about $500,000).

The President's "self-financing" thesis was almost certainly inadequate even so far as the public works and buildings went, as property values would only rise after the infrastructure had been provided. More generally, his defense missed the point that critics, particularly from the opposition UDN which did not gain from the patronage, were complaining at the total diversion of scarce resources. Banks and other firms which would normally have developed elsewhere were put under strong pressure to build in Brasília. Inflation tended to obscure the real costs of the project, and in the surrounding psychological climate there was no chance of a strict accounting.

Jânio Quadros, in January 1961, stated that the total cost by then had reached 72.6 billion cruzeiros (about $266 million). Wild accusations of graft multiplied, but although Quadros and even the military regime of 1964 ordered investigations, these fizzled out. A common assertion was that bricks had been flown into Brasília at the start of construction. Oscar Niemeyer assured the author that this was never true, but if not, it was typical of the legends that flourished at the time.

All the same, in the nation at large the new capital was popular. Even in Rio a public opinion poll in July 1957 produced a small majority in favor of the move, and national enthusiasm reached a climax with the inaugural festivities.

The corruption issue

Almost all his term, and particularly in the debates over Brasília, the President was under fire from his critics for corruption. It was one of the main charges of Jânio Quadros in his campaign in 1960, when his symbol was a broom. As an issue, beautifully generalized but spiced with rumor and malice, it had a strong appeal for UDN moralists who were addressing a middle-class audience. It was a convenient, all-embracing explanation for the inflation, which was paralleled by government supporters in the blame on the IMF.

In a narrow sense the critics were right: Juscelino emerged from ten years at the center of national life a considerably wealthier man than before. Some of this could be put down to the shrewd advice of Julio Soares, who got his brother-in-law to invest in a growing retail chain, Lojas Americanas, and other financial opportunities. But in an administration which obviously depended on a far-flung network of friendships and contacts, it was hard for outsiders to distinguish between legitimate and illegitimate advice from businessmen to the President's associates and between the corrupt transfer of money and the President's prudent investments. In the wider sphere of public contracts, often fulfilled by friends or contacts, the same was true: everything might be above board, but the headlong style of development led to suspicions which in the cynical view of ordinary Brazilians rapidly became accepted facts.

For the professional moralists of the UDN this attack on the Kubitschek government was merely a new version of their critique of the Vargas system whereby the dictator and his henchmen had presided over the setting up of new industries and labor unions with the spoils mentality of the old rural politicians. The PSD–PTB coalition of 1955 was bound to include a lot of people from the Vargas era. The growing middle class was being schooled to demand efficiency and open competition for contracts or positions, and it felt that Brazil, as an underdeveloped country, could not afford waste.

Nevertheless, the friendship patterns of Brazilian social and political life were too deeply ingrained for the UDN to be able to adopt an unambiguous position. In those states—particularly in the more backward regions—where the UDN had elected governors, the same cries of "corruption" could be heard against them and with the same sort of justification. Indeed, in spite of efforts to instill a new morality, it was still broadly accepted that politics in Brazil, like the Church in medieval Europe, offered one of the few well-rewarded careers open to all. In this context Kubitschek himself could not be regarded as notorious, and the quality of many of those he brought into the government was undeniably high. He was particularly skillful at inspiring participation in the development process by younger educated people, and the ISEB (Instituto Superior de Estudos Brasileiros), a research center on the problems of social and economic development, was an excellent example.

Outside the axe-grinding opponents of the Kubitschek Administration's corruption and its obvious beneficiaries the mass of voters could make their own judgment on the development policies and rumors of graft. Quadros's big victory over Lott in the 1960 elections was owing to a much wider arc of support than the usual UDN electors, and this probably had to do with his commitment to continued development, if without inflation. Though corruption, if not in one's own favor, was regrettable, the development was essential and a Brazilian voter could assume under Kubitschek that any kickbacks would be invested locally rather than in a Swiss bank.

After the Presidency

Jânio Quadros, the charismatic political outsider from São Paulo, won forty-eight per cent of the votes in the 1960 elections; but his rule was short-lived. Kubitschek had spent a month in Paris on leaving office and had returned to find investigations going on into alleged use of social security funds to buy votes, falsification of stamps and signatures on loans, and one or two other hangovers from his term which had inspired the new President's moral fervor. The PSD–PTB majority in Congress did its best to damp down the investigations, and Kubitschek, openly declaring that he was looking forward to the 1965 presidential elections, was elected Senator for Goiás, the state which had been put on the map by Brasília.

In August the eccentric Quadros, who had resigned once from his presidential candidacy and who had drifted farther away from his UDN sponsors in office without establishing any firm new support, suddenly resigned. João Goulart, who had again been elected Vice-President in spite of the defeat of his running mate, Lott, was at the time on an official visit to Communist China. His succession was anathema to the military ministers, but the army was not entirely under their control, and the result of a "prolegality" demonstration by General Machado Lopes of the Third Army (in Rio Grande do Sul, where Goulart's cousin Brizola was now Governor) was a compromise. Goulart would be allowed the Presidency on condition that a parliamentary system with a prime minister took much of the real power from him.

Kubitschek, who used part of his first free year traveling in the United States, Japan, the Middle East, and Europe, used his influence in favor of a peaceful succession. Mindful of his own hopes and no doubt aware that Brazil was difficult enough to govern without any extra division of power within the executive, he voted in the Senate against restrictions on the Presidency.

The collapse of Quadros, a figure who personified much of the instability of Brazilian politics, had serious consequences. It encouraged the disillusionment of the UDN, the traditional opponents of Vargas and exponents of liberal democracy, with Brazil's democratic process when they saw the failure of their one clear-cut electoral success. Parallel with this, it was a disappointment to those who believed that strong measures were needed to curb the country's inflation to see as popular a President as Quadros starting to change his tune when he saw the resistance such steps evoked. Above all, the dichotomy of Vargas–anti-Vargas, apparently laid to rest by the conciliatory politics of Kubitschek and the success of Quadros at the polls, broke out again with renewed force under conditions of greater social tension, and underlay the progressive radicalization of politics under Goulart.

The parliamentary experiment, which Goulart had a strong interest in proving unworkable, had reached a point of inadequacy by August 1962, when his military ministers launched a manifesto calling for a plebiscite on presidentialism. Strikes and continued inflation colored the situation. Kubitschek strongly supported the campaign for an early plebiscite, and on January 6, 1963, Brazil voted five to one to end the parliamentary system and to return to a strong Presidency.

Goulart had already spoken of the need for basic reforms—tax reform, land reform, and the nationalization of foreign-owned utilities—and in a trial of strength between his moderate and extreme nationalist supporters the latter had forced through a very tough and somewhat unrealistic law on the remission of profits. As full President he renewed his call for basic reforms, and at the same time experimented with an ambitious three-year program for growth without inflation drawn up by Celso Furtado and San Tiago Dantas, his Finance Minister. But the program, under constant assault from the far left because it seemed to mean coming to terms with Washington and in practice deflation, collapsed by mid-June owing to congressional opposition to land reform and the pressure from civil servants and the military for higher pay. By September the general atmosphere of agitation had led to a revolt of noncommissioned officers in Brasília, Brizola appeared to be gaining more of a hold on the President, and the latter was cooperating closely with the trade-union leaders of the CGT.

In October Goulart asked for, and was denied by Congress, emergency powers to govern. By December Carvalho Pinto, a moderate representative of the São Paulo bankers, had left the Finance Ministry, and Goulart abandoned his attempts to cultivate a broad consensus in favor of reliance on the divided and untested resources of the left. The start of 1964 saw continued inflation and the government wildly trying to cope by direct controls over prices.

Various groups on the right, military and civil, were already plotting Goulart's overthrow when, in March, he challenged them directly. At a Rio rally on the 13th organized by trade unions, he signed decrees expropriating the relatively unimportant oil refineries in private ownership and making underexploited estates close to roads, railways, or federal irrigation schemes subject to take-over by the state. He declared that he was planning rent controls and extension of the vote to illiterates and servicemen, and that he was dissatisfied with the constitution. In his presence Brizola called for a constituent assembly which sounded like the Russian workers' and peasants' soviets of 1917.

The crisis quickly moved to a climax. After a large anti-Goulart demonstration in São Paulo on March 19, there came a traumatic mutiny by sailors in Rio over the Easter weekend, March 27–9, which Goulart resolved by sacking his Navy Minister and replacing him by a retired admiral, one of a short list put forward by the CGT, who at once gave an amnesty. The revolt, starting with an anti-Goulart manifesto by the Governor of Minas Gerais on March 30, was all over by April 2, with only a small amount of bloodshed. By then Goulart was en route for exile in Uruguay, and Brazil had acquired a military government.

Kubitschek's strategy in the closing stages of the Goulart era was to preserve at all costs the chance of free elections in 1965 and to keep the PSD–PTB alliance in working order. Given Goulart's seeming lack of resolution and the strength of the opposite forces working for unconstitutional solutions, this was difficult. The 1962 elections for governorships had already shown the breakdown of statewide PSD–PTB alliances and the trend in congressional elections in the same year suggested that the PTB was growing at the PSD's expense. The alliance in Congress was getting strained by 1964. The growing controversy over land reform put the PSD at a disadvantage.

Though a group of firebrands called the *agressivos* was pressing for land reform within the party, the majority of PSD Congressmen had ties with the beneficiaries of the old system of land tenure. At the PSD convention in late March 1964 which launched Kubitschek's candidacy for the 1965 elections, he had committed himself to a moderate land reform, which would not disturb medium-sized proprietors, as well as to a big urban housing campaign. He was certainly given broad hints that the military were planning a coup, and in March anti-Goulart figures like Adhemar de Barros and Carlos Lacerda appealed to him to come off the fence and join the opposition. But he contented himself with warning Goulart in public that he must observe the constitution.

At the height of the crisis, on March 31, Goulart called him for a long talk, and there were rumors that he wanted Kubitschek to mediate with the Governor of Minas and that JK was proposing another temporary reversion to a parliamentary system. By then, however, the military conspiracy had gone too far, Goulart had made it clear that he would not disavow the Communists and trade-union radicals which would be the lowest price of a settlement, and JK's public calls for peace and reconciliation had a lame, overtaken air.

Within a week or so after the coup it had become quite clear that it was essentially a military operation, that the army intended to retain power, and that along with the Communists and student leaders, the trade-union leaders, and the agrarian agitators, a leading target for the military purges was the UDN's old villains of the Vargas system. Some of the PSD figures, accommodating as ever, coalesced around the UDN in the purged Congress. More stayed neutral. A PSD man, José Maria Alkmim, was chosen Vice-President by General Castello Branco, the military President.

But the whole tone of the new regime, with its economy and morality, its military-police inquiries into graft and Communism, and its contempt for the politicians' search for easy popularity, was bad for Juscelino. His devotion to constitutional government and to national development even at the cost of U.S.–Brazilian relations, and his obvious determination to run a public campaign for the Presidency even after the revolution, brought him into conflict with it. In spite of a petition against his disqualification on June 8, six days before the end of the period that Castello Branco was allowing for the cancellation of political rights, the new government canceled Kubitschek's for ten years.

Kubitschek thereafter, though he tended to travel around, established his base in Paris, where there was a considerable Brazilian exile community. But he continued to keep in close touch with Brazilian politics through his network of old PSD contacts, and his activities abroad continued to be news in the Brazilian press. In 1965, as has been seen, he made an abortive return to Rio. The widespread disillusionment with the PTB leadership provoked by the 1964 disaster and the decimation of PTB personnel caused by the purges improved Kubitschek's standing in that quarter. At the same time the unpopular deflation, which seemed inconsistent with the country's need for development, and the continued military retention of control caused a breach between the soldiers and the civilian politicians who had backed the revolution. In all, the principles and practices of Kubitschek were favorably reassessed across a wide spectrum.

When Castello Branco allowed the experiment of elections for state governors in October, it was not surprising that the PSD in Minas should nominate Israel Pinheiro of NOVACAP (after Sebastião Pais de Almeida had been vetoed as a candidate) and that in Guanabara a PTB–PSD alliance, which was prohibited from putting up Marshal Lott and another more ardent PTB figure, ended up with Negrão de Lima, Kubitschek's ex-Minister and a distant relation of Castello Branco. In the event, Pinheiro won a huge victory and Negrão de Lima a creditable one over two UDN candidates who tried to distinguish themselves from federal policy; the PSD picked up a majority of state governorships.

But Kubitschek's return, though perhaps to the gain of his reputation long-term, immediately resulted in his ignominious withdrawal and a toughening of the extraconstitutional aspects of the Castello Branco regime. However much it was said on

Kubitschek's behalf that his trip home, after the voting but before the results were declared, was not a challenge to the regime,
it had a strong aura of a democratic hero challenging an unpopular dictatorship. But the spirit of the army leadership was
quite different from November 1955 and Kubitschek's challenge,
though less noxious than one from Goulart or Brizola would
have been, had to be stamped on just as firmly.

On December 30, 1965, Sebastião Pais de Almeida announced
in Rio that Kubitschek had now opened a commercial bureau
in New York and had definitely retired from politics. The next
day JK declared: "I consider that the political page of my life is
now turned." In Brazil the PSD governors had been installed on
sufferance, the old parties had been wiped out, and the next
gubernatorial and presidential elections would be indirect. But
veteran politicians don't find retirement easy. In the United
States Kubitschek spoke extensively at universities on the problems of Latin America. He visited Portugal, where, in partnership with Niemeyer who had done the designs, he was responsible for a big seaside hotel development.

The accession to the Presidency of Marshal Costa e Silva in
early 1967 after the retirement of Castello Branco at first raised
the prospect of a return to more open politics. Though a strong
military figure who had been Castello's War Minister, the new
President had links with PSD politicians and spoke of "hu-
manizing" the revolution. In May Kubitschek was allowed back
to Rio after accepting undisclosed restrictions. He at once threw
himself into a "wide front," campaigning for a return to direct
presidential elections and a return to recognizable democracy.
Although all politicians who had lost their mandates were invited to join the "wide front," it was basically an alliance between Kubitschek and his old enemy Carlos Lacerda, sealed in
Portugal, and limited in its objectives. Lacerda was the public
spokesman owing to his greater freedom of maneuver, while
Kubitschek worked behind the scenes.

In late July the ex-President told the author that it was too

soon for him to become an elder statesman. But shortly thereafter, when the Costa e Silva regime started to put pressure on
the "wide front," Kubitschek found it politic to leave Brazil temporarily. In mid-1968, as a by-product of student riots in Rio
and elsewhere, the "wide front" was officially outlawed, and the
regime gave itself more powers, curbing the press in the process,
toward the end of the year.

Friends, family, and style

Kubitschek's style, particularly as President, was that of a Latin
American Kennedy. Brimming with vitality and an extrovert,
he was good-looking too, though he was vain enough to wish
to improve his appearance with plastic surgery on his face. He
dashed around the country, flying 115,000 miles in twelve months
in a specially bought Viscount. His day as President would start
at 7 a.m. with an English lesson and go on with meetings and
conferences far into the night. Yet he still liked to go out to
dinner parties or to his daughters' dances. He was a restless
man, not much given to abstract thought. He had his amours,
like other Brazilian males, but the President's family presented
a respectable and even admirable front to the nation. His wife,
Sara Lemos, who might have looked forward to a life as an
ordinary doctor's wife in Minas Gerais, schooled herself to be a
President's hostess and made sure that her two daughters gained
the social and intellectual benefits of their station. Only one
daughter, Marcia, a dull girl who suffered from back trouble,
was in fact their own. But the adopted Maristela, a live wire
happily integrated in the family, was very much after her father's
heart.

Kubitschek was not a charismatic leader like Quadros, but he
was a very good speaker and he was *"simpatico."* In the construction of the new capital his charm coaxed prodigious ex-
ertions out of the building crews and the organizers. In the
period of exile and military rule after the 1964 revolution his

name brought a moistening around the eyes to many fellow countrymen. Though his own background was humble, he acted in a stylish way, and even when just back from exile in 1967 his household operated appropriately for a former head of state. Kubitschek's election was the signal for a mass descent of *mineiros* on Rio de Janeiro which caused some amusement at the time. The standard of these *mineiro* cadres was on the whole high. An example of how a *mineiro* could join the Kubitschek retinue was provided by Oswaldo Penido, the President's successful press secretary, who had first met him in 1934 when Penido was the district attorney for Diamantina and Kubitschek was just making a name for himself in the Valadares state government. Though Penido was never actually employed by Kubitschek before 1955, his abilities would have been well known to the latter, and he was rewarded for his presidential service by getting the official property registration business for a fashionable part of Rio.

The administration provided facilities for both the national and international press in a manner which, though it would be normal in Europe or the United States, was new to Brazil. Although the Brazilian press was much too partisan for such measures to make a great difference, the press relations effort was one element in the President's campaign to establish himself and his goals.

Other able personalities of the Kubitschek era were Sebastião Pais de Almeida, variously governor of the Bank of Brazil and Minister of Finance, who was a wealthy glass manufacturer, and Francisco Negrão de Lima, a former Prefeito of the city of Rio de Janeiro. Negrão de Lima had not been a particularly good administrator of Rio, but his canniness and closeness to Kubitschek were important when he was Ambassador in Lisbon and when he was Foreign Minister charged with making something of Operation Pan America. Another figure, of legendary astuteness, responsible for keeping Kubitschek's fissiparous congressional support together, was the PSD leader Amaral Peixoto. Married to one of Vargas's daughters, he represented that carry-over of Vargas apparatchiks that UDN opponents held against Kubitschek.

The pragmatic democrat

In Brazilian history Kubitschek has several lasting claims to be remembered. More than Vargas or any previous President, he dramatized Brazil's need for development and the fact that, by the intelligent application of her own resources, she could achieve it. The economic advance visible to all in five years created a new standard of performance for politicians which was reflected in the claims and promises in subsequent elections and debates even at local level. His approach to development, though it may be criticized for paying too little attention to the needs of social justice or the possibilities of a frontal attack on agrarian problems, was characterized by winning a commitment from the whole community to demand and try to achieve higher living standards. Like many Catholic contemporaries, he had been affected by the social encyclicals of various popes. For Brazil there was no future in offering fair shares in poverty, and the obvious way to overcome stumbling blocks was to implant more advanced high-wage industries. This was done, but not always scientifically. In common with other Latin American countries, Brazil's car industry, for example, emerged with too many factories producing at too high a unit cost.

To a certain extent the industrialization boom eroded the old agrarian structure, by swelling the migration to the cities and forcing up demand for food and natural products; but immediately it highlighted the contrast between urban and rural living standards which led to so much rural unrest up to 1964. Kubitschek's setting up of SUDENE, whose work was closely followed by the UN and aid-giving countries, showed an appreciation of the problems of regional imbalance that was of interest elsewhere in Latin America. But the reliance on friendships and connections for effecting a technological transformation, and the disinterest in rationalizing the existing overstaffed administration—though comprehensible in the Brazil of his time —made him a more anachronistic figure than Frei of Chile, for example. (The United States, too, has managed to preserve a traditional patronage system in an advanced industrial society, and there is some similarity between JK's *mineiros* and JFK's "Mafia.")

His development policy, otherwise of interest only to Brazil, became a matter of hemispheric and world concern as a result of Brasília and OPA. Brasília was an advertisement for Latin America as a whole in a world often liable to forget her, and the internal colonization policy—an adaptation of the Iberian Conquest to modern requirements—was to be adopted by nearly every Latin American country. (The "forest road" of President Belaúnde Terry of Peru, intended as a link for all the Andean countries through their deserted trans-Andean forests, was one seminal proposal.)

OPA alone and Brazil's advocacy were not, as has been seen, enough to bring to birth the Alliance for Progress. For that the growing anti-Yanqui sourness of the Cuban Revolution was responsible. Vastly inferior to Marshall Plan aid in amount and restricted by prior U.S. commitments to free enterprise in the area, the Alliance was not all that Kubitschek had hoped of OPA. Yet coming from a nationalist tradition in Brazilian politics and possessed of an American immigrant's dream of the untapped potential of his continent, he was one of the first Latin Americans to grapple responsibly with the traumatic dilemma of underdevelopment: that to raise living standards required a transfer of capital and skills from outside, and particularly North America, which ran the risk of reinforcing patterns of economic dependence. His solution within Brazil was to obtain a high degree of government control over the aims and methods of foreign investment, to attract the support of as many advanced industrial countries as possible, and to arrange, wherever possible, a majority interest for local capital in mixed companies. For Latin America as a whole he wanted OPA to be genuinely multilateral. But the course of foreign relations showed once again the difficulty for any Latin American country, however well disposed to the United States, in maintaining consistently friendly terms with the giant.

In the continuing Latin American dialogue about the place of democratic politics, the armed forces, or revolutionary movements in national life, he stood four-square as a democrat. Brazilian elites had always been believers in paternalist government—the military were profoundly affected by the positivist doctrine of an enlightened dictatorship—and it would hardly be too much to say that Kubitschek's home-grown faith in democracy was one of the most powerful factors behind the mass belief in representative government which survived the successive setbacks of Quadros, Goulart, and a military coup. But, too busy improvising support, he did nothing to cure the defects of existing Brazilian democracy or to strengthen or democratize the shaky party system with which he worked. His kid-glove treatment of the military allowed them to continue thinking they had special privileges in the national arena, and he could never escape the fact that the votes that elected him in 1955 had had to be ratified by a military intervention.

As a democrat Kubitschek could not be a revolutionary; indeed, during his term of office, and arguably in 1964, there was neither a genuine revolutionary situation in Brazil nor anything but microscopic revolutionary movements. But he was a reformist by outlook operating in political surroundings in which some social and economic change was thought necessary. He tried to take the tension out of such change in accordance with Brazilian tradition and Catholic social policy (Minas was known for its Catholicism), but the expectations and discrepancies aroused by the inflationary boom worked in the opposite direction. By capturing Brazil for democracy from 1956 to 1961 in a glamorous way, he set a critical example for other Latin American countries, such as Argentina, which was trying to free itself of the heritage of Peronism via interim military governments, and Venezuela, which was throwing off the dictatorship of

Pérez Jiménez. In Latin America he was an example of that incoherent force, center opinion: he was a pragmatic democrat, sometimes reformist, sometimes conservative, whose overriding aim was to overcome the poverty and narrow horizons of life in a partially developed country.

Carlos Lacerda

The Palácio Guanabara, March 31, 1964

The Palácio Guanabara, the Governor's official residence in the Brazilian state of Guanabara—better known as the city of Rio de Janeiro—is not the best headquarters for street-fighting in a civil war. A sugar-icing edifice dating from the Brazilian Empire, overlooked by hills on two sides, it is a prominent target and would probably tumble from the shock of a near-miss shell. Yet for a period of over seventy-two hours in 1964, as the military revolt that toppled the Goulart government cranked into action, the *carioca* citizens heard and saw by radio and television their Governor, leather-jacketed and armed to the teeth, apparently leading the most desperate resistance to the forces of Goulart from the vulnerable old palace.

Carlos Lacerda was in his element—histrionic, volatile, the schoolboy dramatics carried to extremes. At the beginning of the crisis caused by the sailors' mutiny he had called on the armed forces to re-establish control; then he denied there was any national crisis; then he said Brazil was in the first stage of the Marxists' revolutionary war. Five hundred state military policemen were guarding the Palácio throughout, and volunteers kept arriving at the nearby Anne Frank School, carrying old pistols and weapons, and were handed handerchiefs of blue and white, the state colors.[1]

The Governor and his family had got themselves into a suitably heroic mood by watching the film *PT-109* (about John F. Kennedy's naval experiences in the war against Japan) on the night

---

[1] The following account of Lacerda's behavior during the revolution is partly based on the graphic daily reports in the *Jornal do Brasil* of Rio de Janeiro.

of March 30. On March 31, when the military revolt was breaking out all over the country, there was a rumor that four armored cars from the Ministry of War were coming to take the Palácio. They weren't. They were off to protect the President at his official residence, scarcely a mile away. Carlos had a loudspeaker network rigged up around the Palácio Guanabara, having a strong belief in the effect that his amplified voice might have on enemy troops.

The atmosphere among the group surrounding him was a tense mixture of fear and bravado. Periodically Carlos would speak to other rebel Governors, like Magalhães Pinto of Minas on the phone, and journalists from as far away as Miami—where an enterprising Chicago *Tribune* man with an enormous disregard for the normal limitations of the Rio phone system was operating—called up to keep in touch with developments. The Lacerdistas wondered hopefully whether the neighboring population would offer a house-to-house defense, as in Naples during the war, if it came to the crunch. One humorist, a Major Osorio, speculated on the effect that one helicopter, carrying grenades that would cause instant diarrhea among advancing troops, might have on the enemy. For much of the time Carlos was on the air. In the period leading up to the revolution Abrão Medina, one of Brazil's richest men, had promised him an emergency radio network. During the crisis he broadcast largely by telephone to Minas Gerais for transmission by the insurrectionary "Liberty Network," which was calling for Goulart's overthrow.

It was on April 1, while he was broadcasting by phone, that the Governor's revolution had its apotheosis. Outposts in the Rua Farani thought they saw some pro-Goulart marines on the hill above them. Everyone in the Palácio fell to the floor. Carlos called for the microphone linked to the loudspeakers in the street and, while he told his spellbound audience on the phone that the palace was being attacked by a "band of desperadoes," he was simultaneously calling on the marines to abandon their arms over the loudspeakers. "I have never seen him like this. Today he is terrifying," remarked an associate. The expected attack never came, thus originating a favorite *carioca* joke of the revolution: "Why did the marines never march up the Rua Payssandu to attack the Palácio Guanabara? Because it's a one-way street."

The rest was bathos and TV recordings. When he was told that the tanks which had been guarding Goulart's residence were now clattering around to give him protection, he exclaimed in tears: "Thanks be to God. . . . Thank you, my God." It was, he added, the greatest emotion he had experienced in his life.

Home background

A life stuffed with emotions began for Carlos Lacerda in 1914 in Rio de Janeiro. He was the third child of Mauricio de Lacerda, a professional politician with a good command of rhetoric who, after serving as a cabinet aide to the then President, Hermes de Fonseca, was now engaged in furious opposition to him. Mauricio's father had been a Minister, and the family had been in comfortable bourgeois circumstances for generations. There was a family farm at Vassouras in the state of Rio de Janeiro. Mauricio, an erratic man with whom Carlos was to have lengthy quarrels, dabbled in Utopian Socialism and was imprisoned for over two years without trial by the oligarchic government of Bernardes in the twenties. His wife and children were pressed for money.

Carlos, then, was brought up on rebellion and the fleeting fortunes of politics. His heroes, he has written, were Luís Carlos Prestes and the other active rebels against the Old Republic. He ran away from school. In 1930, after the revolution had swept away the Old Republic, Vargas sent Mauricio as his special representative to attend the independence centenary of Uruguay, and Carlos traveled in the party. He subsequently studied law at the National University in Rio. As a second-year student he and another successfully defended a prostitute on a charge of murdering her baby by asphyxiation. Society had condemned Castorina and six thousand other registered prostitutes in the Zona de

Mangue to their trade, he argued. The prosecution had used only one of over twenty available medical tests to prove the manner of the baby's death.

Communism and journalism

At the age of sixteen Carlos worked for a local paper in Vassouras. In the same year he participated in the revolution which brought Vargas to power by distributing posters urging troops not to bear arms against the rebels and by assisting in the arrest of one of the Senators of the *ancien régime*. His lifelong addiction to journalism and politics was therefore established in his teens. But the ordinary process of earning a living was overcast after he left the university by the complications that arose from his associations with the Brazilian Communist Party. This period in his career was crucial to the formation of his own outlook—particularly his attitude toward Vargas's personal rule and its abettors—and for the lasting suspicion toward him that was a consequence in both the left and the right wings of Brazilian politics.

The various parties have kept the record misty. Carlos himself has denied that he was ever a member of the Communist Party or its youth movement. Other people thought differently, and Lacerda has admitted that it was only by accident of the party's adopting popular-front tactics and submerging its own youth movement that he did not belong to that. In Brazil the Communist Party was as attractive as anywhere else in the thirties, and Carlos met members both at home and in the university. Luís Carlos Prestes, the rebel soldier of the twenties, had joined the party, and for those who wanted a tangible ideology to give point to the vague reformism of the 1930 revolution, it had the right blend of idealism and intellectual rigor.

Carlos Lacerda, after being imprisoned once or twice as a result of participating in Communist demonstrations, was asked as a student speaker to propose the name of Prestes as honorary president of the new National Liberation Alliance in 1935. This popular-front movement—calling for the cancellation of "imperialist debts," the nationalization of foreign firms, and the expropriation of *latifundia* (large estates)—had made considerable progress by early 1935, as had the Integralistas, the Brazilian Fascist movement.

In July 1935 Vargas, who played on the growth of the radical movements to justify his own claim to personal power, suppressed the National Liberation Alliance. In November the Communist Party, which wrongly thought that the revolutionary situation was ripe, organized a barracks revolt among northern garrisons and also in Rio de Janeiro. The revolts were not properly synchronized and resulted in widespread and vicious repression under Vargas's emergency powers. On the morning of November 27, when the Rio uprising took place and Lacerda by chance was due to begin his military service, he has written that the radio announced his capture. He then went into hiding for several months, changing his location when he heard that the police had seen through his disguise at carnival time, and eventually crossing Guanabara Bay into the state of Rio in a coffee smuggler's boat with a false bottom.

Lacerda's position for the next couple of years—during which Vargas was maneuvering to create the conditions for his own coup of November 1937—is obscure, but it is probable that he was lying low. With his Communist connections he was vulnerable, and the actual pretext for the November coup was the forged "Cohen Plan," which was supposed to be a plan for a Communist revolution. But with Vargas's success, and the subsequent repression of the Fascist Integralistas, it was possible for him to emerge in public again.

By 1938 a sufficient change had come in Lacerda's circumstances for him to have a job on the *Observador Economico e Financeiro*, one of the financial journals permitted by the censorship of Vargas's Estado Novo (New State). Among his tasks in this position was to interview the Minister of Education as part of a series of reports paid for by the regime on the first year's achievements of the New State. He was also asked to write a history of Brazilian Communism.

By his own account,[2] he mentioned this to his friends in the party and their view was that it would be a good chance to tranquilize the Vargistas. Hence he wrote an article suggesting that the Communist Party in Brazil was finished. But he went too far in the eyes of the party leadership, which felt that on the strength of his analysis no bourgeois opposition group would think it worth-while to cooperate with them. So they denounced him as an *agent provocateur* and a betrayer in the service of Nazism, American imperialism, and Trotskyism. The police held him for a fortnight on a Communist tip-off and accused him of Trotskyism, and none of his Communist friends would speak to him again. Lacerda has denied that his departure from the ranks of fellow travelers was accompanied by any betrayal of Communists to the Vargas police; but there remains a widespread belief to the contrary which may not have done him any harm later, when he came to trade on his anti-Communism.

This early period in his career taught him a lot. In that mixture of idealists and crude practitioners of power politics—the latter liquidated a mistress of the party's secretary general on mere suspicion that she had leaked information to the police—he acquired a grasp of politics, propaganda, and ideology which was to set him apart from the normal, nonideological run of Brazilian politicians. He also had personal experience of the brutality and corruption of a police state that was to fuel his lasting opposition to Vargas.

His career as a journalist prospered, and by 1942 he was running the Agência Meridional, the news agency attached to Diários Associados, the large Brazilian press chain owned by Assis Chateaubriand. With Brazil gradually veering from a pro-Fascist neutrality to a pro-Allied one, yet still subject to censorship, there were pitfalls for a journalist. When the Agência Meridional

[2] Given in Carlos Lacerda: *Rosas e Pedras do meu Caminho*, serialized in *Manchete* (Rio de Janeiro; 1967).

phoned Radio Tupi with the news that a Brazilian ship had been torpedoed by a German submarine, the unfortunate broadcaster who announced it was suspended by the censorship department. When a Royal Navy ship removed German armaments duly purchased by Brazil from a ship on the high seas, the War Minister briefed journalists on the need for editorials on offended national pride and the possibility of war with Britain. At last, when an expeditionary force was being prepared to fight beside the Allies in Italy, Lacerda tried to join as a soldier. But he failed, and Assis Chateaubriand would not let him go as war correspondent. So instead he had to be satisfied with writing stories about the convoys now zig-zagging up the Brazilian coast, and the huge U.S. air bases in the Northeast.

From his vantage point as a journalist Lacerda could see that the days of the Estado Novo were numbered, and he worked actively for its replacement by a democracy. At the first Brazilian Congress of Writers, held in São Paulo in January 1945, he was on the commission which drafted a declaration calling for democratic legality, liberty of thought and religion, security from violence, and direct secret elections by universal suffrage. These were the principles, the writers concluded, for which the forces of Brazil and the United Nations were fighting.

The following month Lacerda interviewed José Americo, the pro-government candidate for the 1937 presidential election which never took place because of Vargas's coup, and he too called for an elective democracy. It was this influential interview, first published in the *Correio da Manhã* and widely reprinted, which marked the overthrow of the censorship and sped the dismantling of the dictatorship.

With the end of the war and the dictatorship Lacerda, an established journalist, entered the mainstream of his career as an excitable, verbally violent figure forever on the attack against the legacy of Vargas. His contribution to the 1945 election was a vitriolic book about the Communist candidate: "Fiuza the Rat." For Vargas's heirs, conscious of the social security and labor legislation achieved after 1937, this made him an antiworking-class conservative. In his own eyes and in those of his friends, the founders of the UDN party, the trade-union system had been created with built-in corruption and a democratic system showed every sign of being manipulated against themselves, the true democrats. From their point of view the election of Marshal Dutra, the Vargas regime's War Minister, as President in 1945 was a setback; the election of the new, "democratized" Vargas in 1950 was an unmitigated disaster. Lacerda, who had been elected a city councillor for Rio de Janeiro in January 1947, played a prominent role in the opposition to the Dutra government both in the UDN and the press. In the old-established *carioca* paper, *Correio da Manhã*, he ran a controversial column called the Tribune of the Press (Tribuna da Imprensa).

While he was working for the *Correio*, he visited Palestine, then in the last throes of the British Mandate, and argued that Brazil, with its large Arab population and its influential Jewish one, ought to stay neutral on the Zionist issue. He strongly attacked the Brazilian delegation at the United Nations, which, largely on its own initiative, voted in favor of a state of Israel. In spite of some pressure Paulo Bittencourt, the *Correio's* proprietor, gave space to his fiery columnist until the time that Lacerda attacked the Dutra government for granting a monopoly of oil refining in Brazil to two private groups. One of them was run by a childhood friend of Bittencourt's. Lacerda's article did not appear, and he resigned.

Shortly thereafter he was able to set up his own morning paper with the title of his old column, *Tribuna da Imprensa*. This was a mixture of muckraking, scandal-stirring journalism and radical anti-Communism, leavened by the unpredictable feuds of its boss.

Vargas's suicide

After Vargas's return to power in January 1951—wearier, less adroit, and with a very mixed company hanging on his coattails —the tone of *Tribuna da Imprensa* became even more aggressive.

After calling for a military coup to prevent him from being elected, Lacerda called for a coup to oust him. With the army uncertain about the President and economic conditions difficult, Vargas's associates found the opposition of a majority of the press embarrassing. A consortium backed by the Bank of Brazil enabled Samuel Wainer, a brilliant popular journalist who, like Lacerda, had at one time worked for Diários Associados, to set up a new, progovernment paper for Rio, *Ultima Hora.*

The strong financial backing of the new paper—compared with the wobbly position of *Tribuna da Imprensa* and other existing papers—its preferential paper supply, and its politics all combined to bring Lacerda to boiling point. An inaccurate rumor that the Bank of Brazil was having to intervene in the management of *Ultima Hora* as a big shareholder concerned about its finances sparked off Lacerda's bitterest and most far-reaching vendetta. His campaign against *Ultima Hora* was at its height from May to August 1953. Not only was government meddling in the press wrong but, he wrote excitedly, seventy per cent of the federal investment in Brazil in one year had been diverted to the Wainer group. UDN friends set up a parliamentary commission of inquiry, inter-American press organizations expressed concern, and worried press and radio magnates like Roberto Marinho and Assis Chateaubriand gave him air time.

Lacerda's trump card was the claim that the documents attesting to Wainer's birthplace had been falsified. He was not a Brazilian citizen by birth, as was required by the constitution for anyone controlling communications media, but had been born in Bessarabia. There is reason to believe that this allegation was true, and the *Tribuna's* campaign came within an ace of closing *Ultima Hora,* which had meantime been defending itself by ascribing the criticism to foreign influences and ridiculing the *Tribuna's* smaller circulation. In August 1953 the Wainer group's right to a Rio radio station was canceled by the government.

In spite of threats against him and a robbery at his apartment, Lacerda continued, in his paper and on the radio, his attacks on corruption in the government. He gave voice to the fears, particularly of middle-class Brazilians, that Vargas might try a "Peronist" solution. Attacks centered on João Goulart, the Minister of Labor, whose manipulation of the labor organizations was thought to be sinister and whose doubling of the minimum wage would eat into the salary differential distinguishing army officers from manual workers. After a memorandum of protest from eighty-two colonels Vargas dismissed Goulart in February 1954. But both the political and economic situation continued unsettled and the death of a Rio journalist, beaten up by the police, added to the disquiet. Lacerda decided to run for Congress in Rio in the elections scheduled for October. Some young service officers, sympathetic to him, resolved to accompany him on his way home at night from his radio broadcasts.

On the night of August 4 he was brought home by car from a conference by a young air force major, Rubem Vaz. Also in the car with him was his son Sergio, aged fifteen. A little after midnight, as they were saying good night outside Lacerda's home in Rua Toneleros, Copacabana, shots were fired, killing Vaz and wounding Lacerda in the foot. The murderers got away unscathed, and the shock in public life was immense. Vargas admitted that he stood in a sea of mud. The day after the attack, five hundred people demonstrated outside the Catete palace, Vargas's residence, calling for punishment of the assassins. In a signed article in the *Tribuna* Lacerda wrote: "I accuse only one man as responsible for this crime. He is the protector of thieves whose impunity gives them the audacity for acts like that of today. The man is named Getúlio Vargas."

The Inter-American Press Association, of which Lacerda had been secretary from 1951 to 1953, condemned the attack as "reprehensible," and on August 6, two thousand officers of all services met in the Aero Club to discuss how to obtain justice. Two days later the Rio police chief resigned, and the following day the Presidential Guard, an unpleasant assortment of strong-arm men whose leader was being accused of complicity in the murder, was disbanded. On the 10th, Lacerda was allowed to scrutinize forty-seven Presidential Guards at Police Headquarters, and the following day thousands marched on the Chamber of Deputies to demand Vargas's resignation.

For a few days it looked as though Vargas, now seventy-one, might weather the crisis. But by the 17th, army and air force men had picked up Climerio Eurides de Oliveira, the prime suspect, and Lutero, the President's son, felt obliged to report to the armed forces to refute suggestions that he too was implicated. Two former Presidents asked Vargas to resign, and on the 24th, after receiving an ultimatum from the military commanders, he committed suicide. A suicide note accusing foreign influences, whose authenticity has been doubted, was broadcast afterwards and combined with the President's tragedy to produce an astonishing turn of sentiment. A crowd attacked the *Tribuna's* offices, Lacerda was taken to an air force base for his own protection, and he wrote an article in the *Tribuna* saying that it was the people around Vargas rather than he himself who was to blame.

In an interesting cable to the London *Observer* Lacerda compared the corruption around Vargas with King Farouk's court, and described him as a *caudillo* tempered by an acute sense of opportunism and a victim of "the illusion that Brazil could continue to progress under a form of social demagogy in which the unions and an advanced social legislation could serve the kind of paternalism typical of the South American *caudillo.*" [3]

The deaths of Vaz and Vargas gave rise to several legends which it would take a decade and a genuine military revolution to modify. The first was that Lacerda was a hero in the middle-class struggle against corruption, as typified in the workings of Vargista labor legislation. The second was that he had special influence within the armed forces. These two were closely interwoven. The death of the innocent Vaz and the involvement of the young Sergio Lacerda endorsed the real target with a kind of crusader's purity that his erratic and extravagant behavior would not quickly minimize. The third legend, very popular among the

[3] *Observer,* London, August 29, 1954.

working-class PTB stalwarts who had adored Vargas, was that Carlos was somehow their idol's murderer. The drama surrounding his suicide made a scapegoat necessary, and Lacerda, with his venomous press and radio attacks, was the obvious candidate.

For the country at large these traumatic days originated the more generalized legend that Lacerda was a destroyer of Presidents. His militant opposition to Vargas's successors went a long way to substantiating this reputation, but it was solidly based on the political destruction of the man who had been Brazil's authoritarian master for fifteen years and her democratic President for four. That this was a considerable political achievement, and that Lacerda had played a critical part in it, could not be denied.

The attack on Kubitschek

The interim government of Vice-President João Café Filho, though more conservative and open to UDN influence than Vargas's, did not represent a clear-cut victory for the Lacerdista wing. Some UDN spirits wished for a postponement of the October congressional elections and, although Lacerda succeeded in getting elected as a deputy for Rio, the UDN lost some ground. But already eyes were turning to the following year's presidential election which, as the PSD–PTB coalition congealed around the candidacies of Kubitschek and Goulart, was watched by the UDN with growing pessimism. It became increasingly clear that however much President Café was personally opposed to a resurrection of the Vargista spirit, neither he, nor—even less so—his strongly "constitutional" Minister of War, General Lott, was prepared to quash or rig the elections.

Lacerda's disillusion with Café could be observed in his articles. Whereas in September 1954 Café had "an eminently political spirit and a firm democratic conviction," by February 1955 his policy was "doubtful and mysterious, above all inconvenient," and by July Café had a "history of treason . . . to moral imperatives. . . . The Presidency for this man is not a career, it's a lunch." Lacerda's program to pre-empt the election of Kubitschek (whom he charmingly described as the "catalyst of national treachery") harked back to his schemes in 1950 for averting the return of Vargas: there should be an emergency government that would so effectively purge Brazilian democracy that it would be impossible for Vargistas to regain power.

However, the limitations of Lacerda's influence in both the armed forces and the government became more obvious as the army memorandum for a "candidate of national unity" and the subsequent choice of Távora, the chief of Café's military household, to be the UDN and Administration candidate, made it clear that elections would take place. *Tribuna da Imprensa* did its best in the great UDN press game of prominently reporting hints from friendly military figures that the elections would not be allowed to occur. Carlos also conducted vigorous propaganda against the rising star of Jânio Quadros, the new São Paulo Governor ("he has the morals of a Communist"), who played a key role in the maneuvers leading up to the selection of Távora. By September Lacerda was giving Távora his reluctant support.

Kubitschek's narrow victory in the October elections and the fluke by which the anti-Kubitschek president of the Chamber of Deputies, Carlos Luz, temporarily succeeded Café, who had had a heart attack, encouraged Lacerda in his pressure for a coup.[4] The *Tribuna* harped on about Communist support for Kubitschek and Goulart in the elections and published a letter from a Peronist Congressman in Argentina (which many years later Lacerda claimed he still thought was authentic) that suggested that Goulart had been buying arms from Perón two years before to equip a workers' militia. While the UDN was split on the merits of a coup, Lacerda and his friends among the junior officers plotted almost openly.

On November 9, the day of confrontation between Acting Pres-

[4] The *Tamandaré* affair is also referred to on pp. 186–7, in the chapter on Juscelino Kubitschek.

ident Luz and War Minister Lott, who wanted to discipline a junior officer who had publicly called for a coup, the *Tribuna* said of Kubitschek and Goulart: "These men cannot take office, they should not take office, they will not take office." But Lott, for whom the first priority of preservation of military discipline had become inseparable from a guarantee of the election results, even by unconstitutional means, moved faster. Having decided to act after his own dismissal, he carried out a successful "prolegality" coup on the morning of November 11, which was essentially based on the backing of the army command in Rio only.

In rainy weather Carlos Luz, Lacerda, Admiral Pena Boto (head of the Brazilian Anti-Communist Crusade), and assorted government ministers and sympathizers sailed in the cruiser *Tamandaré* from Rio to Santos. The idea was not as harebrained as it might seem, as the "legal" Acting President (then being deposed by a Congress voting under Lott's supervision) and Lacerda hoped for support from Governor Quadros at Santos. The Rio forts fired at the *Tamandaré*, which, so its crew claimed, withheld its own fire in order not to injure the civilian population. This stirring voyage, compounded with lengthy debates on board, satisfied Lacerda's passion for action. But the vital aid from Quadros never came, and although UDN speakers might afterwards rant about Lott's coup and claim that nothing illegal was coming from their side, there could be little doubt that the general acceptance of the "prolegality" coup was a direct consequence of Lacerda's boomerang propaganda.

After some futile steaming about, the *Tamandaré* returned to Rio, and Lacerda took refuge in the Cuban Embassy. From Havana he went straight to the United States and spent roughly a year in exile. Just how necessary this was, given that many in the *Tamandaré* affair were left unpunished, is debatable. For most of his stay he lived in Connecticut, though he visited Portugal too. He maintained himself by translating and other work and wrote a regular column in the *Tribuna* which appeared under the pseudonym "John of the Woods."

Election as Governor

Although an issue of *Tribuna da Imprensa* had been seized by the police only two months earlier, Carlos felt it safe to return to Rio in October 1956, and characteristically announced that Brazil was now in the hands of Communists in the army and that Kubitschek was a "clown" forced to go begging for money in Washington. The optimistic tone of the Kubitschek years, buttressed by Lott's firm stewardship of the armed forces, was unpropitious for Lacerda's brand of extremism. The Lantern Club, the Lacerdista supporters' club which dated from the row with *Ultima Hora*, was closed down by the government. All the same Carlos did his best to stir things up, helping to organize resistance to a press law proposed by the government and creating a furor in Congress by alleging that Vice-President Goulart had fraudulently sold timber to Perón's Argentina, thereby incurring the accusation himself that he had broken the Brazilian diplomatic code. Lacerda beat the anticorruption drum and was an outspoken critic of Kubitschek's obsession with a new capital. "Brasília is the most expensive monument to folly and incompetence erected to this day," he stated. Such a line did not go amiss in Rio, where he did well in elections for the Chamber of Deputies in October 1958. In spite of past differences he played a considerable part in uniting the UDN behind Jânio Quadros as its best avenue to power in 1960.

In the same year the change of capital ironically gave Carlos his best chance to date: the transfer created a new state of Guanabara for the former federal capital, and Carlos Lacerda became the UDN candidate for Governor. With the leftist-nationalist and working-class vote split between two other candidates, Lacerda, with 357,153 votes and 35.7 per cent of the total, won the election. His narrow success in a traditionally radical city was ironic, too, in that the UDN had frequently claimed in its past defeats that only an absolute majority would suffice for victory.

Relations with Quadros

Carlos Lacerda as Governor of Guanabara and Jânio Quadros as President of Brazil took office simultaneously. Yet whereas Lacerda was to serve his term through three Presidencies, Quadros only lasted eight months. The President's eccentricity, indecision, and alcoholism all told against him. It rapidly became clear that he did not regard himself as much beholden to his UDN backers, though the UDN did well in cabinet offices. He had risen as a charismatic outsider in the nonpartisan climate of São Paulo, and he did not expect professional politicians to come between him and his mass audience.

Some of the things he did the UDN could support: his drastic anti-inflation policy, which won him friends in the international counsels of financial orthodoxy, and his attack on government bureaucracy responded to a case the party had been pleading for fifteen years. Even his ludicrous moral exhortation, shown in petty edicts against perfume bombs at carnival time and the wearing of bikinis on the Rio beaches, was a distorted echo of UDN charges of moral corruption.

But on other counts it was noticeable that Quadros was following his own path. He had visited Castro's Cuba before his election and immediately afterward he had gone on a world tour. While the Kennedy government after the Bay of Pigs was trying to organize all friendly Latin American governments to ostracize Cuba, Quadros tried to retain normal relations, and his visits in the Third World had impressed him with the possibility of roads that were neither capitalist nor Communist. As part of a more dynamic Brazilian foreign policy in the Third World he tried to reawaken an awareness of Brazil's African connections. All this diplomatic activity, combined with signs that Quadros was about to adopt a developmental economic policy like Kubitschek's, created growing suspicion in the UDN.

Quadros's sudden renunciation of office on August 25 followed a blistering attack by Lacerda on radio the night before. Lacerda, in his role as the most rigorous anti-Communist in Brazilian politics, had begun to make propaganda against the drift of foreign policy and was brought to high anger by the President's decoration of Che Guevara with a Brazilian order. At meetings in Brasília with Quadros and his aides, Lacerda claimed, the Justice Minister, Oscar Pedroso D'Horta, had asked him to join a plot to enable Quadros to institute an emergency regime like the one he had urged in 1954 and earlier. This would have allowed Quadros to rule by decree without congressional sanction. On the other side the Justice Minister suggested that Lacerda had come to Brasília to get government money to help the *Tribuna*.

Whatever the truth of the matter, there seems strong evidence that a plan of the sort denounced by Lacerda was being mooted in Brasília; for in spite of Quadros's large popular majority he was utterly unskillful at managing a Congress where the majority theoretically opposed him. Lacerda as savior of constitutional democracy was a posture that he had not adopted since the heady days of the overthrow of the Estado Novo, and he was to find it increasingly attractive. But his political instinct was sound. Quadros, by means of his great popularity from left to right of the political spectrum, which tended to supersede the old feuds about Vargas, was perhaps the first person since Vargas in 1937 to be in a position to make a continuist coup[5] if he wanted to.

Had Quadros wished, he could have ignored or fought back Lacerda's attack. But on August 25, without mobilizing any public or Congressional support, he offered Congress his resignation. It was quickly accepted. Quadros's motives remain obscure, although lack of party backing in Brasília had made him frustrated. Maybe he thought Congress and the conservative public were so terrified of his constitutional successor, Vice-President Goulart, then by chance on a visit to Communist China, that they would give him extra powers to remain. He had used the resignation ploy successfully when he had wanted greater freedom as a

[5] "Continuismo," the attempt to extend a President's term beyond his legal mandate, had been successfully achieved by Vargas in 1937, by coup d'état, and was a source of recurring fear in Brazilian politics.

presidential candidate. But his offer merely caused bewilderment in the public, and it was unhesitatingly seized by the hardbitten hostile Congressmen. The UDN Congressmen no longer had particular cause to defend him, and for the PTB and PSD Goulart would be a much better alternative. Military support for Quadros had disintegrated to a point where the War Minister refused to replace the army commander in Rio who had disobeyed the President's order to keep Governor Lacerda off the air. For the latter, of course, the sensational fall of Quadros merely enhanced his reputation as a destroyer of Presidents.

Relations with Goulart

Between Lacerda and the new President, Goulart, there was hostility from the start. Goulart, to both friends and enemies, was the embodiment of the Vargas tradition. But the very accession of Goulart, the result of the inability of the commanding officers to maintain a united veto and his own willingness to accept reduced powers, was a setback to Lacerda and a vindication of more moderate politicians who felt Goulart should have his chance. For the first year and a bit of the new Presidency, in spite of the unsatisfactory working of the imposed parliamentary system and the government's economic failures, Lacerda lost ground. He attacked Goulart as pro-Communist and as plotting a coup, but there was surprisingly little profit for him in the increasing radicalization of politics. As a Governor everything he did was news and he broadcast frequently, but he was no longer able to edit the *Tribuna*. His state government was harried by deliberate noncooperation from the federal authorities, and Rio was racked by strikes.

Guanabara seemed to be slipping out of his hands in 1962, when elections for Lieutenant Governor returned Eloi Dutra, a professional anti-Lacerdista of the left, and the city elected Leonel Brizola, Goulart's violently leftist cousin, as Congressman with a record majority. The UDN could only get twenty-five per cent of the vote. Always ambivalent on nationalist claims to expropriate utilities and economic resources, Lacerda found it convenient to propose the nationalization of the Rio phone services after Brizola had acted similarly in Rio Grande do Sul. Perhaps the nadir of Lacerda's electoral position came in January 1963, when only 21.7 per cent of the Rio electorate could be persuaded to vote against full presidential powers for Goulart in the plebiscite which abolished the parliamentary experiment.

Throughout 1963 Goulart was governing from expedient to expedient—now a gesture to the left, now something for the military, here an attempt at disinflation, there a large wage increase. Disillusion mounted, particularly among those Catholic middle classes which provided the natural basis for the UDN. The embattled Lacerda, managing to run an unexpectedly efficient state administration in conditions of administrative siege, became rather more attractive. His appeal spread beyond Guanabara. In the countryside, where large and small proprietors were getting frightened by a more active peasantry and calls for land reform from the left, he found a new audience.

When the federal government, seeking to head off expropriation of foreign utilities by the individual states, announced plans to purchase the Guanabara telephone system, Lacerda denounced the terms as excessively generous for "old iron." Signs of civilian and military demoralization were growing. While conservative Congressmen were making plans to impeach Goulart, a few hundred NCO's and enlisted men came near to seizing control of the government in Brasília in pursuit of radical claims that troops, like civilians, should have the right to vote. In late September Lacerda gave an interview to the Los Angeles *Times* in which he said that Goulart was an inept pro-Communist and that he was only in office because senior military officers lacked the courage to remove him.[6] The latter remark, though credible enough,

[6] Los Angeles *Times*, September 1963, quoted in Thomas E. Skidmore: *Politics in Brazil, 1930–1964* (Oxford University Press: New York; 1967).

could hardly have pleased the generals with active commands.

On October 4 Goulart, with the support of the military ministers, asked Congress for emergency powers, and about the same time there were somewhat half-hearted efforts to remove both Lacerda and Governor Arrais of Pernambuco—who was crystallizing support on the left for an anti-Goulart movement—by a *coup de main*. Lacerda was tipped off about the attempt, the federal troops supposed to arrest him arrived late, and he was given a propaganda field day. More important, the following month Goulart insisted on disciplinary measures against Colonel Boaventura, the airborne officer who had refused to take part in the attempted arrest. The revolt at Brasília—with its evidence of the potential effectiveness of military action and the dangers of enlisted men slipping out of the control of their officers—combined with the Boaventura incident to provoke much harder thought by anti-Goulart officers on the possibility of a coup. A hard core of civilian conservatives had been plotting for almost a year, even exchanging ideas on the sort of regime which should follow Goulart, and keeping in touch with the military. Lacerda could hardly be unaware of these movements of opinion.

But in the early months of 1964, as the atmosphere of crisis deepened and it seemed that Goulart was opting definitely for the anticonstitutional left and an extension of his own mandate, Lacerda found himself in a difficult position. As a result of his intransigent stand against the President he had high expectations of being chosen UDN candidate for the Presidency in the 1965 elections. His principal rival, Governor Magalhães Pinto, the UDN Governor of Minas Gerais, represented the party's liberal wing, which was being overtaken by events. Hence there was good reason for him to hope that Goulart would complete his term so that he might come to power either as a result of elections or by military action after a highly charged campaign in a more personally successful repetition of the events of November 1955. But this hope rested on the restraint of two groups outside his control: Goulart and the people pressing him on, and the army conspirators centered around the High Command. In so far as he could directly influence events, his militant attacks on Goulart and appeals to the armed forces inevitably contributed to an early showdown.

Most crucial of all, his natural allies—the senior officers led by Generals Castello Branco and Costa e Silva who were planning the revolt—operated independently of him and probably did not even trust him with full details of their plans until within a day of the action. It was very noticeable over the period of the actual coup from March 31 on that Lacerda, like Magalhães Pinto and the other rebel Governors, was subordinate to the rebel generals. Partly this switch of authority to the military was due to the nature of the final *dénouement* of the Goulart saga: in the crisis over the sailors' mutiny during the Easter weekend the constitutional threat posed by the leftist revolutionaries who were egging the President on took the form of a direct attack by NCO's and sailors on discipline and hierarchy in the services.

The Governor's resistance in the Palácio Guanabara, on March 31, with his two submachine guns and a pistol, his *maquisards,* state policemen, and garbage-truck roadblocks, was hilariously melodramatic. But the success of the revolution in Rio, still Brazil's most important political center, owed something to the efficiency of Lacerda's political police, who had rounded up many of the leftist labor leaders on March 30, thus paralyzing Goulart's trade-union support. More generally, the Governor's propaganda triumphs on the air were deserved in that, more than any other civilian politician, he had conditioned the Brazilian middle classes and the army which they so largely staffed, to accept the necessity of force.

But he had succeeded better than he knew. His criticism of the army for not intervening more drastically in 1954 and 1961 and for tolerating for too long "corrupt" and "pro-Communist" governments had found a ready response, particularly among the fervently antipolitical younger officers—the successors of that clique of friendly officers who had vowed to help Lacerda before the attempt on his life in the Rua Toneleros.

Relations with Castello Branco

On April 9 the three military ministers (General Costa e Silva had appointed himself War Minister), who now formed the "Supreme Revolutionary Command," promulgated an Institutional Act which had been drafted by Francisco Campos, the author of the Estado Novo constitution. The executive thereby acquired powers to submit constitutional amendments to Congress which must be voted on within thirty days and need only have a simple majority, to declare a state of siege without congressional approval, and to suppress the political rights of people it disliked for up to ten years. Had Quadros or Goulart claimed such powers, Lacerda would have been on the air within hours to denounce the overthrow of the constitution; but some such program had always been implicit in his calls for an emergency regime. On April 11 General Castello Branco, whose accession to the Presidency had been endorsed by the revolutionary Governors, was duly imposed on Congress. The broad outlines of the Estado Novissimo, as Lacerda was to call it with a vehemence rehearsed against the Vargistas, had already been laid down.

Relations between the new regime and its leading civilian proponent started amicably enough when Lacerda was sent off on a propaganda tour to Europe to "explain" the revolution. It had a skeptical reception from the liberal European press, for whom Goulart's defects did not easily justify the military take-over and a mass of political prisoners. On his arrival in Paris in late April he criticized the "Communist" correspondents of French papers in Brazil for false reporting and said that de Gaulle's prospective visit would be so much banquets and speeches. When he returned to Paris in May he was given strong protection and, in a radio interview on Europe 1, excused himself for being tired before his last French press conference. "When a man who has fought for life and country is called a Fascist and reactionary he must riposte," he said. He described himself as a pragmatic idealist inspired by Christian Democratic doctrine. In Bonn he appealed for private capital for Brazil and claimed that the regime was constitutional, with a President elected by Congress and a free press. In June he was in London to put his case to the Prime Minister, Sir Alec Douglas-Home, in what must have been a fascinating conversation.

Significantly, his warmest reception came in Portugal, where he was greeted by President Tomaz and Dr. Salazar and described in the official press as "one of the most notable Brazilians of all time." The compliments were repaid. On radio he called Dr. Salazar "an extraordinary politician, certainly the greatest political writer in our language and one of the greatest of our times," and attacked the United Nations for wanting to interfere in the administration of Portugal's overseas territories. In July he returned home hurriedly from New York on learning that President Castello Branco was proposing to let Congress choose the next President if there was no popular majority. In its defeats it had always been a UDN claim that electoral winners needed an overall majority of votes cast, a situation that rarely applied. It was highly unlikely that Lacerda, in anything like a free election, could hope to win with an absolute majority, and if the choice were left to the rump Congress, in which the regime, by use of its Institutional Act, had an almost assured majority, anything might happen.

Within fairly few months it became clear that Carlos, the eternal headache of Presidents, was not going to give Castello Branco an easy run. There were small causes of friction, Lacerda was rude to de Gaulle during his visit, and signs of divergence grew. The President, a small, tough Northeasterner, wanted to "clean up" Brazilian institutions, but he also wanted to cool down the political temperature. Lacerda by nature preferred argument and intense excitement. Secondly, the whole approach of the regime, and particularly the "hard line" colonels pressing it on, was ambiguous toward free elections. Partly this was due to distrust of the preferences of the electorate, partly to distrust of even the leading UDN politicians. On the other hand, there was some pressure from the United States to reinstate free elections, and part of the case for the revolution was that Goulart had been tampering with the constitution.

In the circumstances Castello Branco hedged his bets. He extended the unexpired portion of Goulart's mandate, which he was serving, by a year, to the end of 1966, and he permitted elections for state governorships in eleven states including Guanabara in October 1965. While it was always possible that Castello Branco might impose Lacerda as his successor—though the possibility receded in the course of 1965—the latter appeared to be committing himself to open elections when he won the nomination of a UDN convention to the Presidency in November 1964.

Lacerda's big quarrel with the Castello Branco regime broke out in 1965 over its anti-inflation policy. This, directed by an American-trained economist, Roberto Campos, was aimed at reducing by stages the rate of inflation, which had been running at over eighty per cent a year under Goulart. The result was, inevitably, a minor recession by the middle of 1965 which particularly affected cars and consumer durables. With the demand for new jobs then running at 1,100,000 a year in Brazil and widespread underemployment, any check to expansion was bound to be unpopular. Lacerda, receptive to the complaints of his constituents and anxious to get his successor elected in Guanabara, began to protest.

As ever with Lacerda, a policy disagreement rapidly became a vendetta in which issues like Roberto Campos's transparent pro-Americanism began to loom as large as his economics. Nineteen sixty-five was Rio de Janeiro's fourth centenary, with celebrations that any publicity-conscious Governor would find useful. In the middle of the year, with the much-purged PTB opposition in disarray, there seemed a good chance that Lacerda's chosen successor, Flexa Ribeiro, a former headmaster who was then state secretary for Education, might win. Education had been one of the successes of the "New Rio" of which the Governor boasted, but Ribeiro lacked weight as an independent personality.

Lacerda left to Castello Branco the odium of vetoing two contentious opposition candidates—one of whom was his old enemy Marshal Lott, who the Governor said should be free to run—until within a fortnight of the elections the PTB and PSD coalesced around the "acceptable" Negrão de Lima. The Governor had been outmaneuvered. The embarrassing situation for Castello of having an unpopular revolution defended in Guanabara by a Lacerdista against some extreme opponent—so that the army would be forced to save Lacerda and Ribeiro—had been avoided, because in the last analysis the PTB, which provided the voting power for the opposition alliance, hated Lacerda more than the President.

From the moment of Negrão's endorsement the Governor was running scared, and the campaign's tone degenerated. Ribeiro's expensive electioneering—which included constant repetition of the jingle "*Flexa vai ganhar*" (Flexa is going to win), sung by a carnival favorite on radio and TV—was aided by the full force of his master's talents. Lacerda charged that the Communists and the foreign power utility Rio Light were behind Negrão, and that the military would prevent elections. He made a marathon appearance on television to defend his administration. But though Ribeiro did relatively better than Lacerda had in 1960, probably polling the full prorevolution vote, he was beaten by the undistinguished Negrão and the expansionist ghost of Kubitschek which stood behind him.

Lacerda was left angry that he had been defeated by the unpopularity of a program with which he disagreed, while Castello could congratulate himself on severely deflating a firebrand on his own territory, with elections. But the Governor's swan song, coupled with the defeats of UDN candidates elsewhere and the challenge posed by Kubitschek's dramatic return, was responsible for a second Institutional Act soon after. Responding to military pressure, Castello turned away from free elections for the time being—the next President would be chosen by the manipulatable Congress—and established tighter military control at state level.

Quality of Governorship

Many in Guanabara, aware of Lacerda as a journalist or as a demagogue with a variable temperament, were surprised to find that he could turn himself into a capable administrator. He threw himself into the job with enthusiasm. Rio had not, on the whole, fared well with its appointed *Prefeitos*, and its first elected Governor was faced with tremendous pressure on housing in the narrow strip between the mountains and the sea, as well as all kinds of disease and deprivation in the *favelas*, those matchbox slums which climb ever further up the slopes. Basic services like water, electricity, and roads did not meet public needs, and the streetcar service, offered by frail *bondes*, was a byword for antiquity. Of Rio it was said that the setting was devised by God and despoiled by man.

In these circumstances Lacerda at least made a start on some of the problems, in spite of the utter hostility of the federal government for three of the five years of his term.

For his staff he had the pick of the UDN outsiders who had criticized civic administration for so long. Among his appointments was Sandra Cavacanti, a teacher who came to be a regular TV performer, who looked after social services. Flexa Ribeiro, headmaster of one of the best-known city schools, took on education. Lacerda also remembered his friends in the services. Colonel Gustavo Borges, who but for chance might have been with him instead of Major Vaz in the Rua Toneleros, headed the police and security. Colonel Americo Fontenele took over transport and irritated some by his attempts to introduce one-way traffic systems. Each and every one was at times a target for the opposition press, but the general level of ability was high, and there was little hint of the corruption which had characterized earlier administrations.

The New Rio program was accompanied with strenuous publicity, and Lacerda's name was daubed on every project. To replace the *bondes,* the Governor made a deal with Fiat for a large number of municipal trolley buses, and transportation personnel were put into smart uniforms. New tunnels were driven through the Rio rock, one of them named after Rubem Vaz. COPEG, a mixed development company for the state, was set up to promote industrial development and do something to reduce the effects on employment of the transfer of government business to Brasília. To compensate for the enmity of Goulart, Guanabara received rather more than its share of both private and public U.S. aid. The state cleared away some of the *favelas,* and their inhabitants were rehoused in housing projects with evocative names, Vila Kennedy and Vila Aliança. There were, however, inevitable complaints that the *favelados* had to travel a greater distance to work, and other *favelas* expanded.

The Governor tried to improve the meager amount of open space available to the crowded *cariocas.* By artificial means a new beach and seaside park were created within Guanabara Bay at Flamengo, with landscaped gardens by the expert Roberto Burle Marx, and so on. Another park, the Parque Laje, gave new point to Lacerda's intermittent quarrel with the proprietors of *O Globo,* the conservative afternoon paper, as one of the Marinho family was involved in a rival proposal to develop the land for speculative purposes. When the *Globo* group accepted assistance from the U.S. Time–Life group in setting up a new Rio TV station, the quarrel reached a crescendo.

With regard to schools, it was claimed that all children of primary-school age were, for the first time in Rio's history, receiving an education. This was the sort of claim hard to prove, given the dearth of civic statistics, but there was certainly an impressive crash program for schools and teachers. The state government took advantage of the city's quatercentenary to boost its prestige with a film and music festival, extra international soccer matches, and even a night of *macumba* dancing, which the Governor found it inconvenient to attend after such a pagan affair was put under the censure of the Roman Catholic hierarchy.

Opposition to the New Rio was as inevitable as it was to Lacerda's stand in national affairs. One of the less attractive criticisms was that he was a "beggar killer." A scandal broke out in the state police when the bodies of Rio beggars were found floating downstream in a river in neighboring Rio de Janeiro State. Although Lacerda was not implicated, it seemed an inhumane comment on his desire to see his city polish its image. After the revolution there was also criticism of the strong-arm tactics of Colonel Borges and his security officers.

As Governor, Lacerda exercised powers of censorship over the Rio theaters which on at least one occasion brought him into conflict with the usually anti-Lacerdista theater people. In 1965 one Rio theater wished to put on an antimilitarist piece, *Berço do Heroi* (Cradle of the Hero), by a young author, Dias Gomes. While the state censors were willing to permit its performance, the Governor, anxious about army sensibilities, protested so energetically that it was not given. Another criticism, aimed at him personally, was about his "triplex" or three-floor apartment. The maximum permitted by the state was a "duplex" and Carlos built on to it what he described as only a small study. The active opposition in the state legislature made much use of this issue.

More generally, there were complaints that the New Rio was too expensive and resulted in a tax burden which, in combination with the high levels of inflation, added to the difficulties of consumers and businessmen. A press critic[7] claimed that from 1961 to 1964 Guanabara's GNP dropped by sixteen per cent and per capita income fell by twenty-four per cent, whereas the rest of the country was registering an increase. The early sixties were poor for the Brazilian economy as a whole, but there were legitimate fears in Guanabara not only that its traditional rival, São Paulo, was totally outdistancing it but that other centers were making faster progress.

[7] *Correio da Manhã*, Rio.

But the overriding fact about the government of Guanabara was that it was not trying to provide a normal state administration in peaceful times—it was a self-appointed challenge to the federal government of Brazil in the same way that the "free land of America" created in Cuba by the revolution was a total rejection of the Pan-American system supported by the United States. The parallel under Goulart was the more striking in that many better-off Brazilians and North American observers sincerely, if wrongly, believed that Goulart was slipping toward a Communist-dominated dictatorship. Hence a strike of state employees in Guanabara was not just an industrial dispute—it was a blow at the state administration by the aggressive trade-union followers of the President. Hence the Bank of Brazil was ordered by the Ministry of Finance to refuse to cash checks for the state government. Hence U.S. advisers of the Alliance for Progress clustered around the Governor to help make Guanabara a showpiece of the Alliance and free enterprise. Hence, too, the Governor gave state employees the day off on March 13, 1964, when Goulart was expected to sign several radical decrees at a demonstration—in hopes that they would make a long weekend of it and not go.

Guanabara, however, was not an isolated entity. President Goulart spent most of the week at his residence there, the Palácio Laranjeiras. The bulk of the federal civil service and all the diplomats still lived there. It was the center of the trade-union network on which Goulart was coming increasingly to depend. It was the bastion of Goulart's cousin Brizola, who had a radio station there. It was also physically within the power of the local army command, whose attitude became increasingly uncertain as the drama of Goulart continued, and against whom the military police under orders from the state government could offer piddling resistance. So, in the two and a half years under Goulart that provided the centerpiece of Lacerda's stewardship, Guanabara seemed to be the cockpit in which the future of Brazil—possibly even of South America—was being fought out, and all arguments about the state administration became subsumed under the greater controversy.

Politics after the Governorship

In his early fifties, after two decades in the public eye, Lacerda found himself out in the political cold as a result of a military revolution for which he had been a leading apologist. In March 1966, having left the governorship at the beginning of the year, he was on holiday in Nice and told a reporter, "Politics for me is over." It was a most implausible remark. As Castello Branco's rule drew to a close, Lacerda—one of the few civilian critics free to speak his mind—showered the regime with abuse. In its economic policy and its attitude to free elections it had betrayed the revolution. But Carlos's abuse made little difference to a regime solidly supported by the armed forces. In so far as his attacks accomplished anything, they may have contributed to the emergence of the Minister of War, Arturo Costa e Silva, as Castello Branco's successor. As a soldier, Costa e Silva answered the hard-line revolutionaries' demand that there should be no backsliding into the laxer national discipline and softer life of the civilian politicians. On the other hand, Costa e Silva had contacts among the former PSD politicians, ambivalent in their view of the revolution, and he offered a different program from Castello. There would be more emphasis on national independence and less on the U.S. alliance, a drive for development and a six per cent growth rate, and an effort to "humanize" the revolution.

It was, therefore, in circumstances of continued disillusion with the revolution he had helped to father that Lacerda turned to the "wide front" with Kubitschek. It was almost as though, seeing that Castello's successor was anxious to adopt Kubitschekian policies for the revolution, Lacerda had decided to make a pact with the fountainhead itself. But the crucial point about the public reputation of Kubitschek was his tested devotion to free elections and normal constitutional processes, and it was these certainties that the Costa e Silva government still withheld from Brazil. To join up with Kubitschek meant unsaying many harsh words of Lacerdista criticism, and inevitably Lacerda's enemy *O Globo* reprinted a photo of the dead Major Vaz and cried betrayal.

But the alliance was not entirely without precedent. In the chaotic days before the fall of Goulart, Lacerda had appealed to Kubitschek to join other Governors and public figures in statements and public appearances in favor of the constitution which might, if successful, have staved off the military intervention. Latterly, too, Lacerda's career had brought him within striking distance of the Presidency thanks to free elections, and to stand on that platform was consistent with the principles of his old UDN constituents.

In personal terms the "wide front" was very much to Lacerda's advantage. For while Kubitschek was still popular, he was also too old to have a new political career ahead of him and was anyway restricted by the revocation of his political rights. On the other hand, Lacerda was now in touch with groups like the old PSD, and even the old PTB was considering giving the "wide front" temporary support. All this might make it possible for him to work with a wider range of backing than the old UDN if the front succeeded in re-establishing direct elections for the Presidency. Meantime relations between the two principals were said to be surprisingly cordial, even though some in the Costa e Silva government in 1967 seemed interested in trying to detach Carlos and sending him to the United Nations as Brazil's Ambassador. But the banning of the front in mid-1968, after Goulart had joined it, set back the prospects for direct elections.

Style, friends, family

Carlos, who had married Dona Leticia when he was still under suspicion as a Communist, had two sons and a daughter. It was Sergio, the eldest son, who was a witness of the Rua Toneleros attempt and who later helped in running the *Tribuna*. Family life, with a man of Lacerda's uncertain temper, cannot have been easy. At times he would see psychiatrists in an effort to maintain his equilibrium.

Lacerda, however, always had a number of interests aside

from his politics and journalism. He was exceedingly well read and alive to the world of ideas. His translations from English into Portuguese ranged from Shakespeare's *Julius Caesar* to the Broadway hit, *How to Succeed in Business Without Really Trying*. His hobbies included the cultivation of roses and collecting parrots (he kept a selection caged in the grounds of the Palácio Guanabara when he was the tenant). His reconciliation with the Church, which took place after the war, led to a strong identification with Catholicism.

Carlos, nicknamed the "Crow" by his enemies, had a wide smile which displayed a fine set of teeth and was said to have a strong attraction for women. In his youth he had his amorous exploits. Throughout his life he found himself in quarrels of all sorts, escalating from restaurant incidents to the attempt on his life which led to the death of Major Vaz. To be a friend of such a man meant accepting inevitable periods of strain and the risk of total enmity. Even so some of those, military and civilian, who had become his admirers in the early fifties were still devoted to him some fifteen years later.

The *Tribuna* remained a focus for the staunch Lacerdistas. One close supporter from the Lantern Club days was Amaral Neto, perhaps the ablest young politician in the Lacerda circle and regarded by outsiders as the master's heir apparent. But by 1965 he had broken with the Governor, apparently for a mixture of personal and political reasons, and ran as an anti-Lacerdista independent in the gubernatorial elections of that year.

But though political contingencies could make foes of Lacerda's closest collaborators, they could have the opposite effect also. Long before the classic reconciliation with Kubitschek there had been a significant pause in Lacerda's periodic row with the Marinho family which owns *O Globo*. Whereas in 1950 and 1951 he was saying that *O Globo* had sold out to the Prefecture of Rio —and was reminding everyone that it had been one of the most enthusiastic backers of the Estado Novo—in 1953, when the row with *Ultima Hora* was at its peak, he was saying how respected *O Globo* was. By then, of course, he was broadcasting on the

Marinhos' radio. The quarrel with the Marinhos was pursued again later. No close observer of Lacerda could fail to be aware that his hatreds could be inconsistent.

That he is a good orator and journalist is not open to doubt. His platform performance, with simile piled on simile, has been widely imitated in Brazil but scarcely bettered. Because he has hates, not just mild dislikes, gutter language is frequently employed to inflame an audience. But there is also wit and, for instance in the context of a low-keyed press conference, he can be urbane. His journalism is really a condensed form of oratory, using the same kind of invective. He is a skilled wordsmith— "Estado Novissimo" as a depreciation of the Castello Branco regime, with all the worst connotations for Lacerdistas, is one example. "Time–Life–Globo" was an instant invention at a press conference which summed up his attack on the Marinhos for getting American help for their TV station. The oratory, the journalism, the invective, and the wit are all in the service of a master propagandist.

Was Lacerda, the flayer of corruption in government, in any way corrupt himself? His opponents in Guanabara made capital out of the "triplex" flat, and there were some who thought that he was better off than he should be, but the case remains unproven. As state Governor he undoubtedly had considerable powers of financial and industrial patronage, and many jobs, important or humble, were in his gift. He has himself written ironically of the politician who approached his staff asking for a job for the husband of his wife's maid so that he could make sure she did not move. Under Lacerda's auspices the state bank of Guanabara, for example, expanded enormously, but whether this brought any personal benefit to him is another matter. Long before he became Governor, his journalism and books could have brought him a quite reasonable income, and though the *Tribuna* might not always have been a solid asset, it too was worth something.

By the time he left the Palácio Guanabara, he was running a finance house, a public relations firm, and a publishing concern.

Dating back to the early fifties, he seems to have been able to rely on financial backing for political campaigns, as well as air time on radio and television. No doubt the sources of this backing varied over the years, but in 1965, in the crucial governorship election, there was no shortage of money. Later, at the time of the collapse of the Lebanese Intra Bank, it was being said in Brazil that its head, Yussuf Beidas, was one of Lacerda's backers. But the ex-Governor denied it.

Carlos the military politician

For a large part of his career Lacerda's political stance concealed a basic contradiction: he was a civilian politician whose energies seemed bent on transmitting the government of his country to soldiers. After April 1964 the inherent illogic in this situation showed through, but in the fifties the position was not so curious. All Brazilian politicians knew that the armed forces were the final arbiter in their system, and each attempted to court some members of them in his own way. Also, though the armed forces might possess a discipline lacking in other Brazilian organizations, they were officered by the same middle class who operated the civilian political system. (Because of the literacy qualification for voters the middle class has always been overrepresented in civilian politics.) Common to sectors of both the officer class and the civilian middle class were ideas on Catholicism, anti-Communism, nationalism, and democracy on which Lacerda rang the changes.

But what marked him out, even in conservative company, was his readiness to appeal for a military coup d'état to validate opinions which seemed to make little electoral headway. In this, in spite of some military sympathy, he was bound to meet resistance among officers. For while it was true that there had been several military interventions in Brazilian history and the army was strongly imbued with the positivist tradition, it was also true that it regarded itself as the last support of the constitution—a more cautious professional view augmented by contacts with Anglo-American armies from the Second World War on—and was reluctant to see its essential unity undermined by Lacerda's maneuvers. Whatever he might like to say, it would be the army that would have to act, with all the risks of bloodshed, civil war, and loss of the privileged military position that this could entail.

For anti-Vargista and conservative officers, however, particularly the young ones who had less to lose, Lacerda's pre-eminence as a civilian propagandist gave him a certain influence in the early fifties. Inasmuch as these officers were trying to affect national politics, they were bound to depend on someone who was obviously a much better politician than they. In 1952 the anti-Communist Democratic Crusade, Lacerda's ally, was winning battles within the army against the leftist nationalist officers who supported the President. The Crusade forced the resignation of the War Ministers, Estillac Leal, and caused his defeat in crucial elections to the presidency of the Military Club in May. Less than two years later a memorandum signed by forty-two colonels and thirty-nine lieutenant colonels complained to the War Minister about loss of salary differentials with civilians, lack of equipment, and inequality of opportunities for promotion. Such discontents gave Lacerda material for his broader attacks on the Vargas regime and led to his very close cooperation with military men in the period surrounding the Rua Toneleros attempt and Vargas's suicide.

Lacerda was probably never so close to so many serving officers again. The Lott coup, justified as a constitutional move, was a defeat for the Lacerdista position. His election as Governor of Guanabara, in part a response to the frustration of military options and a more universal respect for constitutional forms, tended to commit Lacerda more firmly to the electoral path. When, under Goulart, senior officers started plotting an intervention again, Lacerda's role could only be that of propagandist. Partly this would be because of his erratic behavior in the past, partly because the senior officers, anxious to secure as wide a consensus as possible in favor of a "constitutional" intervention, could not be exclusively linked with a man popularly regarded as an extremist. But above all, the reason lay in the fact that those officers in the High Command belonging to the "Sorbonne" school had developed their own anti-Communist interventionist ideology.

For these men, who stood at the heart of the conspiracy, the civilian politicians as a body had failed to give Brazil the purposeful, pro-Western direction she needed. Only a disciplined group such as they themselves could offer the necessary unity and persistence. Hence the success of the "Sorbonne" in 1964, combined with Lacerda's oppositionist temper, made it almost inevitable that he should break decisively with the military regime. At the time of the crisis over the UDN gubernatorial defeats in 1965 and Kubitschek's attempted return, Lacerda's desperate pleas for a self-protecting coup revealed that the overwhelming majority of the armed forces preferred to serve Castello Branco and Costa e Silva rather than him. This, although enough officers shared his anxieties to force through the second Institutional Act. By 1967 it was said that Lacerda had finally lost his *cobertura militar* (military backing). However he was still mindful of service sensibilities. When Helio Fernandes, the current editor of the *Tribuna*, raised a storm by an extravagantly critical obituary on the death of ex-President Castello Branco in an air crash, Carlos—whose attacks on the live President had been equally vigorous—presented an orthodox expression of the nation's loss.

Carlos the civilian politician

In his own eyes, as he enjoyed telling North American audiences particularly, Lacerda was always a liberal democrat. Any departures from this position had been forced on him by the toll that corruption and *caudillismo* were taking of Brazil. To his domestic opponents of the PTB, however, he was a Fascist and even the *Correio da Manhã* was describing him in 1965 as a Mussolini figure.

According to the occasion, either view could be sustained. The UDN supporters in Guanabara were overwhelmingly bourgeois (the *Tribuna* tended to show more *petit bourgeois* instincts), and the position of the bourgeoisie in Brazil, as in other developing countries, was emotionally insecure. The long Vargas era, in which a combination of state power and specially created working-class institutions had destroyed the old import economy and frustrated middle-class ambitions, left the civilian bourgeoisie as confused as the army officers. They felt they ought to be constitutional and democratic, yet the only force they could ultimately rely on to protect their interests was the military.

Lacerda's instinctive understanding of these ambiguities may well have been sharpened by his acquaintance with Marxism. (Mussolini, of course, had once been a Socialist). Where fears were more important than facts, Lacerda was adept at the language of veiled threats, at the spreading of rumors of what adversaries might do, which could in tense conditions lead rapidly to an atmosphere of hysteria. The Communist bogey, essentially occult because the party was illegal after 1947, became such a standby that any opponent of Lacerda was almost by definition Communist or Communist-supported. Because the party's true strength (damaged in the sixties by divisions in the international movement) was unknown, even the wildest accusations might gain credence, but to anyone not in a mood to believe, some appeared to be sheer fantasy.

Lacerda was hardly a reliable friend of the North Americans, although they took to him during his struggle with Goulart. Nationalist sentiment, and anger at capitalist exploitation, tended to be regarded by the Vargistas as their own monopoly. But Lacerda too could play this tune. His long-standing quarrel with the Rio Light was one example, and while he was Governor, he conducted a hot campaign against the Hanna Corporation, which was involved in a significant iron-mining concession in the Rio Doce valley. In 1957, when President Kubitschek was negotiating the cession of the island of Fernando de Noronha to the United States for a missile-tracking station, Lacerda appeared to wobble in his support when he saw there was some nationalist capital to be made out of it.

Lacerda's nationalism reflected the mixture of feelings among the bourgeois groups. On one hand was a feeling of national pride in a country naturally well endowed, combined with a sense of irritation at its poverty by the side of the United States and envy at the local activities of U.S. groups. On the other was a contempt for the inefficiency and corruption of some of the Brazilian state enterprises which had been set up by Vargas in response to nationalist pressure, and an eagerness to acquire the advanced techniques practiced by U.S. firms.

Though it is clear that Lacerda has at times taken a line that critics have understandably decried as Fascist, he can be clearly distinguished from the European Fascists of the 1930's. First, he has never established a personal movement with its own apparatus of discipline, hymns, and regalia. Though the party system which lasted from 1945 to 1966 was not well defined, his place was always within the UDN. Not even the Guanabara UDN, in the period of his Governorship, was just his personal vehicle. To compare the Lantern Club with a European Fascist group would be unrealistic, and to suggest that "A Cidade Maravilhosa," the sunny theme song of Lacerda's Governorship, had anything in common with the "Horst Wessel Lied" would be preposterous.

Second, there is no evidence that Lacerda is a racist. In spite of centuries of miscegenation involving most varied components —Portuguese, Amerindian, Negro, Japanese, Italian, German, Arab, and others in lesser degree—there are various racial snobberies in Brazil. But Lacerda has not tried to capitalize on them, and in fact, in a broadcast in Portugal in 1964, he cited Brazil's mestizo heritage as an argument for avoiding the fashionable division of Africa into black and white which was challenging Portugal's overseas territories. The row with *Ultima Hora* and its Jewish head, Samuel Wainer, could have acquired anti-Semitic overtones for some readers of the *Tribuna,* but Lacerda himself could hardly be accused of consistent anti-Semitism. In the early thirties he had led a protest at the take-over of a German Brazilian association by Nazis at the German Embassy, and in the sixties he named a new school after Anne Frank.

Many compatriots recognize that Lacerda is perhaps Brazil's ablest politician, with antennae that sense changes in the political temperature with astonishing speed and a power to move people that should never be underrated. In the more secure environment of a Western European democracy he might have grown into more of a creative statesman, less of a volatile whirlwind. He would still like to be President of Brazil and, if he were ever to succeed, it would be interesting to see whether he would be the liberal democrat who did not attempt to exceed his term, like Kubitschek, or the coup-making continuist he saw and destroyed in Vargas, Quadros, and Goulart. Like the older Latin American political elite, he is largely impervious to that obsession with the intricacies of economic management that plays such a large role in European and North American countries. Even his anti-Communism sometimes seems a spurious front; it is hardly a program of government. His administrative aims in Guanabara were the simple Kubitschekian ones of more, better, faster. Perhaps the only change obtainable by political action about which he feels strongly is in education. As a Congressman he worked for the passage of a long-delayed education bill, in Guanabara he made it his goal that at least all children of elementary-school age should get some schooling, and he has condemned the learning by rote of valueless information which has too often passed as education.

Personalism personified

Lacerda is too much himself to be described as typical of anything. Yet his career illustrates vividly the tensions common to many Latin American countries in which the armed forces hold a privileged place and social pressures are great. In countries as diverse as Argentina, Bolivia, and Peru, to take only three examples, the timing and purpose of military intervention in government have been constantly discussed in recent years. The dilemmas of the UDN voters in Brazil—should they accept defeat at the polls or request a military coup which defied liberal principles —were scarcely different from those which faced Radical voters in Argentina frightened by the prospect of Peronist successes. Essentially these middle-class parties did not trust their labor-oriented opponents to play by the democratic rules, but neither could they hope to keep the same control over a military regime that they might over their own leaders. Lacerda, personifying the fears of conservative bourgeois groups both within and outside the services, merely intensified antidemocratic trends in the PTB and an independent will to intervene by military commanders. Whether the realization that Castello Branco's and Costa e Silva's technocratic military regime, paralleled by the Onganía government in Argentina, was not the answer to all Brazilian problems would cure Lacerda forever of his attraction to the military, only time would tell.

With all Lacerda's inconsistencies, his dialectical oppositionism has yet succeeded in clarifying a number of political phenomena for Brazil. He showed that the statist, welfare, and labor policies of Vargas masked an urban *caudillismo*—a new patronage relation between leader and led that was unlikely to produce the industrial efficiency through competition or the wage improvements through independent bargaining that Western models of industrialization required.

Latterly, in his attacks on the Castello Branco regime and Costa e Silva, he has shown that a military technocracy that deflates a developing economy is irresponsible and that a plural society deserves the greater control over its affairs that direct elections of its leaders permit. Steadily over the years too he has attacked Brazil's oligarchy—to which he must belong himself—and has brought home to people that in spite of the apparent changes of the last forty years the country's affairs are still managed by a relatively small, interrelated group of politicians, soldiers, industrialists, and landowners that has failed to give Brazil either the economic strength or the status in the world that she deserves. In other countries other people have made similar points—about Perón or Ibáñez as urban *caudillos* in Argentina and Chile respectively; about the limitations of the Onganía regime in Argentina; or the purblind character of the Peruvian oligarchy (a favorite theme of the APRA in the past). Nor was Lacerda the only man to make such points in Brazil. It was just that his gifts for publicity have rammed them home.

Throughout his career as an "anti," Lacerda has exemplified a very prominent feature of Latin American politics: its basis in personalities. In Brazil people talk as freely of "Lacerdismo" and "Lacerdistas" as Argentines talk of Peronismo or even Uruguayans of Batllismo. Lacerda's reputation grew by defining and indicting personalities. Enough has been written to indicate that Lacerdismo is hardly a full-fledged political doctrine, and the Lacerdistas were a handful of friends rather than the mass organization of Perón.

Historical and social causes in Latin America help to explain the usual superiority of a man to either a political doctrine or organization—though there is evidence that this state of affairs is by no means absent in either North America or Western Europe today. The "wide front" of Lacerda and Kubitschek was a typically personalist understanding, underlined by the fact that both the parties within which they used to operate had by then been abolished. But the question about this sort of personalism—given armed forces prepared to intervene, a weak institutional framework for open politics, and widespread doubts about electoralism within civilian political elites—is what kind of limits will it accept on its power? In Lacerda's case, had he become President on the death of Vargas or the fall of Goulart, would he merely have installed a new form of the *caudillismo* he so abused? Until the Latin American countries have evolved systems in which personalism is controlled to permit regular changes of leadership and an even political growth (the Mexican one-party system has produced one model), such questions must get uncertain answers.

Eva Perón

The march on Rome

The Plaza de Mayo, the great square outside the Casa Rosada, Argentina's pink presidential palace, had often been crowded for political demonstrations before. But on October 17, 1945, it was filled with perhaps fifty thousand people from the working-class suburbs of Buenos Aires shouting for the man who had until the beginning of the month been Vice-President, Minister of War, and Secretary for Labor and Welfare: Juan Domingo Perón. They were *descamisados*—shirtless ones—and it was the day of Perón's march on Rome. Later his wife, Eva, never one to play down the claims of the movement, would describe it as the day that Argentina acquired her economic freedom.

The military and pro-Axis regime set up by a coup d'état in 1943 had become increasingly unstable. In February 1944 its third President, General Edelmiro J. Farrell, took office, and by July the rising strength of Perón—made Minister of War after the change of President—was recognized by giving him the Vice-Presidency. Its unpopularity was growing. In August 1945 Farrell lifted a state of siege that was almost four years old. Within weeks Radical, Conservative, Socialist, and Communist oppositions had joined forces in a Board of Democratic Co-ordination which staged a huge protest march in Buenos Aires. By the end of September Farrell had reimposed the state of siege and said that the constitution would remain suspended until the country knew how to use its rights of citizenship. There was a general roundup of opposition leaders. Service jealousy of Perón combined with the public unpopularity of the regime to make him an obvious target for a coup.

On October 1 Radio Belgrano, Buenos Aires's leading radio station, announced that Perón had been asked for his resignation. In the afternoon his mistress, Eva Duarte, took part in the station's science-fiction serial as usual, but it broke up in a row and was never broadcast again. On the next day Perón incautiously said, "Everybody is demanding my head but thus far no one has come to get it." But by October 9 it was announced that he had resigned his posts, that his henchman Colonel Filomeno Velazco had resigned as police chief in the capital, and that the commander of the Campo de Mayo garrison, General Eduardo Ávalos, was the new War Minister. But if Ávalos could make his coup, he did not have enough support in the armed forces or outside it to make it stick. Four days later a desperate series of cabinet changes left President Farrell with a cabinet of only two—General Ávalos and Admiral Hector Vernengo Lima.

On the night of October 1 there had been rumors that a group of captains and majors planned to attack the building in the Calle Posadas, in which Perón and Eva had adjoining flats. Furniture was stacked against the windows and food bought for a siege. But nothing happened, and before midnight they were driven by a German industrialist friend out of the center of the city and spent the night in the house of Eva's sister Elisa and Major Arrieta. From it they moved to a property belonging to the same friend at Tres Bocas, Tigre, and it was there, at one in the morning of the 13th, that Colonel Perón was detained by the new Buenos Aires police chief, Aristóbulo Mittelbach. He requested permission for Eva to accompany him, but this was not allowed. Perón was then taken to a naval vessel and imprisoned on Martín García Island in the River Plata, where he vainly asked to be put on trial or told the charges against him.

There are conflicting accounts of how Eva spent the days following Perón's capture. According to the preferred Peronist account, she charged round factories and trade-union meeting places in the car of the Spanish singer Conchita Piquer and in the company of Peronist henchmen like Cipriano Reyes, the meat workers' leader, and Colonel Domingo Mercante of the Secretariat of Labor and Welfare. Together they organized the pro-Perón demonstrations which led to the successful climax of the 17th. According to the anti-Peronist version, she spent the time doing her best to pull strings to obtain *habeas corpus* for her lover so that they could go off into exile. In this version Juan Atilio Bramuglia, a Peronist protégé in the Secretariat of Labor and Welfare who had been government interventor in Buenos Aires, told her firmly that Perón's place was in Argentina and thereby laid the basis for an enmity that would remove him from the Ministry of Foreign Affairs some years later. Knowing Eva's energy and the always unresolved dilemma between her simultaneous roles as adorer of a man and as political activist, it is not impossible to imagine that she followed both lines of attack in the hectic days of Perón's imprisonment. On the 16th she got punched in the course of an argument with a taxi driver, and that night the only man to walk through the ring of troops around the house in Calle Posadas to call on her was the perceptive Brazilian ambassador, Lazardo.

On October 17, the Peronist day of days, Eva stayed in her apartment while the drama was played out in the Plaza de Mayo. In the morning Perón, who said that he was suffering from pleurisy, was moved to the military hospital in Buenos Aires. The shouting mob in the square overawed Farrell and his tottering cabinet in the course of an all-day demonstration, and Farrell gave in. On leaving the hospital, Perón called Eva to tell her he was going to the Presidency. To the delirium of the crowd, Perón suddenly appeared on the balcony of the Casa Rosada in the company of the President. They embraced. Farrell said he had nothing but the closest friendship for Perón. Perón made a speech praising the workers, and in reply to periodic shouts from the crowd asking where he had been, he made the classic statement:

I ask you not to question me nor to remind me of questions that I have already forgotten. Because men who are incapable of forgetting do not deserve to be loved or respected by their fellows, and I want to be loved by you. I do not want to tarnish this occasion with a bad memory.

But to drive home his victory, he called on them to take a one-day holiday the next day.

A great deal of mythologizing surrounded October 17, not least contributed by Eva herself, who was to claim a much wider spread of social and occupational support on that first-ever Day of the Descamisado than seems to have been the case. The basis for the demonstrations had been carefully laid in the Secretariat of Labor and Welfare in its general work over the previous eighteen months and, almost certainly, specifically in the early days of October, when Perón could see he was threatened. Avellaneda, a working-class suburb of Buenos Aires in which there were several meat-packing factories and the meat packers' union, on which Perón through Cipriano Reyes had strong influence, appear to have played a big part.

Perón's triumph had a mixture of causes. First, Argentina was not conducting anything like an open political system and the widespread hostility to the regime, running the gamut of traditional parties, could not come to a focus. Second, the revolution of 1943 had failed to throw up a leader or a coherent doctrine of government: the Nazi-Fascist inspiration for appeals to order, work, and the greater Argentina looked tawdry with the doom of the Axis and the absence of local results, and the officer class was demoralized. Third, Perón, whose nineteen months in the Ministry of War had given him a considerable base in the army, had fashioned a labor machine strong enough to provide crucial outside support; hence he could offer a way out for the 1943 revolution to which so many officers had been committed. It may also have been true, of course, particularly for the groups opposed to Peronist labor policies, that Perón himself was a positive cause of the unpopularity of the regime; and there is every reason to suppose that the Ávalos coup was a last effort within it to stop him. But he publicly recognized one person to whom he owed the happy issue of October 17—his mistress Eva Duarte.

Five days later, in the town of Junín where her mother was still living, they were married in a civil ceremony. Colonel Mercante and Eva's brother Juan were witnesses. She wore an ivory-colored suit, and after the wedding they went to her mother's house and later to a friend's *estancia*. In December they were married in a church in La Plata.

Origins and first meetings with Perón

María Eva Duarte was born on April 26, 1919, in a house in Los Toldos, a small country town in the province of Buenos Aires. In 1945 the entry in the civil register would be switched to indicate that she was born in 1922. She was the daughter of an unrecognized union between Juana Ibarguren and Juan Duarte and was their fourth child. She had two elder sisters, Elisa and Blanca, an elder brother, Juan, and a younger sister named Herminda. Her father belonged to an upper-middle-class landowning family and was a conservative in politics. Her mother was the daughter of a coachman, a background that lay somewhere in that borderland between the lower middle class and the rural proletariat; and her politics were Radical. The family situation was not prosperous, though when Eva was to come before the microphones later, she may have exaggerated the degree of poverty. When she was seven, a disaster occurred which worsened it and whose memory would be vividly recalled: Her father died, and she and her brother and sisters and mother were subjected to the most painful humiliation when they wanted to attend his wake at the house of his "legal" family in Chivilcoy. They were only let in at the insistence of the intendente of Chivilcoy, who was a relative of the Duartes. Illegitimate children were not rare in the countryside, but the "legal" Duartes were no doubt specially affronted that Juan had largely deserted them. The experience of class prejudice they gave her would haunt Eva, helping to make her conscious of herself as an outsider. As her authorized book, *La Razón de mi Vida*, put it:

I remember very well that I was sad for many days when it occurred to me that in the world there were poor and there were rich; and the strange thing is that it was not so much the existence of the poor that made me sorry as the knowledge that there were rich at the same time.[1]

Three years later Juana Ibarguren moved to the town of Junín, leaving her elder daughter Elisa, who had a job in the post office, behind in Los Toldos. Soon after, Juana started taking paying guests of the wealthier sort, and among them was Major Arrieta, who was to marry Elisa, and a lawyer who was to marry Blanca, a schoolteacher. Eva remained at the Escuela Normal while Blanca qualified, and Elisa's transfer to Junín was wangled by a congressional deputy. She fell in love with the theater. When the singer Agustín Magaldi arrived in Junín on a tour in 1934, she tried to persuade him to take her to Buenos Aires and introduce her to the theatrical world. As she was only fifteen, he wasn't too keen on the idea, but Eva's mother added her voice in favor and on January 3, 1935, she reached Buenos Aires with Magaldi. For a starry-eyed girl of her age Buenos Aires, cosmopolitan, bustling with automobiles, must have seemed paved with gold. The city had plenty of theaters, and the arrival of motion pictures, and the first wave of national as well as international film stars, must have given the overlapping worlds of show business a particular glitter. By comparison the unimportant places in which she had grown up, Los Toldos and Junín, with their firmer class distinctions, stereotyped entertainments, and limited prospects for a working girl, could hardly be duller.

But even with Magaldi to help her begin, it was not easy for an inexperienced youngster to break into the magic world of the theater. Eva must have looked attractive—though she may not yet have acquired the blond hair which became a trademark—and she was as keen as mustard. On March 28, she joined a comedy in a bit part, but when in the middle of the year the company went on tour, she was not asked to go with it. She rejoined it when it returned to the capital in November and studied drama in the meantime. Professionally her first few years in Buenos Aires were a slow grind, a slow progression from the smallest parts balanced by the inevitable periods of resting. It was from these years that wealthy Argentine women—whose bitterness against Eva in her days of power would know no scruple—obtained the legend that she had been a prostitute. That she had several lovers, some of whom were able to help her in her career, such as Olegario Ferrando, the boss of Pampa Films, was hardly surprising. But she was not a prostitute. Inevitably, however, the professional freedom and public appeal of a woman in the theater, contrasted with the severely restrictive social code by which the Argentine oligarchy confined its women, made the first a subject of shock and jealousy for the second.

In 1937 Eva had a tiny role in a comic boxing film entitled *Seconds Out,* and the following year she did some modeling as well as acting. In 1939, through the medium of the same friend, Emilio Kartulovich, who had got her the part in the film, she had her first worth-while part in radio theater, heading a cast on Radio Prieto. She was so carried away with the idea of being a star that she put up at Buenos Aires's Savoy Hotel for a few days. That year and the next she had parts in two more films and was linked with a producer on Radio Argentina for whose program about films she worked. In 1941 she had a better part in a film called *A Bride in Trouble,* which was directed by a North American, John Reinhardt, and the next year she persuaded "Jabón Radical"—a brand of soap—to sponsor her radio dramas. Her brother, Juan, came to work for the soap firm. After the successful military revolution in June 1943 Eva became friendly with a number of officers, particularly with Lieutenant Colonel Aníbal Francisco Imbert, the Director of Posts and Telegraphs, whose permit was necessary for her "Jabón Radical" shows, which were now on Radio Belgrano. For the first time her economic position was really secure, eight years after reaching Buenos Aires, and she could afford a luxury flat in the Calle Posadas close to Radio Belgrano. Toward the end of the year she began to collaborate with the writer Francisco José Muñoz Azpiri, who wrote for her a series of dramatic biographies of famous women, including Queen Elizabeth of England and Napoleon's Josephine. He also encouraged the use of a musical background to cover up any weaknesses in Eva's diction. This fantasy series took on an extra meaning after she had met Perón.

This epoch-making event is still hidden in uncertainty. But the most satisfactory explanation is that it occurred on January 22, 1944, a week after the disastrous earthquake of San Juan, which caused Eva Perón and many others in the acting profession to take to the streets of the capital to collect money for the victims. The then President Ramírez and Colonel Perón visited on January 22 a charity performance to raise funds for San Juan at which Eva was present in the front row with Lieutenant Colonel Imbert. The momentous introduction took place there. Gossip adds that Perón's previous mistress, a youthful sixteen-year-old, was on holiday in Mendoza at the time, and it was not too hard for Eva to displace her. Shortly afterward the forty-nine-year-old widower disposed of his own flat and took the twin apartment in the Calle Posadas.

Various points need to be made about the two parties at this stage. Eva, twenty-five, was an actress with no previous record of mixing in politics or trade-union affairs. She was not a first-rank Buenos Aires actress, but she had a secure niche in the steady field of radio drama. She was no longer the provincial ingénue of ten years before. Perón, on the other hand, might already be described as the *eminence grise* of the military government, he had had plenty of political experience, and he had already discovered the possibilities of a labor organization. His first wife, Aurelia Tizón, whom he had married in 1926, had died long before, in 1938.

Perón's career had been a successful one in the army, but like Eva he was a natural child. His father, Mario Tomás Perón, was a rich landowner whose own father had been a well-known doctor; but Juan's mother was a poor girl, probably of Indian origin. As a young man he was lively and personable and became famous as an army ski instructor. He was sent as a military attaché to Santiago, from which he was withdrawn after a spy scandal. But this did not stop him from going as a military attaché to Rome. Here, undoubtedly, he was affected by Mussolini's Fascism, then at its zenith. Its relevance must have seemed more immediate in that Argentina and Italy, two Catholic countries, were then at a more similar stage of economic development than might be imagined later. On his return home in 1939 he went to the Andean garrison of Mendoza, where he became a founder of the GOU group of officers, which was authoritarian, patriotic, and unashamed in its admiration for Nazism and Fascism. GOU represented "Government, Order, Unity," and the group was the force behind the overthrow of the shaky civilian government of President Castillo in 1943. A manifesto issued at the time illustrated GOU thinking: the era of nations had given way to the era of continents; as Germany was making a titanic effort to dominate Europe, so Argentina should ensure, Brazil notwithstanding, its guardianship of South America; there would have to be an arms program, and the right spirit must be instilled into the nation through the radio, controlled press, education, and the Church; "Hitler's fight in peace and war shall be our guide." [2]

After the 1943 coup it was Colonel Perón, as Undersecretary of War, who was responsible for the critical GOU take-over of the army. By October he had taken over the National Department of Labor, renamed the Secretariat of Labor and Welfare the following month, and had started work in removing existing labor leaders and promoting those dependent on himself, and in establishing a propaganda machine. The practice of staging pro-Perón demonstrations dated from early on. Perón's bid for labor support was not original in Latin America—a similar effort in Brazil was being made on Vargas's behalf simultaneously—and he must have noted in Italy the importance of trying to incorporate labor into the Fascist regime. But though GOU officers may have approved

[2] Quoted in George I. Blanksten: *Perón's Argentina* (University of Chicago Press), 1953, p. 48.

the principle of organizing labor within the dictatorship, there appears to have been no great competition for his job. In dealing with labor, the peculiar circumstances gave him plenty of advantages: he could use the army's dictatorial power to dismiss uncooperative labor leaders and to press employers for pay raises or social benefits at the same time. He was therefore in an enviable position to get results for labor while scarcely damaging his position in the officer class, whose ideology was such that all civilians—employers as well as employees—must expect to suffer, and whose social roots lay rather among landowners than in the newer class of manufacturers. Such was his strength in the army in fact that in 1944, as Minister of War, he was able to claim of ninety per cent of active officers that their undated applications for retirement were on file, ready to be enforced at a moment's notice.

When Perón met Eva, there is no reason to believe that the most important factor involved was not simple sexual attraction: he was a handsome forty-nine, she was a vivacious five-foot-two blonde. But what made it stick was probably her flattery, originating in his undoubted power and her ability to instill the permanent myth of him as hero and her as privileged mistress; and his recognition that her confidence and histrionic skill would be valuable acquisitions.

The politics of the Peronist dictatorship

Eva's initiation in politics took place gradually in 1944. On radio she had a show called "Toward a Better Future," written by Muñoz Azpiri under a pseudonym, which consisted of propaganda for Perón and the Secretariat of Labor and Welfare. In June Muñoz Azpiri was made director of propaganda for the Secretariat of Information and began work on Perón's presidential campaign. Eva's professional life continued to be busy, and she was given a considerable part in a film called *Cavalcade of the Circus*, allegedly because one individual hoped this might ease his problems in importing films and running a casino at Mar del Plata. Shooting was difficult, as Eva would often arrive late or break off to go to the telephone, arriving much later to explain that her work as collaborator of Perón was much more important than the film. In 1945 Eva continued her radio dramas about famous women—including Isadora Duncan, Madame Chiang Kai-shek, and Anne of Austria—and also took a big step forward in the trade-union world by becoming president of the Actors' Association. She starred in another film, *The Wastrel,* of which she chose the director, but although it had been expensive to make, it was never allowed to appear because of Eva's political eminence. Meanwhile Perón had been sponsoring a campaign for votes for women, and his mistress's unpopularity with the armed forces had already been drawn to his attention. General Fortunato Giovannoni, the Director of the Gendarmerie, had complained to him formally that he was setting a bad example by bring Eva to his official residence at the Campo de Mayo barracks. His reply to the critics was that at least he was normal and she was not an actor. This army suspicion was intensified shortly before the Ávalos coup when Oscar Nicolini, an old friend of the Duarte family who was a lowly employee in the post office, was suddenly named Director of Posts and Telecommunications.

After October 17 and marriage Eva interred one career to take up another, as wife of the President-to-be. In January and February of the following year, amidst unfounded rumors that she was pregnant, she accompanied Perón on his election tours in the interior. Perón's Labor Party, created in the Secretariat of Labor and Welfare, was backed by some of the Radicals, various Church officials who were worried about the anticlericalism of the opposition, and Nazi funds. On the other side were most of the Radical Party, the Socialists, the Communists, and, unofficially, much of the Conservative Party. Their candidates were two Radicals, Dr. José Tamborini for President and Dr. Enrique Mosca for Vice-President, while Perón's vice-presidential candidate was a dissident Radical, Juan Hortensio Quijano.

The campaign, which had been advanced six weeks to suit the convenience of the "official" candidate, was violent and murky. The opposition was not homogeneous anyway, and the government used all its resources to defeat it. The army and federal police, riots and terror, and even Argentina's powerful elements of anti-Semitism—deprecated to some extent by Perón—were employed on his behalf. A government bonus law of December 1945, calculated to impress labor and to cow the Radical and Conservative employers, required all establishments to pay a thirteenth-month bonus to employees. In January this resulted in a three-day lockout by employers, and in the same month the stock exchange was bombed. In February, in a counterproductive effort to influence the elections, the United States government released a "blue book" entitled *Consultation Among the American Republics with Respect to the Argentine Situation*. Primarily the work of Assistant Secretary of State Spruille Braden, it said that since 1943 Argentina had been governed by a Fascist-type military dictatorship which had consistently failed to cooperate with the rest of the Western Hemisphere in efforts to set up the United Nations. Such interference in Argentine concerns gave the Peronistas an excellent nationalist issue. At length, after various incidents which included firing on and setting on fire the Tamborini–Mosca campaign train, the voting on February 24 gave Perón a margin of about eleven per cent. He won 1,527,231 votes to Tamborini's 1,207,155 and thereby gave himself democratic cover. He was duly inaugurated President on June 4, 1946, the third anniversary of the revolution, and Eva rode in a coach behind him.

Eva's period of real power was short—little more than five years—but she made the most of it. Under the Argentine constitution the President's wife has of course no powers, and because her position as active political partner of her husband had no statutory basis and few precedents it was subject to little restriction. In fact, though she maintained a general interest in the affairs of state, her prime concerns were three: labor, her Social Aid Foundation, and the Peronist women's party. Eva took an office in the new Ministry of Labor and Welfare (the former Secretariat) after Perón became President, and rapidly became the effective head of the department, although a worker, José María Freyre, was the official Minister.

The Social Aid Foundation was started in 1946, partly out of spite. The aristocratic Sociedad de Beneficencia traditionally invited the President's wife to be its president. But it could not stomach Eva. When it apologetically explained that it could not invite her because of her youth, she suggested her mother instead. The Foundation quickly became a massive operation, the Sociedad de Beneficencia closed, and the degree to which the welfare activities of the Foundation were personalized in "Evita" had an important part in the creation of her legend. From 1946 she headed the Asociación Pro Sufragio Femenino and, after September 9 in the following year, when the Argentine Congress approved a law giving votes to women, she proceeded to organize the Partido Peronista Femenino. The women's vote, so carefully sought by the Peróns, would be one of the factors in the even greater victory in the 1951 elections.

Eva made sure that all her doings were suitably publicized. In 1947 she bought the daily paper *Democracia,* in which a column appeared over her name; she ceaselessly addressed workers, women, and other groups, and radio brought her passionate demagogy into millions of homes. In December 1951 her official book of philosophy and autobiography, *La Razón de mi Vida,* appeared and was made into a textbook for primary and secondary schools and universities.

Her major appearance before the world outside Argentina was in her trip to Europe in 1947. On her arrival in Spain she was met by General Franco and 200,000 cheering people at the airport, and her stay was a paean to Spanish–Argentine relations and the similarity of the two regimes. In Rome she had an audience with the Pope, wearing the cross of Isabella the Catholic. In Paris she was present at the signing of a Franco–Argentine trade treaty by which Argentina loaned France over 150,000,000 pesos (about $22 million) to help in postwar reconstruction. In Paris, too, she wore some of her most gorgeous jewelry and clothes. People on the left suggested that she would have done more to please the French workers if she had come dressed in meat. In Switzerland her car was pelted with tomatoes, and a projected visit to Britain was canceled after MP's had made it clear to the Labour government that with tensions over meat quotas, expropriation of British utilities, and the Fascist parentage of the Peronist regime, she would be rather unwelcome. After being civilly received in Brazil, she arrived home two and a half months later, by sea, being met by Perón on his presidential yacht. "After these several months of absence it is with profound emotion that I return to the country of my three loves: my fatherland, my *descamisados,* and my beloved General Perón," she said. The trip, underlining Eva's own quasi-presidential status, may have done some good in reminding Europe of Argentina's existence. But it also served to emphasize what a strange concoction was Perón's Justicialism and how alien the Peronist regime was in the postwar comity of nations.

The oppressive features of Peronist rule, including arbitrary arrest, expropriation, the use of a secret police, and so on, went unopposed by Eva. The general theme of the *descamisados* versus the oligarchy, with the myth of Perón as the universal savior, justified anything. She played a crucial part in the final stages of the regime's battle with *La Prensa,* the reputable and critical journal of the wealthy whose closure in January 1951 led to widespread condemnation of the regime abroad. It was the officially sponsored demand of the news vendors' union for a large pay raise and a fifth of the paper's advertising revenue that brought it down, and it was Eva's Foundation which provided for all the workers put out of jobs by the closure. She also played an important role in unseating potential threats to Perón's control within the Peronista hierarchy. Colonel Domingo Mercante, by then the Governor of Buenos Aires province and hopeful of succeeding Perón if the 1949 constitution could be prevented from going through, went into alliance with Juan Atilio Bramuglia, the Foreign Minister. Both had strong roots in the CGT from the old days of the Secretariat of Labor and Welfare, but both had access to other sources of support. As a result of Eva's vigilance they were dismissed. It is likely too that she had a hand in another internecine mystery: the sudden discovery in September 1948 of a plot to assassinate Eva and Perón which was headed by the former meat workers' leader and Peronist member of the House of Representatives, Cipriano Reyes. He was thrown in jail. Whether or not there was any sort of plot, he too was a rival for the affections of labor.

The labor movement

In the labor movement Eva wanted to be an absolute mistress. She built up her own machine of clients and used her allies, like Angel Gabriel Borlenghi, the Minister of the Interior, against rivals and enemies like Mercante and Bramuglia. As the President's wife she obviously had tremendous powers of patronage. To a large extent the battle for labor had already been won by her husband. At the time of the 1943 revolution, unionization was by no means universal, and the union movement itself was split into two general confederations, one more right-wing and Socialist and the second dominated by the Communists. The first thing Perón did was to disband the second and to intervene in the first. Eva always attacked the Socialists and Communists on the grounds that they were antinational and ineffective, but by the time she was Lady Bountiful in the Ministry of Labor and Welfare they had been largely crushed. In the first two years after the revolution unions were merged and their leaders jailed and replaced, but there was considerable opposition. Although a decree of January 1945 had made strikes illegal as crimes against the security of the state, there were major stoppages by packinghouse workers, railwaymen, and port workers later that month. The 1949 constitution incorporating the "rights of the workers" more or less made strikes illegal, but even the combination of repression, client leaders, and generous wage settlements could not entirely remove labor unrest. Two important strikes by railwaymen in 1950 and 1951 showed a persistence of Socialist influence and the dangerous potential of intra-Peronist bickering in the labor field. In 1950 180,000 of them struck when Eva installed the unwanted Pablo López in their union as part of her drive against Mercante and Bramuglia. The following year she went around the main railway stations appealing to the men to go back to work.

Eva and the Peronist CGT took advantage of the regime's pro-industrialization, prolabor bias to build a much stronger position for organized labor in Argentina than it had ever had before. From only 330,000 in the CGT in 1943 the membership had more than doubled to 800,000 ten years later. With the passage of a "statute of the farm laborer" the first hesitant steps were taken to organize the workers of Argentina's most important economic sector. But on the whole the regime treated its farm sector, source of nearly all its foreign exchange, with kid gloves, and unionization, like talk about agrarian reform and expropriation, never got very far. Eva's significance in the labor world was that she understood and was keen to channel the aspirations of those farm workers who had come to the cities in that growing urban explosion which was occurring in Argentina as in most other Latin American countries. In an article in *Democracia* she wrote that the *descamisado* was the descendant of the *gaucho*, the Argentine cowboy, and this could either be a matter of one generation or of the boy being father of the man. Awareness of this social force, of which Eva was in a sense herself a part, distinguished Peronism from the older labor ideologies of Socialism and Communism which had grown up in the early industries of Buenos Aires among people who were more often immigrants from European countries with a history of another type of trade unionism. The land workers coming to the cities shared a tradition in which authoritarian leadership and protection, nationalism, and strong-arm methods all had a place. Peronism was able to mediate between them and their insecure urban environment. On the other hand, the close connection of labor with the government had the consequence, familiar in Communist states, that the government tried to use union organizations to increase production. Eva herself wrote that low productivity, absenteeism, and indifference to results were ways of sabotaging General Perón's work of social justice and of joining his enemies.

Eva's Foundation

Eva's Social Aid Foundation became one of the most all-embracing welfare bodies of Peronist Argentina, cutting across established departmental boundaries, conducted in a whirl of Evita publicity, responsible to no one but its autocratic boss. The Foundation, which had begun with about $2,000 of her own money, received juridical recognition in July 1948 and snowballed in size. By the time of her death in 1952 it was reckoned to have an annual budget of $100 million. She had said at the beginning that it would operate on voluntary contributions from herself and others. Later, however, it did nothing of the sort. Though funds came from many sources, the common element was usually some form of compulsion. In July 1949 the Foundation was exempted from taxation, government funds were frequently transferred to it for particular projects, and by 1950 Congress had provided that it could share in the government's budget, though it was carefully explained that the Foundation was not to be regarded as another government agency. A fifth of the proceeds of the national lottery went to it, unions made "voluntary" contributions, and in 1950 the CGT deducted two days' pay from all workers, which was refused and then accepted by Eva in rather disingenuous circumstances. It became the practice that the first payment of any raise went into her coffers. Business firms and the stock exchange too were mulcted. The sort of thing that could happen to a firm which refused to donate was illustrated by the case of the Massone Institute, a pharmaceutical firm directed by the anti-Peronist Arnaldo Massone. When it proved obdurate, the firm was fined over $54,000 and the directors were sentenced to from forty-five

to ninety days imprisonment on charges of falsifying descrip-
tions of products. The large funds that passed through the Foundation were not systematically organized in either their getting
or their spending, and the country had to take it on trust from
Evita that it was getting value for money.

The Foundation's aims were constantly expanding, ranging
from disaster relief and Christmas presents for poor children to
the building of schools, hospitals, and houses and the training
of nurses. Its achievements were considerable. It had built about
a thousand schools by the end of 1950—a quarter of the total
constructed by the revolution up to then. It played a big part
in the doubling of the number of hospitals between 1943 and the
end of 1949. In 1951 its nursing schools were training 1,300
nurses, and it had opened thirty-five clinics in the same year.
In 1951, also, it went into the retail business, setting up a chain
of stores selling food and other articles cheaply. Naturally this
did not please fearful and antagonistic businessmen overmuch.
Eva built three holiday camps, planned student cities for Buenos
Aires, Córdoba, and Mendoza, built transit homes for women,
and several old people's homes. She had a special interest in
children. One of the Foundation's proudest monuments was the
"children's city" in the Buenos Aires suburb of Belgrano,
set up to provide a home and schooling for poor and orphan
children. When Fleur Cowles visited it, however, she found the
whole thing lifeless and theatrical.[3] "The country which forgets
its children and does not supply their needs is a country which
denies itself a future," Eva said once. She patronized a junior
sports championship. Over Christmas 1950 the Foundation distributed millions of toys and traditional seasonal goodies—cider
and sweet bread—to poor families with children. Its disaster-relief
work was not restricted to Argentina and could sometimes be
embarrassing to recipients. It sent clothes, medicines, and nurses
to Ecuador in August 1949, when a major earthquake killed eight

[3] Fleur Cowles: *Bloody Precedent: The Perón Story* (Frederick Muller:
1952), pp. 181–2.

thousand people, and this was no doubt warmly received. But it also sent clothing for six hundred poor children in the District of Columbia, United States, which caused something of a rumpus, and a shipment of clothes for needy Jewish immigrants at Tel Aviv. Broadly speaking, the Foundation's relief work caused little ill feeling in Latin America, where the needs were so evident and all succor was welcome, but elsewhere it was suspect as Peronist propaganda. In January 1950 Pope Pius XII sent a message congratulating the Foundation on its works of charity.

The description "social aid" was applied to the Foundation because Eva, like welfare enthusiasts in other countries, was anxious to get away from the traditional concept of charity sponsored by the oligarchy and accepted by the poor. The "Rights of the Worker" and the "Rights of the Aged" proclaimed by the regime were in large part rhetorical (the first five rights of the aged were to assistance, to lodging, to sustenance, to clothing, and to medical care) and represented aspirations rather than the guaranteed pensions and health service that the British Labour government, for example, was developing contemporaneously. Nonetheless, the Social Aid Foundation did change the attitude of the working classes toward the acceptability of welfare as well as making some provision for the most glaring needs. In some of her attitudes, like the importance of making institutional "homes" homelike and of brightening up hospitals, Eva was fully modern, and bodies like the Inter-American Conference of Social Security—of which she took the chair in Buenos Aires in March 1951 —showered her with praise.

But everything that the Foundation touched became part of the Peróns' propaganda machine. Many of the clinics, schools, and housing estates were named after them. As Eva said in a speech in 1949:

In Argentina the beggars, tramps, and vagrants have disappeared and we owe this to the untiring and patriotic work of our illustrious President, General Perón. Until his advent little or nothing had been done in our country for the Argentine populace. That is why the Fund had to start by organizing everything down to the smallest unit.[4]

Eva herself saw many of the poor and distressed at her office daily, and her working day, much of which was spent on Foundation business, lasted anywhere up to eighteen hours. She spoke of burning herself out in the process of eliminating poverty and, messianically, of a time when the Peronist Movement would have succeeded and there would no longer be a need for the Foundation. But in fact, though it had a lot of achievements to its credit, it was unstable, bureaucratic, and too personal to offer more than a transitional panacea for Argentine social problems.

The feminist movement

If labor and welfare policies had had, through the activities of Perón himself, a place in the 1943 revolution almost from its beginning, there was one field in which the influence of Eva was responsible for a sharp break in the revolution's social thinking. This was in its attitude to women—which was profoundly antifeminist, in accordance not only with Nazi–Fascist models in Europe, but with the actual status of women in Argentina historically. General Ramírez, in pursuit of his aim to renew the national spirit, discouraged the government and business from employing women and urged them to keep to their homes, their children, and their religion. This was an approach with which Eva, by temperament, could have little patience, and she made it her business to get women the vote, to make it easier for them to work, and to enhance their status.

Both legally, as far as civil, property, and political rights were concerned, and also socially, the women of Argentina were in a subordinate position in 1946. They were objects to be protected

[4] Speech at the first Inter-American Congress of Industrial Medicine, December 5, 1949. *The Writings of Eva Perón*, a collection of articles written for *Democracia*, Subsecretaria de Informacion de la Presidencia de la Nación, Buenos Aires, 1950.

or desired, but neither they nor the men gave them much room for independent judgment or careers. Very few received higher education. All the same, since 1889, when Dr. Cecilia Grierson became Argentina's first woman doctor and started campaigning for political rights for women, various groups had been chipping away at prejudices over sex education, the divorce laws, and protection for female workers. In 1926 Congress passed measures to improve the legal status of women, and time saw more pressure for changes. If the suffragettes were in sympathy with one party more than another, it was perhaps with the Radicals, and some of them were bitterly opposed to getting the vote from the military revolution of 1943. In 1945 a National Assembly of Women was organized, addressed by well-known women like Victoria Ocampo, to refuse the vote. In this, the small group of professional suffragettes played into Eva's hands, and over the next two years she was able to reach beyond them to create a much more popular campaign for the vote. She presented herself as a typical career girl and the vote as an essential part of the social justice pursued by Peronism. From being included in the 1946 Five-Year Plan votes for women became a promulgated law in September 1947. From then on, women citizens had the same rights as men and those over eighteen could run for office as well as vote. But a charming amendment of October 1948 provided that women voters would not be required to disclose their ages to polling officials, who would have to accept their oral statements that they were over eighteen. Women were not to be exactly like men.

Eva became president of the Peronist Women's Party, set up in 1949, which was designed not only to organize women voters behind the Peróns but to act as a continuing pressure group for women's rights. It pressed for educational and cultural centers for women. But along with the emphasis on opportunities for women workers went a much more traditional respect for woman's place in the home, as expounded by Eva:

The home—the sanctuary of motherhood and pivot of society—is the appropriate sphere in which woman, for the good of the country and her own children, fulfills this duty daily and it is the home which offers the best prospects for her to make her contribution by rearing men who are worthy of the historic times we Argentines are passing through.[5]

Mary, the mother of Christ, remained the acme of womanhood. If the dual emphasis on a woman's rights and her family duties reflected the changing attitude of the revolution and the limited social progress of women until then, it may also have had roots in Eva's experience of her own family situation. Like the First, the Second World War, for the combatant countries, marked a new step forward for women in industry and in other responsibilities. Awareness of what had been happening abroad, plus the long-time existence of indigenous suffragettes, undoubtedly helped to make Argentina in the forties a country ripe for feminism. Yet, thanks very largely to Eva, it was the Peróns who took the credit for a substantial change in the country's social climate. In purely political terms this was not irrelevant either. At the 1951 elections it was estimated that two million women voted, and six women senators, and twenty-four women deputies —all Peronists—were sent to Congress.

Eva and Justicialismo

Justicialismo, the official doctrine of Peronism, was in its origins probably more the creation of Perón, who felt that any self-respecting movement should have some ideological basis, than of his wife. But it was Eva as much as he who gave it flesh and blood. Justicialism was supposed to be the "third position" between capitalism and Communism, the United States and the Soviet Union. It was capitalism modified by the needs of social justice. Perón's own period of government lasted into the era when countries like Egypt, Yugoslavia, and India would be leading the Third World in experiments that attempted to adapt the best features of both capitalism and Communism for developing

[5] The Writings of Eva Perón.

states. But Justicialism was not admitted as having influenced them. The status of Justicialism and the Peróns had been seriously damaged on both sides of the Cold War by their association with Fascism, and by the time the Third World was an established concept and the membership of the United Nations had multiplied with new nations, the Argentine regime was being dismissed as just another corrupt South American government.

Whereas Justicialism for Perón was a pretentious statement of the compromises involved in his mixed structure of economy and government—though Argentina tried to hawk it around Latin America in an attempt to extend its influence, especially among the working class—for Eva it was a genuine idealism. She really believed that the advent of Perón had brought social justice to Argentina. There were plenty of people getting annual bonuses and pensions, or on officially supported strikes, who were ready to agree with her. Perón himself, a more practical and less visionary person, accepted the propaganda she had created. Her myth-making transmuted Perón into "the first Argentine worker"—a kind of worker's Napoleon with semidivine attributes—and made the word *descamisado* into a synonym for class-consciousness.

According to Eva, *descamisados* was the contemptuous description that newspapers tied to foreign interests had applied to the groups that demonstrated on October 17, 1945, for the release of Perón. The Peróns pounced on the term, and Eva, particularly, brandished it at every subsequent opportunity. Words like "worker" and "proletariat" had been monopolized by the traditional labor groups which had looked abroad for their inspiration—*descamisado* was home-grown. This did not mean that every card-carrying Peronist had to go shirtless to prove his allegiance, but the word allowed everyone with a sense of deprivation to join the movement. It had a special attraction for the very poorest, those outside the traditional unions, and also perhaps encouraged some sense of identification among the frustrated *petit bourgeois,* who were obviously poor by comparison with the oligarchs but were naturally estranged from organized labor.

In *La Razón de mi Vida* and her *History of Peronism* Eva wrote that her three guiding loves were the People, Perón, and the Patria—a mixture highly similar to that of Italian Fascism or the Spanish Falange. *Justicialismo* for her could not be separated from Perón, the genius who was his people's leader, although Perón himself had said that Justicialism and the Peronist movement would survive him. Her desire was to see the oligarchy and the imperialists with which they were tied—and she was harsh on the popularity of the "Made in England" tag in the homes of the oligarchy—overthrown and replaced by the single-class state of the workers. For her the antiworking-class and antinational approach of the oligarchy undermined its protestations about democracy and individual liberties; the line-up of the Communists and Socialists with the bourgeois parties in the 1946 elections destroyed their claims to represent the workers. Eva's faith placed little emphasis on the "golden mean" aspect of Justicialism that was promoted by its would-be philosophers; on the contrary, she was proud of her fanaticism in the cause of the *descamisados* which, in theory at least, would give few rights and no privileges to either private capital or private property. She admitted that the revolution of 1943 was not popular and that the majority of those who had carried it out were not interested in profound social change. She dated the start of Peronism from Colonel Perón's move to the since-renamed Secretariat of Labor.

Eva in decline and Peronism without her

Ever since Eva had been just Perón's mistress, she had been an object of annoyance among some military officers. The growth of her own power as wife of the President, her demagogy about the oligarchy, and the arrival of the CGT as a privileged group which might challenge the armed forces all combined to intensify hostility in the latter. This feeling had been shown, for instance, in her 1947 trip to Europe, when the navy had refused to take her in a vessel of the fleet and she had been forced to fly out by

Aerolíneas Argentinas, allegedly at her own expense. But it came to a head in 1951 in the peculiar sequence of events by which Eva was asked to accept nomination as Vice-President and then refused. In July of that year the parallel esteem in which the two Peróns were held had been shown when Congress had approved the conversion of two federal territories, La Pampa and the Chaco, into provinces with the names of Eva Perón and Presidente Perón respectively. On August 22 an open council of Justicialism, called by the CGT with at least a quarter of a million workers present after a spate of Perón posters had appeared on Argentine streets, asked the two of them to accept nomination as President and Vice-President respectively. It seems likely that if Eva had not actually suggested the idea, she had done nothing to discourage it. She was not present at the assembly but was called to appear before it. In what at first appeared to be a rhetorical exchange with the audience she initially asked for four days in which to consider the offer, then until the following day, then a couple of hours, before she accepted nomination.

But a large number of officers on whom Perón depended in the armed forces were totally opposed to making Eva Vice-President, and hence, in the event of the President's death, their own Commander in Chief. Not only was there a class and policy bias against her, but the possibility of being commanded by a woman challenged all their conservatism. On August 31 Eva, who may also have been thinking of her own ill health, announced on the radio that she would renounce the nomination. It was an effective performance. "I do not renounce my work, I'm only refusing the honors," she said. "All I ask is that history record that there was at the side of General Perón a woman who brought to him the hopes and necessities of the people and that this woman was called Evita." At once the CGT suggested that the 31st be celebrated every year as the "Day of the Renunciation." On September 28 the army's irritation with the Peróns found vent in an attempted uprising, led by General Benjamín Menéndez. Although she was already ill, Eva that night made a dramatic popular appeal for loyalty.

Rumors that Eva was suffering from cancer spread around Buenos Aires, but the regime was extremely secretive about her illness. Undoubtedly the disease was responsible for the increasingly erratic nature of her working life in her last couple of years. In November 1951 Eva went into the Policlínica Presidente Perón in Avellaneda for a four-hour operation in which the American cancer specialist George Pack took part. Pack's role, which was partially paid for in the form of pedigreed bulls, was hidden from Eva. She voted while in the hospital in the presidential elections of November 11. Although she was allowed out in early December, the operation had failed in its goal. The last months of her life must have been painful, though public deification reached new heights. On October 17 Eva, who had had the saintly title "Capitana" bestowed on her, had been exalted at a mass meeting where Perón called her "not only the standard bearer of our movement, but one of the greatest women of humanity." She was given the Peronist medal, and that year October 18 was named Saint Evita Day. In December *La Razón de mi Vida*, the statement of faith edited on her behalf, became an instant best-seller. Early in 1952 Congress in extraordinary session gave her the unprecedented title of Spiritual Chief of the Nation. Her last public speech was on May 1. On June 4, when Perón assumed the Presidency for the second time, she courageously stood in the open coach on the ride from the Congress building to the Casa Rosada. But she collapsed in the Casa Rosada during the swearing-in ceremony. In July national life was overshadowed by the final stages of her illness. Prayers were said for her in the churches, and people came to Buenos Aires from distant provinces to accompany her last struggle. On July 26, with Perón, the Duartes, and Padre Benítez, her confessor, at her side, she entered a coma and died.

Official mourning was taken to unusual lengths. Her body was embalmed and lay in state on the first floor of the Ministry of Labor and Welfare. Vast crowds queued up to pay their last respects, and sandwiches were distributed by the Foundation. The coffin was taken to Congress and the CGT. Perón occupied symbolically the deceased's office at the Ministry for several days, memorials were planned, a record of her voice was released, the CGT organized a torchlight procession with Perón on August 26, and the October 17 celebrations were consecrated to her memory.

The Peronist regime survived Eva's death by three years. Her disappearance removed a lot of its glamor, genuine or manufactured, and the aging Perón, with his youthful mistresses, offered uninspired leadership. After the alleged suicide of Juan Duarte in 1953 the Duartes lost any influence. The closing stages of Perón's rule were marked by changes of policy on foreign private investment and Church matters which offended both nationalist and Roman Catholic opinion. During the period of a wage freeze, from 1952 to 1954, the regime passed Law 14222, specifically designed to attract foreign capital. In late 1954 Perón became involved in a battle with the Church which, though it was a logical extension of Peronist social policy, had the effect of destroying the tacit Roman Catholic support the regime had always enjoyed, and it developed political overtones. The quarrel arose when Congress passed a law giving illegitimate children full rights. This was followed in December 1954 by decrees abolishing religious education in schools and legalizing prostitution, and a bill legalizing divorce.

Early in 1955 most Christian festivals lost their status as public holidays, and in May Congress passed a bill to disestablish the Church. Purges and public insults to Church leaders led to the deportation of the Auxiliary Bishop of Buenos Aires in June 1955 and to Perón's excommunication. After a failed coup in that month, to which Perón skillfully reacted, rioting continued in Buenos Aires and the CGT offered to distribute arms to the workers. After four days of confusion a military rising in September, which began in the staunchly Catholic city of Córdoba, forced Perón into exile. Had Eva lived, it is possible that his policy would have stayed more nationalist, more prolabor, and that the offensive against the Church would have been reduced. In the course of this revolution Eva's body, which was supposed by some to have had miraculous powers, was removed from its resting place in the CGT and disappeared mysteriously. Different rumors suggested that it had been thrown into the River Plata or buried secretly outside Buenos Aires. But the only effect of this attempt to bury the legend of Evita was to add an extra twist of romance.

In spite of Eva's death and Perón's absence—after savoring dictatorial hospitality in Paraguay and Nicaragua, he eventually established residence in Spain—the Peronist movement continued to play a significant role in Argentina. Although Major General Lonardi, who led the coup which overthrew the regime, began by being conciliatory, wage restraints for urban workers, and liberal and proagricultural economic policies under General Aramburu (1955–8) allowed the purged Peronists to regroup as a labor movement. To a large extent Peronist strength, increasingly autonomous from the maneuvers of the old gentleman in Madrid, was the factor which underlay the succeeding confusion of Argentine politics. The traditional Radical Party fractured into two, the Unión Cívica Radical del Pueblo—more liberal and anti-Peronist—and the Unión Cívica Radical Intransigente, which was more nationalist in economics and willing to cooperate with the Peronists. Even in disarray the blank, largely Peronist vote for a convention after Perón's fall was 24.31 per cent, compared with 24.20 for the UCRP and 21.3 for the UCRI. It was thanks to Peronist votes that Dr. Arturo Frondizi and the UCRI were elected to power in 1958 with forty-three per cent of the votes. However when, in fulfillment of his bargain with them, the Peronists were allowed to run their own Justicialist Party in the March 1962 elections, they terrified the military by winning nearly thirty per cent of the vote, compared with less than twenty-five per cent for the UCRI.

At this point the military dismissed Frondizi. After service dissensions Frondizi's legal successor, Dr. José María Guido, was permitted to take office. He held fresh elections in July 1963, with the Peronists not allowed to take part, Frondizi arrested, and a newly introduced system of proportional representation in force. In these conditions the UCRP, led by Dr.

Arturo Illia, was able to win. Illia justified his weak government on the grounds that it was contributing to national pacification, but there were mounting strikes and he too was brought down by the military–Peronist confrontation. In the March 1965 Congressional elections the Peronist Unión Popular led with nearly 31 per cent of the votes to 28.5 for the UCRP and barely 10 per cent for the Intransigentes and their splinter groups. After the Peronists continued to lead in provincial by-elections, it seemed likely that they would win the elections for half the Chamber of Deputies and many provincial governorships in March 1967. Before that could happen, on June 28, 1966, there was a military coup which brought General Juan Carlos Onganía to power. The Peronists, who, in spite of dissensions, control the majority of trade unions, had wanted an army coup, and although existing parties were forced to cease operating, the trade unions were not at first touched. But the regime showed no desire to come to terms with the Peronists—or the "Peronists without Perón," as many termed themselves—and efforts to redeploy labor out of the nationalized industries and railways tended to weaken the trade unions. In mid-1968 Onganía changed his cabinet and chief military commanders, and his regime entered a more nationalist phase.

The phenomenon of Peronism

The Peronist movement is an unusual phenomenon. Its Fascist associations and *petit bourgeois* supporters mix strangely with its role as a working-class party. But it is as Argentina's biggest working-class party, which has survived the exile of Perón and suppression and divisions among the subordinates he left, not to mention free competition with Socialists and Communists, that it has a lasting significance. Compared with the state-approved syndicalism of Franco's Spain or Mussolini's Italy, it is quite apparent that the Peronist trade unions of Argentina are much more responsive to the needs of their members. Where the trade-union wing of Justicialism is concerned, nothing could have been better than the disappearance of the Peróns, with the belief that the conditions of the working class had been depressed under succeeding governments to nourish it instead.

The movement's peculiar origin, spawned by a military dictatorship, appears less odd when the strength of the military tradition in Argentine life is appreciated. Even now a considerable portion of Argentine industry is under the direct control of the armed forces. In conditions of an agricultural economy's relatively rapid acquisition of an industrial sector, organized labor is rarely strong, but unorganized labor risks serious exploitation. The Second World War, cutting off South America from traditional suppliers of manufactured goods in Europe and impairing supplies from the United States, encouraged extensive import substitution in Argentina and the other stronger countries. In these circumstances it was understandable that working-class support could be organized for a military leader who was able to throw the weight of the state and its strongest power element, the armed forces, behind the demands of labor. The chance by which, on that famous October 17, the demonstrations of labor supporters gave Perón the crucial edge over a demoralized military regime, entitled them to a continuing share in the spoils of Peronism. And the fact that in the mid-1940's the exhausted state of the industrialized countries combined with their urgent need for Argentina's food to give that country an enviable economic situation, ensured that—for a time anyway—the spoils were real. But by the 1950's the terms of trade were turning against Argentina, capital was apprehensive, and inflation—which had cut the value of the peso by seven eighths between the end of 1947 and the end of 1951—was harmful. The dichotomy between the claims of the military officers, associated with the nervous rural proprietors and traditional import merchants who were collectively abused as oligarchs, and the labor wing of Peronism had destroyed its fragile consensus.

As a personal movement Peronism was in a central Latin American political tradition: personalities appear to offer more tangible protection than institutions or ideas and provide a simpler focus for human emotions. In Argentina, where the strongest base for the Peronistas lay among the unstructured *petit bourgeoisie* and the unorganized workers, such a personal appeal could have its greatest strength. But the oddity about Peronism, at least during Eva's life, was that it was a two-headed personal movement. In theory this could have been confusing, but in practice it was on the whole an advantage. This was because Eva, in her rhetoric, always boosted Perón and offered herself as a humble intermediary between the *descamisados* and their leader. Without Eva the adulation for Perón would almost certainly have existed, but it might not have reached such phenomenal heights. She also, as Compañera Evita in her plain dresses, offered workers and women a human bond with what might otherwise have been a distant leader. On the other hand, as the glamorous wife of the President, dressed in the most expensive Paris dresses and with costly jewelry, she also offered ordinary people a colorful fantasy for their own escapist dreams which reinforced the image of the Compañera Evita. In her skillful playing on the class and anti-foreign phobias of Peronists and her highly dramatic stance as Perón's wife it is hard to resist the notion that she was fulfilling some of her ambitions as an actress. The striving for popular effect was blatant near the end of her life, when she sponsored her own sainthood, a move which was perhaps particularly popular among the Catholic *petit bourgeois*. The whole campaign would have seemed odious in a more advanced Catholic country, and in fact it gravely affronted pious middle- and upper-class Argentines. But it undoubtedly hit a chord among unsophisticated people brought up on the saintly legends and miraculous interventions of folk Catholicism.

The real relationship between Eva and Juan Domingo Perón was a fruitful ground for speculation. Her public manner was so aggressive that he was often supposed to be henpecked. But even if, as seems likely, Eva's influence was responsible for policy taking turns that it otherwise would not have done, the pair preserved an outward unity. One of the few occasions on which they appeared to clash—over a grant of 70,000,000 pesos to the Social Aid Foundation from the Chamber of Deputies which President Perón vetoed in 1949—seems to have been as much a calculated gesture to indicate the Foundation's independence as a genuine disagreement. "I am content with the veto," Eva said at the time. "It shows the unlimited faith of President Perón in the spiritual force of the Foundation."

Eva's power in the Peronist movement and the country at large was as far-reaching as it was ill defined. Cabinet ministers had reason to be as frightened of her as of her husband. In May 1950 Dr. Oscar Ivanisevich, then Minister of Education, was forced to resign after operating on her for acute appendicitis. It was said that Eva had had a blazing row with him and had accused him of exaggerating her illness, which he may already have suspected was cancer, in order to remove her from political activity. One of the weapons of the regime against dissent was the law of disrespect (*desacato*) under which public criticism of heads of state was illegal. Eva was sensitive on this score. When, in 1949, a photograph from a magazine of 1941 showing the actress Eva Franco with her husband and daughter was reprinted with the wrong identification of her as Eva Duarte, the reaction was vindictive. Eva's old friend of her filming days, Kartulovich, was accused of distributing the photo and was summarily deported to Chile, where he continued to protest his innocence. Grudge-bearing and a lack of humor were part of Eva's reputation.

The significance of Eva

As a Latin American personality, possibly Eva's most revolutionary significance was that she was a woman. The fact that a woman was so obviously playing a leading role in one of the area's biggest countries opened up new horizons for women in every field. She deliberately set out to shatter the conservative protectionism which had cooped up her sex in her own country, which had wasted the potential of wealthier women and denied rights to hard-working poorer women like her own mother. As a crusade Eva's feminism was logically entwined with an attack on the oligarchy and a drive for industrialization and labor benefits; for the countryside, to the traditional eye of the rural landowners, was a man's world, and increasing industrialization must call on female labor which must itself get near-to-equal rights if male labor was not to suffer. The virulent dislike of Eva among wealthy women—though it focused on superficialities like her opulent jewelry and her decolleté dresses—testified, along with the latent hostility to her in the officer class, to the revolutionary nature of her role. Women had been important, even in politics in Argentina, before. Encarnación Rosas, wife of the nineteenth-century dictator, Manuel Rosas, had been one such. But as the protagonist of a new sort of woman, free to pursue any occupation she might fancy in a mass society, Latin America had never seen anyone like Eva.

In conjunction with Perón, she was also responsible for giving a new dimension to the continent's tradition of military authoritarianism. This was to frighten the rich and their officer relations outside Argentina. The archetypal military *caudillo* was not interested in class differences in any positive way, though he might have to take them, as he took geographical rivalries, into tactical account. His prime purpose was to get and hold personal power. Having succeeded in this, it was only by chance that the *caudillo* altered class relationships.

The triumph of the Peróns—and in this Eva was as much the evangelist as Juan—lay in the creation of a movement based on class antagonism by a military leader which would be sufficiently tough to survive the effective demise of the leader. The easy equation of the Latin American officer class with political and social conservatism, good for many countries for much of the time—and an explanation for the enduring rift between Argentine voters and the military, following Perón's exile—fell down at this point. Had the GOU officers in 1943 realized that they were fostering the launching of Peronism, they might have acted differently; but their crude form of Fascism, influenced by foreign models and the wave of Catholic thought that was seeking routes to class reconciliation instead of warfare, temporarily undercut their social prejudices. For if Argentina was to become the strong united state they desired, it would have to be more economically advanced and independent than it was then and its labor force would have to work and be disciplined.

Yet Perón, in the Secretariat of Labor and Welfare, could have told them that it was not enough to intervene in unions and remove existing leaders. Simple repression could offer peace only in the short term. To provide for the future, it would be necessary to establish a new labor leadership and to enable it to show sufficient results to outbid alternative leaders. This was what happened, and Eva urged Perón to this end. The evolution of Peronism to a point at which the labor tail seemed frequently to be wagging the military dog reflected the fact that Perón's winning of strength in the armed forces preceded that of his strength with labor, and that the ethic of authoritarian officers was obedience whereas the ethic of militant trade unionism must inspire disobedience. In Spain, where General Franco came to power after victory in civil war, it would have been unthinkable for the Falange to become so class-conscious and powerful. In Argentina, where the Colonel came to power as a result of a street demonstration in which no troops were involved—where the demonstrators could tip the balance in an internal armed service power struggle—subsequent developments were likely. He became President after elections which showed support far beyond the armed forces. Eva, by her strong identification with the labor wing of Peronism, discouraged any retreat from the "Day of the *Descamisados*."

Eva, along with Perón, was responsible for giving the movement the heady but blurred class-consciousness that distinguished it. Her attacks on the oligarchy and British and American capitalism were demagogic. But they made it possible for anyone who agreed, *petit bourgeois* or unionized or nonunionized workers, to include themselves among the deprived *descamisados*. If Argentina in the early forties had had a stronger industrial and trade-union system, it might have fathered a more purely working-class party, and it would have been less easy for the Peróns to have inserted their own concoction. But for much longer the rural sector would predominate in economic status, even though it employed a diminishing proportion of the labor force, and, for obvious reasons, it would have been quite impossible for the Peróns to have based their strength on the organization of rural workers. The populist appeal of the Peróns, a combination of glamor, nationalism, and labor benefits, was not so different from what other Latin American politicians had tried or would try, though without the Fascist-military trappings. It corresponded to a social reality in which a relatively small elite, associated with foreign economic imperialism, seemed the most important fact to the bulk of the population, and other social gradations counted for little. Where institutions catering to the majority of the population were absent, the personal appeal of Eva and Juan Domingo Perón could burgeon largely unopposed.

Peronism, like Haya de la Torre's theories of Indo-America which had originated in Peru in the thirties, and Castro's Marxist variant of the late fifties, aspired to be an original Latin American contribution to politics. As has been seen, it borrowed from foreign models, but a desire to differentiate itself, not only from the North American capitalism of the Western Hemisphere but also from Stalinist Communism, was inherent in the movement. Independence and originality in dealings with the rest of the world have always been attractive to Latin Americans but, although the Peróns certainly aroused interest outside Argentina, there were two basic limits to their influence. First, Eva and her Colonel were not themselves transferable. Second, whatever might be claimed for Justicialism, the movement owed so much to the nationalism of one country that dealings with others were bound to have an air of chauvinism that would be unacceptable. Hence, although the Peróns could command attention, and their specific policies, such as the expropriation of foreign railways and other utilities, would reinforce trends elsewhere, their movement had the look of a blind alley for future generations of Latin Americans. The example of a colonel who had set up a following on the basis of social discontent might inspire or frighten officers, but there was a clear boundary to his social revolution: the privileges of the armed forces, the ultimate arbiter of power in so many countries, would not be disturbed. However disappointing this might have been to Eva, it was a constraint she and the *descamisados* had had to accept from the moment they started to worship their Leader. Hence the example of the Cuban Revolution, which began with the destruction of Cuba's professional army, was to prove so much more exciting.

Conclusion

Personalism

Throughout this book the strong role of personalities in Latin American politics has been emphasized. This is as true of the Peróns, who gave their name to a political party, as it is in different ways of Stroessner, Fidel Castro, and Carlos Lacerda. Even in the case of Che Guevara, who believed that he was of no account beside the cause for which he worked, there were personalist overtones: as he made clear to Mario Monje, he intended to be the personal commander of the army of continental liberation, and most of his Cuban comrades seem to have been drawn to the Bolivian expedition out of admiration for Che himself. It is time, therefore, to examine more closely what is meant by personalism, and its causes and consequences.

Personalism in Latin America refers to a state of politics in which an individual appeals for public support or wins power primarily on his own merits, and only secondarily on the basis of party or military support or on the basis of a particular philosophy or program. Obviously these different elements cannot be entirely separated; when Juan Perón first ran for the Presidency in Argentina, he had organizational support from the Peronist Party, from within the armed forces, and from the trade unions, and he also had a distinct program, including woman suffrage. But what would have seemed peculiar outside Latin America in the mid-forties, and yet was entirely successful in those Argentine elections, was the projection of a personality divorced from the traditional parties.

The significance of personalities in Latin America—and of the characters examined in this book, only Frei lacks the personalist appeal—has varied roots that include both the need for protection in a frontier society and Roman Catholic emphasis on the worth of an individual. It both reflects and reinforces a usually weak party system, which in many countries is subject to military veto. It may well lead to corruption; in the cases of both Stroessner and Kubitschek the existence of friends around a leader who had few defined institutional curbs on the exercise of his power led to complaints of graft. It may litter national politics with the hulks of fading heroes, where a dynamic party system would have displaced them. In Peru and Venezuela both Haya de la Torre and Rómulo Betancourt have exercised influence over APRA and Acción Democrática, respectively, long past their prime; Juan Perón has attempted to manipulate Argentine politics from his exile in Madrid; and, the Brazilian military would argue, Kubitschek and Lacerda have gone on being a nuisance in national life long after they should have accepted supersession by the 1964 revolution. But polarizing politics around personalities has its advantages as well: It may be easier to change political course for a leader who is not strictly bound by ideology or party supervision than for an Anglo-Saxon politician, who is. It may also be easier to identify a politician with unusual talent and to give him a chance at an early age; though the circumstances of the Batista regime were extraordinary, the habit of recognizing and giving loyalty to an individual undoubtedly assisted the youthful Fidel Castro in his rebellion.

The projection of personalities, like the advertising of goods in a consumer society, tends to lead to simplifications of the image that may distort or falsify the facts. Eva Perón was anxious to appear three years younger than she was, and the entry in the civil register at Los Toldos had to be altered to follow suit. Those aspects of a personality or career that will produce the widest and most favorable identification are projected most strongly: the childhood hardships of Eva or Kubitschek, the narrow escape of Carlos Lacerda when Rubem Vaz was murdered. The most striking case of a personality become myth is of course Che Guevara, and it shows how myths develop without the conscious help of the individual. After his death, features of his life and attitudes were remolded to create something new which was wanted by students nearly all over the world. They wanted, and found in Che, someone heroic, the intellectual become man of action, a Communist opposed to bureaucracy and Stalinism, and an anti-imperialist of the Third World. Interwoven with these factors were Che's good looks, his death in a losing cause, his role as a wanderer, and his epic, if not apocalyptic, view of the freedom of Latin America. Students in many countries wanted some of the things from Che that sections of the British population had wanted from Lawrence of Arabia in the twenties and thirties, but the Che myth was incomparably wider and more popular. Nevertheless, the myth submerged other aspects of the historical figure: his incompetence in the Bolivian campaign, his role and errors in the collectivization and industrialization of Cuba, his support for the creation of a secret police and his condoning of the mass executions of Batistianos after the fall of Havana. The power of personalities in Latin American politics, one may contend, leads into myth and simplistic equations of the "Fidel Sí, Yanqui No" variety. It distracts attention from analysis of the morality or efficacy of policy decisions.

Finally, it is worth emphasizing how easily the power of personalities can break through constitutional or institutional bounds to result in personal rule of an authoritarian sort. "Give me a balcony and Ecuador is mine" is supposed to have been the florid boast of Velasco Ibarra, a "democratic" politician. The demagogic crowd appeal of the Peróns, unchecked by civic restraints on crowd behavior, led to riots, the destruction of property, and coercion of opponents. General Stroessner of Paraguay has no magnetic crowd appeal, and the 1940 constitution endowed him with enormous powers, but even he, in his determination to stay in power, broke through the constitutional limit on the length of one President's tenure. Combining his grip on the services with his alliance with the Colorado Party, he has used the state of siege and other presidential powers to the full. It is arguable that most Latin American constitutions assume a strong personality will be President, that Presidents are often left untrammeled by design, and that the system tends to break down when weak figures become President—like Guido and Illia in Argentina. But in fact many Latin American states have borrowed the checks and balances of the U.S. Constitution, so that powerful executives are matched by powerful legislatures, and in Chile Frei was never able to reform the constitution while his party was in a minority in the Senate. (In Peru President Belaúnde Terry was severely circumscribed because the APRA–Odriista opposition was in a majority in Congress.) The frustrations of trying to govern within a U.S. constitutional pattern in a system that may embrace many parties and proportional representation can tempt Presidents to use their personal appeal to find shortcuts. In Brazil this temptation helped to bring down both Presidents Quadros and Goulart. Where personalism is pronounced, the head of a government need accept only those limits on its own activities, and permit only such liberties to other citizens, as may please him.

The military

Many books on Latin America now stress the role of the military as being purely a force of internal occupation. Though this is an attractive theory as far as Batista or Stroessner or even the Argentine military is concerned, it is obvious from the case of Chile that it cannot be universal. What does seem clear, from looking at the careers of Eva Perón and Carlos Lacerda, is the deep-rooted sense of shadow sovereignty among the armed forces of both Argentina and Brazil. While their apologists describe them as influences for stability, they are really highly disruptive. Even when there is a civilian government in these countries, and the soldiers are in their barracks, it is evident that the officer corps is holding itself responsible to its own concept of the state and constitution, which may not coincide with the upholding of legally constituted authorities. It was this feeling that Lacerda was constantly playing on when he appealed for coups against the Vargistas; it was this feeling that the Argentine military acted on when they refused to let Eva run for Vice-President and when they finally overthrew her widower.

This whole conception may seem strange to Anglo-Saxons, who do not assume that a person holding the means of physical violence, whether a policeman or a soldier, is thereby better qualified, let alone allowed special rights, to manage the government. Carlos Lacerda now regrets the 1964 coup in Brazil and the technocratic character of both the Onganía and Costa e Silva governments reflects civilian opposition to military governments of the old sort. Nevertheless the idea, typified by the claims of Stroessner, that the military embody patriotism in an exclusive way, is central to their political interventions. It is also central to their recruiting appeal and their internal discipline and training, so it is unlikely to ebb rapidly. In spite of the social and industrial changes that have accelerated throughout the region, the military have benefited by the time lag that preserves the standing of all high-status occupations beyond their deserts. The existence of nationalist and Nasserist sectors among the military prevents them from being purely conservative bodies and tends to postpone confrontations between populace and soldiery of the sort that brought down Batista. General Perón, whatever Argentine officers may have said about him and his movement after his fall, was a crucial factor in the preservation of their public authority.

Another significant point about the military in Argentina and Brazil is that, as public sector employees, they are in direct competition for salaries and equipment with bureaucrats and trade unions servicing the government and nationalized industries. This competition was one of the irritants that sapped the Peronist regime and Vargas's and Goulart's also. The dilemma is inescapable for a popular government that wishes to extend state employment and enterprises, and in a crude way most Latin American governments are simultaneously pressed to make uneconomic investments in the armed forces and in other public services.

This uneconomic aspect of the military is doubly significant in terms of the poor economic performance of most Latin American states. Not only does the diversion of funds to noneconomic military purposes create a drain on national resources, but the whole value structure of the military tied to patriotism may be a total influence against material advancement. The story of Stroessner's Paraguay seems to indicate this clearly. On the other hand, nationalist, interventionist officers may try to assuage their guilt for taking a large slice of national resources by adopting planning and trying to present military activities as of benefit to the nation as a whole. The military-planning syndrome in Brazil which emerged in 1964 but which predated that revolution, and which has emerged in Argentina under Onganía, is the product of relatively advanced countries; at a humbler level, General Barrientos's use of troops for civil roadbuilding in Bolivia is another attempt to justify military spending in economic terms. The career of Che, who combined a concern with nonmaterial incentives in industry with a devotion to guerrilla warfare, illustrates to a fascinating extent the relationship between militarism and spiritual, nonmaterial goals. Fidel Castro, who has spoken hopefully about the possibility of abolishing money, simultaneously presides over a country which maintains large standing forces and popular militias, and where the revolutionary martial virtues are frequently extolled. In Cuba, as in Paraguay, the military influence, like the influence of Catholicism, has helped to preserve national life from economic materialism.

Stroessner, the Peróns, and the recent Brazilian military Presidents inspire one difficult question: why are these soldiers so much more involved in political activity than their counterparts in Chile and Uruguay? The contrast between Paraguay and Uruguay, both of which had a sanguinary history in the nineteenth century, has been remarkable in recent years. One could point to the contrast between the large-scale European immigration into Uruguay, compared with the enduring Guaraní influence on Paraguay; one could compare the geographical and economic positions—Paraguay's isolation and backwardness and Uruguay's dependence on international trade focusing on the prosperity of the port of Montevideo; one could compare the influence of Uruguay's reformer Batlle with the successive military leaders of Paraguay and the legacies of the War of the Triple Alliance and the Chaco War against Bolivia. But when all is said and done, it is doubtful whether one would arrive at a completely satisfactory explanation. In the case of Chile, other factors, including the prestigious position of a large navy, may help to explain the lesser involvement of the armed forces in politics.

There is, in addition, no doubt that military interventions in politics are a habit particularly hard to break. The chapter on Carlos Lacerda indicates clearly enough that the knowledge that the military might intervene becomes a central consideration for civilian politicians, who deliberately act in such a way as to either encourage or tranquilize the officers. The military factor tends to divide and unsettle public opinion so that it is rare to get unanimity among civilian politicians and the public at large against a coup: but only this sort of unanimity, accompanied by doubts among the troops themselves, would ever banish the risk of a coup. On the other side are the expectations and habits of the military themselves. It must be wondered whether someone like the young Stroessner would have entered the Paraguayan army if it had merely had the professional home-guard functions of its small Uruguayan counterpart. If Latin American forces had the small political influence of the British army, without the latter's expectation of combat, their recruiting attraction would be negligible.

Roman Catholicism

All the personalities described in this book must have been affected by their faith in Catholicism, with the exception of Che Guevara, who had none. Yet to probe more deeply into the effect of religion or the organized Church leads into a complicated maze. Stroessner, for example, a believer in an ordered, hierarchical Catholicism to match his military and patriotic sentiments, has been criticized by the prelates of Paraguay for the lack of civil liberties and social backwardness of the country. Some of the more vigorous opponents of his regime are Christian Democrats. Carlos Lacerda, another conservative Catholic, was, as Governor of Guanabara, closely involved in the interplay between Church and national politics. Until just before the 1964 revolution the Archbishop of Rio de Janeiro was one of the Brazilian Church's most notable progressives, Dom Helder Camara, which was inconvenient for Lacerda. However, Dom Helder's was a minority position and there were plenty of conservative clergy in Rio who were prepared to cooperate with the Governor. Even more significant, in the demonstrations that led up to the 1964 revolution, were Catholic lay and women's organizations. They organized marches for God and the Family which, while ostensibly religious, were definitely political in intent. They were warnings to the Goulart government that it must not tamper with the constitution and, among the more conspiratorial organizers, they may have been deliberately designed to make conditions propitious for a coup d'état. But although the lay organizations were valuable to Lacerda in 1964, they seem to have been largely independent of him, and their success then was a product of circumstances which could not be repeated. When Lacerda attempted another ostensibly religious march in 1965, as part of the campaign for Flexa Ribeiro's election, it was a flop. Lacerda's campaigns against corruption and Communism in the fifties and early sixties tied in closely with his conservative Catholicism, and his religious stance was probably a factor in his successful appeals for women's votes. He was much too independent to be a tool of the Church, but he had to observe its prejudices, as his withdrawal from a state *macumba* demonstration—organized by his state tourist department but put under ban by the local Archbishop—showed in 1965.

Kubitschek claimed that he had been affected by the social

encyclicals of the 1930's, but he was in no way associated with the organized Church in his career. His attitudes, favoring social reconciliation rather than direct social confrontations in the cause of reform, may have owed something to religious conviction, but they also owed much to the conservatism and property holding in his own party, the PSD. Whereas Goulart boldly made an issue of agrarian reform and made a political appeal to the disfranchised laborers and progressive urban voters—even while he was still accumulating estates himself—Kubitschek tried to sidestep discontent with his projects for Brasília and SUDENE. His real hope probably lay in the nationalist, industrializing movement in São Paulo and Minas Gerais, and in the creation of a mixed economy capable of generating greater domestic wealth and encouraging social mobility. In this kind of philosophy he was not far from the more openly Catholic Frei, or the other conservative Christian Democrats in Chile. In the widest sense, it is probable that the conciliatory element in Catholic social policy—though it was being replaced by a sharper, more militant spirit in the 1960's—coincided with an influential outlook in Brazilian society that was disposed to compromise and anxious to dissipate antagonisms. From this viewpoint it is interesting that Magalhães Pinto, the UDN leader from the same thrifty Catholic state as Kubitschek, represented a more liberal attitude to social questions than the bulk of his party.

The relation of the Argentine Church to the Peronists was one of close cooperation in the 1940's followed by outraged hostility in the 1950's. While Eva was alive, the crisis was never reached, but after her death the conflict over the divorce issue, and the pro- and anti-Catholic demonstrations that ensued, were significant contributors to Perón's downfall. At the start of the regime, however, the cooperation of the clergy was valuable to the Peronists: clergy with authoritarian and Fascist views underpinned the concept of a strong military state and assisted in the construction of a workers' organization. Although some of the clergy may have disliked woman suffrage and Eva's own flamboyant role—particularly as she began to give herself saintly airs—Eva's ambiguous stance helped to prevent a rift with the Church. In spite of her role as social reformer and her grandiloquent talk, she was a loyal Catholic herself and she did not lose sight of the fact that the majority of women would be nonrevolutionary mothers of families, deeply grateful for their religious faith. She did not dispraise religion.

Although Frei is a man of religious conviction, and his outlook is shaped by Catholicism, it would be hard to prove that the Church in Chile now has exceptional influence over the Christian Democratic Party there. Clearly the links of Frei and the young Falangists with the Church were highly significant in the 1930's, when the movement was developing; and in the late forties, when the party broke off its alliance with the Communists, clerical influence was still strong. But ever since the Christian Democrats became a major party, they have been competing for votes in areas of the population which are less committed to the Church, and their overt religious appeal has been played down. The situation in Chile is not comparable with that in Italy between 1945 and 1956, when the full apparatus of the Church—pastoral letters and all organizations of the faithful—was thrown behind Christian Democrat electoral campaigns to obstruct the Communists. Priests are still active among the Chilean party members, but the party is too big for them to be more than one among a number of voices, and even that may stutter. Young radical priests, anxious to demolish the old structures of the Church, have combined with the young activists in the party who have fought Frei for not going fast enough with his reforms. Though Frei was motivated by his religion to be concerned with social injustices —poverty, poor productivity, social outcasts, and the problems of nitrate workers and agrarian reform—the Church could not give him detailed political solutions for these problems. The dreamy, spiritual idealism of communitarianism among some of his supporters was a response to the political intractability of Chilean social problems, at least when attacked from a right-wing, private-propertied voting base.

Revolutionaries

Most of the figures studied in this book have claimed to be revolutionaries: Che, who believed that the duty of a revolutionary was to make revolution, died in consequence; Frei claimed that he was providing a revolution in freedom; Eva Perón, at first a revolutionary by adoption as she began to boost the achievements of the 1943 revolution, became a full-throated convert as she magnified the stupendous changes wrought by President Perón; and Carlos Lacerda, the broadcaster of impending revolutions, lived as a revolutionary in taut hours of fantasy in early 1964, and then lived to regret it. The two who have not professed to be revolutionary, Kubitschek and Stroessner, could each have done so had they wished—both of them in connection with the way they came to power, and Kubitschek, had he wanted to be a propagandist, in terms of his political program. But it was not part of Stroessner's philosophy to claim to have initiated any revolution; rather he would have preferred to be identified with all that was best and unchanging in Paraguayan history. Kubitschek disclaimed revolutionary rhetoric—though he was grandiloquent enough about his program—for other reasons. He wished to be classed as an observer of the constitution, in contrast to UDN malcontents who were always itching for a coup, and in his view the intervention of Lott in 1955 was not a revolution but a constitutional act to protect the popular mandate from being overthrown by plotters.

The attraction of the term "revolution" is clearly considerable, even though the phenomena to which it is attached may vary enormously in social and political consequences. It expresses a preference for rapid and violent change, and it endows with unlimited powers any individual who describes himself as a revolutionary. In these aspects there is a connection between the most unpopular military coup and the social upheaval in Cuba after 1959. The preference for rapid and violent change may answer the frustrations of living in a stagnant and unjust society, such as Chile's seemed in the 1960's and Cuba's was in the 1950's, or it may just be a response to the absence of more relaxed ways of changing the government where a regime has no constitutional origins and its rule is based on force. That the revolutionary is responsible only to the revolution is almost tautologically true; this does not mean that he may not be under orders from a superior who defines the purposes of the revolution, but it does mean that the revolution is bound to no laws or current practices of the state. In Latin America it is hard to imagine any revolution which does not have a leader; in fact, in the cases of both Fidel and Che, the leader came first and the revolution or attempted revolution was fashioned around him. But there is a sense in which, by declaring that he is a revolutionary, each man becomes his own *caudillo*—an outlaw who uses force to attain his ends. The civilian revolutionary, responsible to his own view of the revolution, joins hands with the army officer, responsible to his own view of patriotic duty. Popular consent, though it may be claimed, is secondary to the free actions of revolutions and revolutionaries.

Che was an honest revolutionary when the orthodox Communists of Latin America were dishonest; for years they had tacitly regarded the capture of state power in their own countries by revolutionary means as being so remote as to play no part in their tactics. They were in a ludicrous position. While their talk of revolutionary philosophy meant that in many countries they were deprived of political rights, they did not dare to unsay it and participate in the political game. The actual coups and self-styled revolutions were left to others of many complexions. Che took part in a revolution which gave new meaning to the word and at the same time showed what little right most Communists in the region had to use it. In Cuba the Fidelistas made a Latin-American-style revolution first, and it was immensely lucky for the Communists that the *Jefe Máximo* and Cuba's geopolitical situation combined to make Communism the official philosophy. Che's view of revolutionary action as an end in itself, and his methodology of revolution in Latin American countries, had their weaknesses; but his aim for a revolution that crossed national boundaries, burning through Latin America and provoking many

Vietnams, was a radical extension to the idea of revolution in the region. That it ignored the massive tradition of one-nation nationalism, that it challenged both the vastness of Latin America and the problems of succeeding everywhere at once (for the revolutionary war would be a coordinated campaign on many fronts) and that it rode roughshod over the political jealousies of potential leftist revolutionaries in every country—these things only showed that Latin America was not yet ready for the new concept of revolution. For what Che was asserting was that, with modern communications and the worldwide competition of political systems, there could no longer be an isolated revolution in one Latin American country that was worthy of the name.

Frei's revolution in freedom, by contrast, was an electoral strategy, an attempt to offer rapid and sweeping change while at the same time assuring everyone that laws would be respected. Had the program not been described as revolutionary, the disappointments of the Christian Democrats in office might have been less. But though there may have been voices urging Frei to take extraconstitutional shortcuts, he did not do so, and delays regarding the copper law, the agrarian reform, and even the austerity measures of 1967–8 followed inevitably. In the circumstances, then, a revolution in freedom was a natural slogan for a party relying on the votes of conservative forces. But, interestingly enough, the Partido Nacional, which equated private property with freedom, was still able to complain that Frei's program had restricted freedom. Although the loss may not have been marked—for Frei was reducing the freedom of landowners to hold untilled lands and the freedom of copper companies to conduct their business without taking Chilean national interests into account—it was a reminder that even a nonrevolutionary government is almost bound to remove the privileges of some groups by law. While Frei is not offering a revolution, the attraction of the word has bitten deep into his party, and there might be others who would. One of the most fascinating problems for the Chilean Christian Democrats is whether, as some young radicals desire, they will become a genuinely revolutionary party with all the shattering consequences for the present commitment to democracy that this implies.

Eva Perón, with her husband and associates, managed to change the direction of a revolution, while still making it sound revolutionary. For the conservative militarism of the 1943 coup she substituted the labor and feminist campaigns of Justicialism. The Peronists were certainly revolutionary in their unwillingness to be bound by law and in their use of political violence; there was a radical streak in the attack on the Church, and in the friction between the labor wing and the military. But in the last resort, the potentially revolutionary attacks on private property had personalist limits—typified by Eva's Foundation, which was selective in its mulctings—and the military remained undisturbed. After the fall of Perón the Peronists became frankly nonrevolutionary, although they still frightened their neighbors in Argentine politics. To some extent, it seems, the normal solidity that overcomes erstwhile revolutionary parties may in fact be abetted by an atmosphere of personalism. Thus, it is notable that the growing conservatism of APRA in Peru is associated with the aging process of Haya de la Torre.

Carlos Lacerda's desired revolutions were really counterrevolutions, designed to anticipate or counterbalance the power of populist politicians. The revolution that never was aboard the *Tamandaré* was wholly negative; it was an attempt to gain power ahead of Kubitschek, and, apart from a campaign against corruption, it presaged no particular program. The revolutions of the *Tribuna* would have been real enough in that they anticipated taking power, displacing Vargista politicians and their friends from executive positions, in a period in which the government had extralegal powers. In fact, after the Goulart regime had sufficiently frightened sections of the armed forces and of civilian opinion, this was the formula adopted by the Castello Branco revolutionary government. In concentrating on power, and men rather than measures, Lacerda's views were those of many planners of coups in Latin American history. What was significant was the small response his appeals evoked for most of the time, which indicated that, whatever the defects of the existing Brazilian constitution, only a minority among the armed forces and public could be attracted to that sort of revolution in normal conditions.

Summary—past and future

Eva Perón with her shrill demagogy and her private vendettas; Eduardo Frei with his sober, intellectual appeal to an electorate; Stroessner with his toughness and industry; Che with his utopian vision; Lacerda and Kubitschek—contrasts in excitement and political coolness: such personalities represent the great diversity in Latin American politics, its top–down structures of political organization, and its contrast between an idealist rhetoric and a mode of politics that encourages corruption and inefficiency. But these names are products of a particular era, and their successors, while social changes in Latin America continue and the region becomes more open and self-confident in its attitudes to the world outside, are bound to be different. It is worth examining further some factors which are changing the character of Latin American politics, and which may shape different political personalities in the future.

First, there is the youth factor. Of the leaders in this book, only Che represented an appeal to youth; though the rebels in the Sierra Maestra were a young group backed by youngsters, Che's greatest attraction for youth came posthumously. Yet the demographic structure of Latin America means that youngsters, even though they may be disfranchised by age restrictions, have an unusual weight if they care to use it. In demonstrations in Mexico City, Rio de Janeiro, and Montevideo in 1968 it was clear that students and schoolchildren were discovering their strength. Although there is a long tradition of student political activity in Latin America, family structures supported by Catholic teaching have in the past inhibited the growth of a special youth constituency, comparable to the Anglo-Saxon cult of the teen-ager. But if this is changing, it is clear that those politicians —students or their elders—who can weld youth support together with backing elsewhere in society will have a bright future; and radicalism and idealism must figure strongly in their creeds. By the end of the century—when the population of Latin America may possibly exceed 500,000,000—this demographic process may have reversed and altered the atmosphere again. Chile, which with Argentina has a population growth rate more akin to Northern Europe than to Third World countries, has taken the lead in holding international conferences on birth control in the region; within the next twenty years population control is likely to become official policy throughout the area.

Another factor altering the outlook of succeeding generations of politicians is likely to be the need to concern themselves much more with international and hemispheric affairs. Of the figures examined here, only Frei and Che have a truly international outlook, although Kubitschek tried to take a hemispheric initiative with his Operation Pan America. Kubitschek, Lacerda, Eva Perón, and General Stroessner all respond, in different ways, to a sense of nationalism. Nationalism, or patriotism, is still a vibrant sentiment in all Latin American countries. Better communications of all sorts are making Latin American countries more aware of the world outside and of each other, and will force politicians to choose between trying to create an independent role for their country in the world as a whole and trying to make something meaningful out of a Latin American bloc. In the past, limited travel between Latin American states and colonization limited to certain areas of national territory meant that contacts between different countries were restricted in scope; already the increasing trade and road and air traffic, and projects of internal colonization like the Brazilian move to the west or the trans-Andean forest road, are giving international relations a more immediate flavor. Latin America was as involved as North America or Western Europe in the student unrest of 1968; domestic political events are gradually acquiring a greater outside echo and more of a basis in contemporary political vocabulary. A typical example occurred in July 1968, when Antonio Arguedas, Bolivia's Minister of the Interior, fled to Chile and then Britain after admitting passing a copy of Che Guevara's diary to the Cubans. He promised that he would go back to Cuba if the Cuban Revolution was under military attack, but he refused an invitation from Fidel Castro and returned to Bolivia to explain himself. Almost certainly the Minister's action in releasing a copy of the diary had its roots in the minutiae of Bolivian politics, if not in some desire to embarrass President Barrientos, but explanations were presented in terms of the Cuban Revolution. Whereas at present Latin American integration tends to be a rather airy topic, the concern of bureaucrats and conferences, it is not hard to see that in the future it may become a real issue for the man in the street also.

If one Latin American country depended more on another for basic raw materials or food supplies, as a result of coordinated economic planning, it is clear that a strike or sudden price rise could bring a sharp reaction in the public of the dependent country. Even more significant could be the consequences of greater military integration in the region if this were to result in the use of an international force to intervene in any country pursuing a policy disliked by the others. In this context, of course, one of the objectives of Che Guevara in Bolivia was to provoke U.S. intervention against his movement and, preferably, intervention also by forces from other "reactionary" states. Although informal relations exist between Latin American armed forces—in 1965 the then Argentine Chief of Staff, Onganía, met the then Brazilian Minister of Defense, Marshal Costa e Silva, in talks which observers knew had political connotations—the military has been slow to espouse integration, and pressures from the United States and Brazil have failed to create a permanent international peacekeeping force on the 1965 Santo Domingo pattern. In some cases nationalistic military men have been obstructing prospects for international agreement. Thus, by objecting to the nuclear nonproliferation treaty, the Costa e Silva government in Brazil has effectively killed the hopes for a nuclear free zone in Latin America.

A third factor which may create different horizons among later generations of Latin American politicians is the growth of the cities. Cities of over ten million are a distinct prospect for Latin America in the 1970's. The concentrated tensions of poverty, poor job opportunities, and an indifferent quality of life helped to produce urban riots in 1968. Although there is plenty of space in all Latin American countries for internal colonization, with potential agricultural land available, the attractions of the cities are in most places drawing population from the countryside. As a result the nature of politics is being radically altered; in Peru, for example, every Indian who comes down from the Andes to adopt Spanish speech and ways in the outskirts of Lima is tending to upset the Indianist philosophy on which APRA was founded. This social drift by no means diminishes the arguments for land reform—in fact, it redoubles them, for it is the disparity in living standards that causes the movement of population, a greater urban public needs more food, and urban strength may impose property changes. But urban problems themselves are likely to throw up their own leaders and solutions in a way which could make Che's philosophy of agrarian revolution anachronistic and Eva Perón's urban mass movement of the 1940's seem surprisingly contemporary.

Régis Debray has written: "History advances in disguise; it appears on stage wearing the mask of the preceding scene and we tend to lose the meaning of the play." [1] Nowhere is this truer than in Latin America, where old structures may conceal new attitudes and generalizations go astray. But the six influential persons of this book indicate the content and methods of politics in the recent past, and this is part of the heritage that new political leaders must adopt or reject.

[1] Régis Debray: *Revolution in the Revolution?* (Monthly Review Press: New York; 1967), p. 19.

Bibliography

General

Alexander, Robert: *Prophets of the Revolution*. Macmillan: New York; 1962.

Beals, Carleton: *Latin America: World in Revolution*. Abelard-Schuman; 1963.

Blakemore, Harold: *Latin America*. Oxford University Press; 1966.

Clissold, Stephen: *Latin America: A Cultural Outline*. Hutchinson; 1965.

Debray, Régis: *Revolution in the Revolution?*. Penguin Books; 1968.

Dell, Sidney: *A Latin American Common Market?*. Oxford University Press; 1966.

Gerassi, John: *The Great Fear*. Macmillan: New York; 1963.

Goldenberg, Boris: *Cuban Revolution and Latin America*. New York; 1955.

Herring, Hubert: *A History of Latin America*. Alfred A. Knopf: New York; 1965.

Lieuwen, Edwin: *Arms and Politics in Latin America*. Revised Ed. Praeger: New York; 1961.

Pendle, George: *A History of Latin America*. Penguin Books: 1963.

Rippy, J. Fred: *Latin America: A Modern History*. University of Michigan Press: Ann Arbor; 1958.

Véliz, Claudio (ed.): *Obstacles to Change in Latin America*. Oxford University Press: 1965.

Véliz, Claudio (ed.): *Latin America and the Caribbean*. Blond: 1968.

Wionczek, Miguel S. (ed.): *Latin American Integration: Experiments and Prospects*. Praeger: New York; 1966.

Che Guevara

Draper, Theodore: *Castroism: Theory and Practice*. Praeger: New York; 1965.

Guevara, Ernesto Che: *Reminiscences of the Revolutionary War.* Translated by Victoria Ortiz. Monthly Review Press: New York; 1968. Also Penguin Books: 1969.

Guevara, Ernesto Che, and Mao Tse-tung: *Guerrilla Warfare.* With a foreword by Capt. B. H. Liddell Hart. Cassell: 1962 (two sections published separately by Praeger: New York; 1961).

Guevara, Ernesto Che (ed. Daniel James): *The Complete Bolivian Diaries of Che Guevara and Other Captured Documents.* Stein & Day: 1968.

Guevara, Ernesto Che: *Bolivian Diary.* With introduction by Fidel Castro, translated by Carlos Hansen and Andrew Sinclair. Jonathan Cape/Lorrimer; 1968.

Guevara, Ernesto Che (ed. John Gerassi): *Venceremos! The Speeches and Writings of Ernesto Che Guevara.* Macmillan: New York; 1968.

Huberman, Leo, and Sweezy, Paul: *Cuba: Anatomy of a Revolution.* Monthly Review Press: New York; 1961.

Peredo, Inti: "From the Bolivian Guerrilla." 1968 letter published in *New Left Review* 51.

Alfredo Stroessner

Amnesty International: *Prison Conditions in Paraguay.* A report prepared by Amnesty Delegate Anthony Freire Marreco, 1966.

Pendle, George: *Paraguay: A Riverside Nation.* Oxford University Press for Royal Institute of International Affairs: 1966. Third ed.

Stroessner, Alfredo: "His Life and Thoughts." Asunción; 1958.

Stroessner, Alfredo: *Biografía,* Comando en jefe de las Fuerzas Armadas de la Nación, Dirección General del Personal. Asunción; 1963.

Zook, Capt. David H. Jr.: *The Conduct of the Chaco War.* Bookman Associates: New York; 1960.

Eduardo Frei Montalva

Butland, Gilbert J.: *Chile.* Royal Institute of International Affairs: London; 1956. Third edn.

Frei Montalva, Eduardo: *La verdad tiene su hora.* Editorial del Pacífico SA: Santiago.

Frei Montalva, Eduardo: *Sentido y Forma de una Política.* Editorial del Pacífico SA: Santiago; 1951.

Frei Montalva, Eduardo: *Pensamiento y Acción.* Editorial del Pacífico SA: Santiago; 1958.

Frei Montalva, Eduardo: *La Universidad en Tiempos de Cambio,* chapter by Frei: "La Universidad, Consciencia Social de la Nación." Editorial de Pacífico SA: Santiago; 1965.

Halperin, Ernst: *Nationalism and Communism in Chile.* MIT Press: Cambridge, Mass.; 1965.

Mello Mourão, Gerardo: *Frei y la Revolución Latinoamericana.* Editorial del Pacífico SA: Santiago; 1966.

Juscelino Kubitschek and Carlos Lacerda

Bello, José Maria: *History of Modern Brazil, 1889–1964.* Stanford University Press: California; 1966.

Costa, Licurgo: *Uma Nova Politica para as Americas.* Livraria Martins Editôra: São Paulo; 1960.

Dell, Edmund: *Brazil: The Dilemma of Reform.* Fabian Society: 1964.

Dines, Alberto, et al.: *Os Idos de Março e a Queda em Abril.* Rio de Janeiro; 1964.

Dulles, John W. F.: *Vargas of Brazil: A Political Biography.* University of Texas: 1967.

Kubitschek de Oliveira, Juscelino: *A Marcha do Amenhecer.* Bestseller SA: São Paulo; 1962.

Lacerda, Carlos: *Brazil entre a verdade e a mentira.* Bloch Editôres SA: Rio; 1965.

Lacerda, Carlos: *Palavras e ação.* Distribuidora Record: Rio; 1965.

Lacerda, Carlos: *Critica e autocritica.* Editôra Nova Fronteira: Rio; 1967.

Lacerda, Carlos (compiled by E. Caó): *Carreirista da traição.* Editôra Panfleto: Rio; 1960.

Da Rocha, Munhoz: *Radiografia de Novembro.* Editôra Civilização Brasileira: Rio; 1961.

Skidmore, Thomas E.: *Politics in Brazil 1930–64.* Oxford University Press: New York; 1967.

Eva Perón

Alexander, Robert J.: *The Perón Era*. Victor Gollancz: 1952.

Blanksten, George I.: *Perón's Argentina*. University of Chicago Press: 1953.

Cowles, Fleur: *Bloody Precedent: The Perón Story*. Frederick Muller: 1952.

Owen, Frank: *Perón: His Rise and Fall*. Cresset Press: 1957.

Pendle, George: *Argentina*. Oxford University Press: 1963. Third ed.

Perón, Eva: *La Razón de mi vida*. Ediciones Peuser: Buenos Aires; 1951. Translated by Ethel Cherry: *My Mission in Life*: Vantage Press: New York; 1953.

Perón, Eva: *Historia del Peronismo*. Escuela Superior Peronista: Buenos Aires; 1951.

Perón, Eva: *The Writings of Eva Perón* (articles for *Democracia*). Subsecretaria de Informaciones de la Presidencia de la Nación: Buenos Aires; 1950.

Perón, Eva: *Eva Perón and Her Social Work*. Subsecretariat of Information of the Presidency of the Nation: Buenos Aires; 1950.

Perón, Juan Domingo: *The Theory and Complete Doctrine of General Perón*. Ministerio del Relaciones Exteriores: Buenos Aires; 1946.

Sebreli, Juan José: *Eva Perón—Adventurera o Militante?*. Ediciones Siglo Veinte: Buenos Aires; 1966.

Index

A Note About the Author

Richard Bourne was born in Surbiton, Surrey, in 1940, and studied at Uppingham School and Brasenose College, Oxford, where he took an honors degree in modern history in 1962. He then joined the *Guardian* and for two years was a general reporter in Manchester. In 1965 he was awarded a Brazilian government scholarship to study Brazilian politics and economics, and spent six months in Latin America. He began work on the present book in 1966 and returned to Latin America in 1967 to collect material. Early in 1968 he wrote a series of articles for the *Guardian* from Spain and Portugal. Since February of that year he has been the *Guardian*'s education correspondent. He is a regular contributor to educational journals in Britain and is coauthor of *Struggle for Education, 1870–1970*, a history of Britain's National Union of Teachers.

A Note on the Type

*The text of this book is set in Caledonia, a Lino-
type face designed by W. A. Dwiggins. It belongs to
the family of printing types called "modern face" by
printers—a term used to mark the change in style
of type-letters that occurred about 1800. Caledonia
borders on the general design of Scotch Modern, but
is more freely drawn than that letter.*

*The book was composed, printed, and bound by
The Colonial Press Inc., Clinton, Massachusetts.*

*The typography and binding design are by
Richard-Gabriel Rummonds.*